First World War

and Army of Occupation

War Diary

France, Belgium and Germany

61 DIVISION
184 Infantry Brigade,
Brigade Machine Gun Company
1 January 1916 - 28 February 1918

WO95/3067/2

The Naval & Military Press Ltd
www.nmarchive.com
Published in association with The National Archives

Published by

The Naval & Military Press Ltd

Unit 10 Ridgewood Industrial Park,

Uckfield, East Sussex,

TN22 5QE England

Tel: +44 (0) 1825 749494

www.naval-military-press.com

www.nmarchive.com

This diary has been reprinted in facsimile from the original. Any imperfections are inevitably reproduced and the quality may fall short of modern type and cartographic standards.

Contents

Document type	Place/Title	Date From	Date To
Heading	WO95/3067/2		
Heading	61st Division 184th Infy Bde 184th Machine Gun Coy. June 1916-Feb 1918		
War Diary	Grangham	16/06/1916	16/06/1916
War Diary	Southampton	16/06/1916	16/06/1916
War Diary	Havre	17/06/1916	19/06/1916
War Diary	Lagorgue	20/06/1916	20/06/1916
War Diary	Lestrem	20/06/1916	22/06/1916
War Diary	Laventie	23/06/1916	30/06/1916
Heading	War Diary of The 184th Machine Gun Company. From July 1st To July 31st 1916 Volume 3		
War Diary	Laventie	01/07/1916	03/07/1916
War Diary	Lestrem	04/07/1916	06/07/1916
War Diary	Richebourg St. Vaast	07/07/1916	18/07/1916
War Diary	Laventie	19/07/1916	23/07/1916
War Diary	Le Drumez	24/07/1916	31/07/1916
Heading	War Diary of 184 Company Machine Gun Corps From Aug 1st To Aug 31st 1916		
War Diary	Le Drumez	01/08/1916	01/08/1916
War Diary	Lestrem	02/08/1916	10/08/1916
War Diary	Laventie	11/08/1916	31/08/1916
Miscellaneous	Appendix A	28/08/1916	28/08/1916
Miscellaneous	Appendix B 2/4th R.F.C. Oxf. Bayle.	28/08/1916	28/08/1916
Heading	War Diary Of 184 Company Machine Gun Corps Sept 1916		
War Diary	Lavantie	01/09/1916	11/09/1916
War Diary	Le Drummy	11/09/1916	30/09/1916
Heading	War Diary of The 184 Company Gun Corps From 1st October 1916, To 31st October 1916 Volume V		
War Diary	Laventie	01/10/1916	03/10/1916
War Diary	Laventie (Moated Grange Sector)	04/10/1916	30/10/1916
Miscellaneous	Appendix I	27/10/1916	27/10/1916
Miscellaneous	Appendix II	28/10/1916	28/10/1916
Heading	War Diary of The 184 Company Machine Gun Corps From 1-11-16 To 30-11-16 Volume 6		
War Diary	Robecq	01/11/1916	01/11/1916
War Diary	Robecq to Auchel	02/11/1916	02/11/1916
War Diary	Auchel to Houvelin	03/11/1916	03/11/1916
War Diary	Houvelin to Tinquette	04/11/1916	04/11/1916
War Diary	Tincquette to Roziere	05/11/1916	05/11/1916
War Diary	Roziere to Ransart	06/11/1916	06/11/1916
War Diary	Ransart	07/11/1916	15/11/1916
War Diary	Ransart to Canaples	16/11/1916	16/11/1916
War Diary	Canaples to Contay	17/11/1916	17/11/1916
War Diary	Contay	18/11/1916	18/11/1916
War Diary	Contay to Albert	19/11/1916	19/11/1916
War Diary	Albert	20/11/1916	20/11/1916
War Diary	Albert to Trenches	21/11/1916	21/11/1916
War Diary	Mouquet Farm Sector	22/11/1916	26/11/1916
War Diary	Mouquet Farm Trenches	26/11/1916	27/11/1916

War Diary	Mouquet Farm Sector	28/11/1916	30/11/1916
Heading	War Diary of The 184th Company Machine Gun Corps From 1.12.16 To 31.12.1916 Volume No.7		
War Diary	Martinsart	01/12/1916	01/12/1916
War Diary	Hedauville	02/12/1916	11/12/1916
War Diary	Martinsart	11/12/1916	19/12/1916
War Diary	To The Trenches In Mouquet Farm Sector	20/12/1916	20/12/1916
War Diary	In The Trenches	21/12/1916	27/12/1916
War Diary	Mouquet Farm Sector	28/12/1916	28/12/1916
War Diary	Martinsart	28/12/1916	29/12/1916
War Diary	Hedauville	30/12/1916	30/12/1916
Map	Appendix 1		
Heading	War Diary of 184 Company Machine Gun Corps From 1st To 31st January 1917. Volume 8		
War Diary	Hedauville	01/01/1916	08/01/1916
War Diary	Martinsart	08/01/1916	15/01/1916
War Diary	Pounvillers	15/01/1917	17/01/1917
War Diary	Longuevillette	17/01/1917	18/01/1917
War Diary	Domqueur	18/01/1917	19/01/1917
War Diary	Maison Ponthieu	19/01/1917	31/01/1917
Miscellaneous	Appendix I Company Movement Grader.	06/01/1917	06/01/1917
Miscellaneous	Appendix II Company Orders by Lt. H G. harcourt Commanding 184 Coy. M.G.C.	14/01/1917	14/01/1917
Miscellaneous	Appendix III Company Orders by Lieut HG. Harcourt Commanding No 184 M G.Coy.	16/01/1917	16/01/1917
Miscellaneous	Appendix IV Company Orders by Lieut HG. Harcourt Commanding 184 Coy M.G.C.	17/01/1917	17/01/1917
Miscellaneous	Appendix V Company Orders by Lieut HG. Harcourt Commanding 184 Coy M.G.C.	18/01/1917	18/01/1917
Miscellaneous	Appendix 6 Programme of Traning 184 Company Machine Gun Corps.	22/01/1917	22/01/1917
Miscellaneous	Appendix 7 Programme of Traning 184 Company Machine Gun Corps.	29/01/1917	29/01/1917
Heading	War Diary of The 184 Company Machine Gun Corps From 1/2/17 To 28/2/17 Volume 9		
War Diary	Maison Ponthieu	01/02/1917	04/02/1917
War Diary	Argenvillers (Abbeville 14)	04/02/1917	05/02/1917
War Diary	St. Firmin	05/02/1917	07/02/1917
War Diary	Map Lens II Abbeville 14 1:100,000	08/02/1917	08/02/1917
War Diary	St. Firmin	09/02/1917	09/02/1917
War Diary	Buingy	10/02/1917	11/02/1917
War Diary	Moufflers (Lens. II)	11/02/1917	11/02/1917
War Diary	Moufflers	12/02/1917	13/02/1917
War Diary	Weincourt	13/02/1917	14/02/1917
War Diary	Trenche Refs Rosiers (Comb)1:40,000	14/02/1917	18/02/1917
War Diary	In The Line Deniecourt Sector	18/02/1917	28/02/1917
Miscellaneous	Appendix I	03/02/1917	03/02/1917
Miscellaneous	Appendix II Company Orders by Lieut S.S. Worth Commanding 184 Coy M.G.C.	09/02/1917	09/02/1917
Miscellaneous	Appendix III Company Orders by Lieut S.S. Worth Comdg 184 Company Coy M.G.C.	10/02/1917	10/02/1917
Heading	War Diary Of 184 Company, Machine Gun Corps For Period 1st March 1917 To 31st March 1917. Volume X		
War Diary	Deniecourt	01/03/1917	15/03/1917
War Diary	Harbonnieres	15/03/1917	17/03/1917
War Diary	Herleville	19/03/1917	25/03/1917

War Diary	Pertain	25/03/1917	28/03/1917
War Diary	Athies	28/03/1917	30/03/1917
War Diary	Caulaincourt	30/03/1917	31/03/1917
Heading	War Diary of 184th Company,Machine Gun Corps. From April 1st, 1917 To April 30th, 1917. Volume XI		
War Diary	Caulaincourt	01/04/1917	02/04/1917
War Diary	Vermand	03/04/1917	10/04/1917
War Diary	Maraucourt	11/04/1917	12/04/1917
War Diary	Hombleux	13/04/1917	19/04/1917
War Diary	Foreste	20/04/1917	20/04/1917
War Diary	(Raily Embt) X.11.D.2.0	21/04/1917	24/04/1917
War Diary	Railway Embankment	25/04/1917	30/04/1917
Miscellaneous	Appendix I		
Miscellaneous	Appendix II		
Miscellaneous	Appendix III Not to Re Taken in to Action	06/04/1917	06/04/1917
Map	Map A		
Operation(al) Order(s)	Q.N.A Operation Order No. 1	08/04/1917	08/04/1917
Miscellaneous	Appendix V Lt. Parsons O.C Q.N.A	08/04/1917	08/04/1917
Miscellaneous	Appendix VI	08/04/1917	08/04/1917
Miscellaneous	Appendix VII To O.C. 3 Q.N.Q.	08/04/1917	08/04/1917
Operation(al) Order(s)	Q.N.A. Operation Order No. 4	18/04/1917	18/04/1917
Operation(al) Order(s)	184 M.G. Coys Operation Order No. 5	18/04/1917	18/04/1917
Operation(al) Order(s)	Operation Order No. 6 184 Coy M.G. Corps	18/04/1917	18/04/1917
Operation(al) Order(s)	184 Coy M.G. Corps Operation Order No. 7	19/04/1917	19/04/1917
Map	Map B.		
Miscellaneous	Appendix XII	24/04/1917	24/04/1917
Map	Map C		
Operation(al) Order(s)	Operation Order No. 8	24/04/1917	24/04/1917
Miscellaneous	Appendix XIV G.N.Q. Operation Orders No 8	25/04/1917	25/04/1917
Operation(al) Order(s)	Q.N.A. Operation Order No. 11	27/04/1917	27/04/1917
Miscellaneous	Ref Operation Order No. 10	27/04/1917	27/04/1917
Miscellaneous	Reference Q.N.A. Operation Order No. 11	28/04/1917	28/04/1917
Miscellaneous	Appendix XVI Q.N.A. Operation Orders No 11	28/04/1917	28/04/1917
War Diary	War Diary Volume XII Of 184th Company, Machine Gun Corps For Period May 1st To May 31st 1917		
War Diary	Railway Embankment X 11 D 20 Sheet 66 D.S.E. Near	01/05/1917	01/05/1917
War Diary	Foreste	02/05/1917	13/05/1917
War Diary	Manicourt	14/05/1917	17/05/1917
War Diary	Talmas	18/05/1917	20/05/1917
War Diary	Ransart	21/05/1917	23/05/1917
War Diary	Duisans	24/05/1917	31/05/1917
War Diary	N10 G77	31/05/1917	31/05/1917
Map	Appendix A		
Miscellaneous	Appendix 1		
Operation(al) Order(s)	Operation Order No. 14 184 Coy M.G. Corps	12/05/1917	12/05/1917
Miscellaneous	Operation Order No. 14 184 Coy M.G. Corps	12/05/1917	12/05/1917
Operation(al) Order(s)	Operation Order No. 15 184 Coy M.G. Corps	14/05/1917	14/05/1917
Operation(al) Order(s)	Operation Order No. 16 184 Coy M.G. Corps	16/08/1917	16/08/1917
Miscellaneous	Operation Order No. 16 184 Coy M.G. Corps	20/08/1917	20/08/1917
Operation(al) Order(s)	Operation Order No. 17 184 Coy M.G. Corps	22/05/1917	22/05/1917
Operation(al) Order(s)	Order No. 18	23/05/1917	23/05/1917
Miscellaneous	Operation Order No. 18 184 Coy M.G. Corps	30/08/1917	30/08/1917
Miscellaneous	Attachment No.4		
Heading	War Diary of 184th Company, Machine Gun Corps From June 1st, June 30th,1917. (Volume XIII)		
War Diary	Arras Gambrai Road Sector	01/06/1917	12/06/1917

War Diary	Berneville	13/06/1917	20/06/1917
War Diary	Frohen Le Grand	23/06/1917	27/06/1917
War Diary	Vaulx	27/06/1917	30/06/1917
Operation(al) Order(s)	Operation Order No. 19 App I	04/06/1917	04/06/1917
Operation(al) Order(s)	Operation Order No. 20	09/06/1917	09/06/1917
Operation(al) Order(s)	Operation Order No. 21 184 Coy M.G. Corps	10/06/1917	10/06/1917
Miscellaneous	Appendix 4.		
Miscellaneous	Amendment To Operation Order No. 24	22/06/1917	22/06/1917
Miscellaneous	184 Coy M.G. Corps Operation Order No. 24	21/06/1917	21/06/1917
Operation(al) Order(s)	Operation Order No. 25	26/06/1917	26/06/1917
Miscellaneous	184 Company M.G Corps.		
Heading	War Diary of 184 Company, Machine Gun Corps From 1st July 1917 To 31st July 1917 Volume XIV		
War Diary	Vaulx	01/07/1917	31/07/1917
Miscellaneous	Special Order	07/07/1917	07/07/1917
Miscellaneous	Barrage Demonstration	07/07/1917	07/07/1917
Map	Map		
Operation(al) Order(s)	Operation Order No. 21	20/07/1917	20/07/1917
Miscellaneous	?		
Operation(al) Order(s)	184 M.G. Company Operation Order No. 28	24/07/1917	24/07/1917
Heading	War Diary of 184 Company, Machine Gun Corps From 1st August, 1917 To 31st August, 1917 Volume XV		
War Diary	Buysscheure	01/08/1917	24/08/1917
War Diary	Brandhoek	25/08/1917	29/08/1917
Operation(al) Order(s)	Operation Order No. 30	08/08/1917	08/08/1917
Miscellaneous	M.G. Barrage Time Table		
Miscellaneous	Appendix 3		
Operation(al) Order(s)	184th Brigade Order No. 1000	31/07/1917	31/07/1917
Miscellaneous	General Notes		
Miscellaneous	184th Infantry Brigade Instructions		
Operation(al) Order(s)	184 M.G. Corps Operation Order No. 31	14/08/1917	14/08/1917
Miscellaneous	Appendix III 184 Machine Gun Company Operation Order No	17/08/1917	17/08/1917
Operation(al) Order(s)	184 M.G. Coys Operation Order No. 33	17/08/1917	17/08/1917
Miscellaneous	Appendix V Frezenberg 1/10.000	29/08/1917	29/08/1917
Operation(al) Order(s)	Operation Order No. 34	20/08/1917	20/08/1917
Miscellaneous	Appendix VI Report and action by 184 M G Coy During Operation from 22-8-17. 29.8.17.	22/08/1917	22/08/1917
Operation(al) Order(s)	184 M.G. Coys Operation Order No. 35	24/08/1917	24/08/1917
Miscellaneous	Operation Order No. 35	24/08/1917	24/08/1917
Heading	War Diary of 184th Company, Machine Gun Corps From 1st Sept, 1917 To 30th Sept, 1917 Volume XVI		
War Diary	Wieltje Sector	30/08/1917	04/09/1917
War Diary	Brandhoek G 5c 64	04/09/1917	10/09/1917
War Diary	Wieltje Sector	11/09/1917	11/09/1917
War Diary	Watou A63	17/09/1917	17/09/1917
War Diary	Wormhoudt	17/09/1917	18/09/1917
War Diary	Gouves	19/08/1917	19/08/1917
War Diary	St Nicholas	24/08/1917	30/08/1917
Operation(al) Order(s)	Operation Order No. 37 184 Coy M.G. Corps	04/09/1917	04/09/1917
Miscellaneous	Operation Order No. 37	04/09/1917	04/09/1917
Operation(al) Order(s)	Operation Order No. 38 184 Coy M.G. Corps	07/09/1917	07/09/1917
Miscellaneous	Operation Order No. 38	07/09/1917	07/09/1917
Operation(al) Order(s)	Operation Order No. 39 Terror	09/09/1917	09/09/1917
Miscellaneous	Messages And Signals		
Diagram etc	Diagram		

Operation(al) Order(s)	Operation Order No. 40	12/09/1917	12/09/1917
Miscellaneous	Operation Order No. 40	12/09/1917	12/09/1917
Miscellaneous	Handing Over		
Operation(al) Order(s)	Operation Order No. 41	14/09/1917	14/09/1917
Miscellaneous	Operation Order No. 41	14/09/1917	14/09/1917
Operation(al) Order(s)	184 M.G. Coy Operation Order No. 42	16/09/1917	16/09/1917
Operation(al) Order(s)	184 M.G. Coy Operation Order No. 43	18/09/1917	18/09/1917
Operation(al) Order(s)	Operation Order No. 44 184 Coy M.G. Corps	23/09/1917	23/09/1917
Heading	War Diary of The 184 Company M.G. Corps From 1st October 1917 To 30th October 1917 Volume 17		
War Diary	St Nicholas	01/10/1917	03/10/1917
War Diary	Greenland Hill Sector	04/10/1917	28/10/1917
War Diary	Arras	28/10/1917	30/10/1917
Operation(al) Order(s)	Operation Order No. 45 184 Company M.G. Corps	03/10/1917	03/10/1917
Operation(al) Order(s)	Operation Order No. 47	09/10/1917	09/10/1917
Operation(al) Order(s)	Operation Order no 48	15/10/1917	15/10/1917
Operation(al) Order(s)	Operation Order No. 49	16/10/1917	16/10/1917
Operation(al) Order(s)	Operation Order No. 50	21/10/1917	21/10/1917
Operation(al) Order(s)	Operation Order No. 51 184 M.G. C.	26/10/1917	26/10/1917
Heading	War Diary Of 184th Company, Machine Gun Corps. From 1st. Nov To 30th. Nov. 1917. Volume XVIII		
War Diary	Arras	01/11/1917	21/11/1917
War Diary	Chemical Works Sector	22/11/1917	28/11/1917
War Diary	Arras	29/11/1917	30/11/1917
Operation(al) Order(s)	Operation Order No. 52 184 M.G. C.	09/11/1917	09/11/1917
Operation(al) Order(s)	Operation Order No. 53	27/11/1917	27/11/1917
Miscellaneous	Details		
Operation(al) Order(s)	Operation Order No. 54 184 M.C. Coy	29/11/1917	29/11/1917
Heading	War Diary of 184th Company, Machine Gun Corps From 1st Dec. To 31st. 1917. Vol. XIX		
War Diary	Bertincourt	01/12/1917	01/12/1917
War Diary	Fins	02/12/1917	02/12/1917
War Diary	Havrincourt	03/12/1917	03/12/1917
War Diary	Gonnelieu Sector	04/12/1917	11/12/1917
War Diary	Metz	12/12/1917	24/12/1917
War Diary	Suzanne	25/12/1917	31/12/1917
Heading	War Diary Of 184th Company, Machine Gun Corps From 1st. January 1918 To 31st. January 1918. Volume XX		
War Diary	Vrely	01/01/1918	07/01/1918
War Diary	Pargny	08/01/1917	09/01/1917
War Diary	Beuvois	10/01/1917	10/01/1917
War Diary	Fresnoy (sector)	11/01/1917	11/01/1917
War Diary	St Guentin	11/12/1918	11/12/1918
War Diary	Fresnoy	12/01/1917	26/01/1917
War Diary	Vaux	24/01/1917	31/01/1917
Heading	War Diary of 184th Company, Machine Gun Corps From 1st Feb. 1918 To 28th Feb. 1918 Volume XXI		
War Diary	In The Field	01/02/1918	19/02/1918
War Diary	Vaux	20/02/1918	28/02/1918

61ST DIVISION

184TH INFY BDE

184TH MACHINE GUN COY.

JUNE 1916-FEB 1918

Folio I

Army Form C. 2118. 61

Instructions regarding War Diaries and Intelligence Summaries are contained in F. S. Regs., Part II. and the Staff Manual respectively. Title Pages will be prepared in manuscript.

WAR DIARY OF 184 MACHINE GUN COMPANY

~~or~~

~~INTELLIGENCE SUMMARY~~

(Erase heading not required.)

Vol 1

Place	Date	Hour	Summary of Events and Information	Remarks and references to Appendices
Grantham.	16/6/16	7.30 AM	The Company entrained at the MILITARY DOCK. TIME TAKEN 18 MINUTES.	
"	16/6/16	8.45 AM	The Company proceeded to Southampton. where they Disentrained at 4.30 P.M.	
SOUTHAMPTON	16/6/16	8-30 P.M.	TUG CAME ALONGSIDE THE S.S. BELLEROPHON. WHICH HAD 4 Officers and 103. O.R. AND TRANSPORT ON BOARD	
"	16/6/16	9-30 P.M.	do do do do S.S. CESAREA. WHICH HAD 6. Officers and 39 O.R ON BOARD	
HAVRE	17.6.16.	4.45 A.M.	S.S. CESAREA arrived at HAVRE. after a rough crossing.	
"	"	8.30 AM.	Officers and men disembarked a	
"	"	10. A.M.	S.S. BELLEROPHON arrived. reported having seen Destroyer H.M.S. EDEN. CUT IN HALF	
"	17.6.16	1. P.M.	The Company formed up in column of Route. and marched through Havre to No 1 REST CAMP	
"	17.6.16	4. P.M.	" " ARRIVED AT No 1 REST CAMP. WHERE THEY WERE INSPECTED BY THE COMMANDANT OF THE CAMP	
"	18.6.16	7.30 AM.	G.S. WAGON AND PARTY. CONSISTING OF 2. OFFICERS AND 8 O.R. PROCEEDED TO BASE SUPPLY HANGARS AT HAVRE AND DREW STORES TO COMPLETE THE UNIT.	
"	18.6.16	10.30 P.M.	THE COMPANY PARADED AND MARCHED IN COLUMN OF ROUTE TO THE RUE des. MARCHANDISES. WHERE THEY ENTRAINED AT POINT ~~[illegible]~~ 3. RATIONS WERE DRAWN FOR TWO DAYS AT POINT IV. CONSIDERABLE DIFFICULTY WAS EXPERIENCED IN ENTRAINING THE MULES.	
"	19.6.16	3. A.M.	THE TRAIN MOVED OFF. ~~AT~~ A. GOOD JOURNEY WAS MADE TO RAILHEAD LA GORGUE	
LA GORGUE	20.6.16	2. A.M.	THE TRAIN ARRIVED AT LA GORGUE. THE COMPANY AND TRANSPORT, WERE THEN ~~DISEMBARKED~~ DISENTRAINED AND PROCEEDED UNDER A GUIDE TO LESTREM. WHERE BILLETS WERE FOUND FOR OFFICERS AND MEN	

184 MACHINE GUN COMPANY

FOLIO II

Army Form C. 2118.

WAR DIARY

of

~~INTELLIGENCE SUMMARY~~

(Erase heading not required.)

Instructions regarding War Diaries and Intelligence Summaries are contained in F. S. Regs., Part II. and the Staff Manual respectively. Title Pages will be prepared in manuscript.

Place	Date	Hour	Summary of Events and Information	Remarks and references to Appendices
LESTREM	20-6-16	10.A.M.	THE C.O. AND 2ND IN COMMAND AT DIVISIONAL HDQUARTERS. BRIG. GENERAL MACKENZIE WAS INTERVIEWED AND INFORMATION OBTAINED.	
do	21-6-16	10 A.M.	THE COMPANY WAS INSPECTED BY G.O.C. DIVISION. INSPECTION PROVED SATISFACTORY.	
do	22-6-16	5. P.M.	THE COMPANY VACATED BILLETS. AND MARCHED TO LAVENTIE. WHERE BILLETS WERE OCCUPIED BELONGING TO 106. M.G. COY COMMANDED BY. CAPT MERISON. ON. REPORTING TO THE BRIGADIER. SIR COLIN. MACKENZIE. ORDERS WERE GIVEN. THAT THE COMPANY WERE TO BE ATTACHED TO NO 106 M.G. COY FOR INSTRUCTION OUR TRANSPORT WAS PACKED ALONGSIDE THE TRANSPORT OF NO 106 M.G. COY. AND GUARDS WERE MOUNTED OVER THE LIMBERS CONSIDERABLE DIFFICULTY WAS EXPERIENCED IN FIND ROOM FOR THE DRIVERS	
LAVENTIE	23-6-16	10. A.M.	GUIDES ARRIVED FROM 106 M.G. COY. AND COMPANY WENT INTO THE TRENCHES BY. SECTIONS. FOR 36 HOURS INSTRUCTION. THE DISPOSITION OF THE COMPANY WAS AS. FOLLOWS. NO I SECTION HELD THE RIGHT SECTOR FRONT NO IV SECTION " " RIGHT SECTOR REAR POSTS NO II SECTION " " LEFT SECTOR FRONT. NO III SECTION " " " " REAR POSTS.	
do	24-6-16		OFFICERS. N.C.O.s AND MEN WERE INSTRUCTED IN TRENCH WARFARE. THE C.O. AND SECTION COMMANDERS. VISITED THE FRONT LINE, AND WERE SHEWN THE VARIOUS BATTLE EMPLACEMENTS BY THE O.C. NO 106 M.G. COY. SECTION OFFICERS NO 106 M.G. COY MADE A DEMONSTRATION TO THE SECTIONS OF NO 184 M.G. COY ATTACHED TO THEM, OF INDIRECT FIRE. SOME OF THE I.F.P EMPLACEMENTS WERE DIFFICULT TO FIRE FROM OWING TO THE PRESENCE OF CORDITE GAS.	

2449 Wt. W14957/M90 750,000 1/16 J.B.C. & A. Forms/C.2118/12.

184 MACHINE GUN COMPANY

Folio III

Army Form C. 2118.

Instructions regarding War Diaries and Intelligence Summaries are contained in F. S. Regs., Part II. and the Staff Manual respectively. Title Pages will be prepared in manuscript.

WAR DIARY

~~or~~

~~INTELLIGENCE SUMMARY~~

(Erase heading not required.)

Place	Date	Hour	Summary of Events and Information	Remarks and references to Appendices
LAVENTIE	25/6/16		IN THE MORNING FURTHER INSTRUCTION WAS GIVEN. TO THE COMPANY	
			THE .O.C. 184 M.G. COY HAD A MEETING WITH THE COLONEL COMMANDING THE LEFT GROUP, AND AN EXAMINATION WAS MADE, OF THE GAPS AND ENEMY'S WIRE, FROM VARIOUS POSITIONS	
		2 P.M.	THE COMPANY CAME OUT OF THE TRENCHES TO FETCH GUNS	
		6. P.M.	THE COMPANY RETURNED TO THE TRENCHES AND WERE PLACED IN VARIOUS POSITIONS	
			INDIRECT FIRE WAS AGAIN DEMONSTRATED. AND OUR GUNS WERE USED	
	26/6/15		106 M.G. COY WERE RELIEVED BY US AT 12 NOON AND REMAINED THE NIGHT IN LAVENTIE	
			INDIRECT FIRE WAS DELIVERED FROM A NEW I.F.P AT N.4 B.4.3. NEAR JOCKS POST	
			AT NO1 I.F.P. GUN TEAM WERE UNABLE TO FIRE, OWING TO ENEMY SNIPERS, BELIEVED TO BE BEHIND OUR LINES.	
			NOS 1 AND 2 GAPS WERE STRENGTHENED.	
	27/6/16		INDIRECT FIRE WAS DELIVERED FROM NO 4A I.F.P. ON N15. A. 4.5. THIS IS BELIEVED TO BE A FORT.	
			do do WAS ALSO DELIVERED NO 4A I.F.P. ON POSITION N19. B.3.9.9. THIS IS BELIEVED TO BE A BRIDGE.	
			THE GAPS IN ENEMY'S WIRE AT POINTS. F.2A AND F2B WERE KEPT OPEN. BY INTERMITTENT BURSTS OF FIRE FROM BAY 48	
			OPEN EMPLACEMENT AT BAY 28 WAS REPACKED	
	28/6/16		THE GAP AT F.6. WAS KEPT OPEN BY VICKERS GUN FIRING FROM BAY 28.	
			THE GAPS AT F2A AND F2B WERE KEPT OPEN FROM DUSK UNTIL MIDNIGHT.	
			AT 12.10 AM. THE RAIDS BY OUR TROOPS WERE COVERED BY CROSS FIRE AND OVERHEAD FIRE. ~~FROM THE FRONT LINE~~. ON TO THE ENEMYS COMMUNICATION TRENCHES BEHIND F2B.	
			GUNS WERE FIRED FRONT LINE FROM THE FOLLOWING POSITIONS. N.8.D.1½.8. 14A.5.9. 14A.1.2. N13.D.4.0.	
			THESE GUNS CEASED FIRE AT 1.10 A.M.	
			A NEW I.F.P. EMPLACEMENT WAS PUT UP NEAR JOCKS POST. AND PROVED VERY SATISFACTORY IN THE SCHEME	

2449 Wt. W14957/M90 750,000 1/16 J.B.C. & A. Forms/C.2118/12.

184 Machine Gun Company

Folio IV

Army Form C. 2118.

Instructions regarding War Diaries and Intelligence Summaries are contained in F. S. Regs., Part II. and the Staff Manual respectively. Title Pages will be prepared in manuscript.

WAR DIARY

or

~~INTELLIGENCE SUMMARY~~

(Erase heading not required.)

Place	Date	Hour	Summary of Events and Information	Remarks and references to Appendices
LAVENTIE	29/6/16		A RAID WAS CARRIED OUT BY THE 3/5TH OXFORD/BUCKS BATTALION SUPPORTED BY THE FIRE OF VICKERS AND LEWIS MACHINE GUNS.	
			THE GAPS AT F2A AND F2B. WERE FIRED AT FROM DUSK UNTIL MIDNIGHT.	
		12-10.A.M.	AN ATTACK WAS LAUNCHED BY THE 3/5TH OXFORD/BUCKS WHO WERE TO ENDEAVOUR TO CAPTURE 11 PRISONERS. AND DESTROY ENEMY MINE SHAFTS AND MACHINE GUNS	
			SMOKE BOMBS WERE TO BE THROWN. TO DECEIVE THE ENEMY INTO BELIEVING THAT GAS WAS BEING USED.	
			THE FOLLOWING SIGNALS WERE BEING USED :-	
			1 RED ROCKET ATTACK WAS OVER.	
			BOUQUET OF RED ROCKETS BEFORE 12-10 A.M. ATTACK WAS OFF.	
			" " " " AFTER 12-10 A.M INFANTRY UNABLE TO PROCEED.	
			VICKERS GUNS. SUPPORTED INFANTRY BY CROSS FIRE AND OVERHEAD FIRE. ON THE ENEMYS COMMUNICATION TRENCHES BEHIND F2B.	
			GUNS WERE FIRE FROM FRONT LINE.	
			ONE GUN FIRE FROM N8.D.1½.8.	
			" " " " 14.A.5.9	
			" " " " 14.A.1.2.	
			" " " " N13.D.½.1½.	
			GUNS FIRING IN FRONT LINE. CEASED FIRE AT 1.10. A.M.	
			AN AVERAGE OF 1500 ROUND WERE FIRED.	
			A BARRAGE OF FIRE WAS PLACED IN THE AREA OF THE COMMUNICATION TRENCHES IN REAR OF THE POSITION ATTACKED.	
			THESE GUNS KEPT UP A STEADY FIRE FROM 12-10 A.M. TO 2.A.M.	
			THE INFANTRY ADVANCED UP TO ENEMY'S WIRE. WHICH THEY WERE UNABLE TO PENETRATE, OWING TO ENEMY M.G. BEING PLACED IN A POSITION COVERING THE GAPS AT F.2.A AND F2B.	
			INFANTRY RETIRED LEAVING. 1 OFFICER KILLED. 8 MEN KILLED. AND BROUGHT BACK 1 OFFICER AND 25 MEN WOUNDED.	
	30/6/16		VICKERS GUNS MOUNTED ON BAY 46 AND BAY 28. FIRED RAPID BURSTS AT GERMAN PARAPET AT STATED INTERVALS UP TILL 4·30 P.M.	
			SMOKE BOMBS WERE AGAIN USED.	
			INDIRECT FIRE WAS BROUGHT TO BEAR ON DISTILLERY. NEAR POINT N19.3.5.1.	
			VICKERS GUNS ALSO FIRED AT HEAD OF ENEMY'S COMMUNICATION TRENCH N.19.A.5.0.	
			THESE POSITIONS WERE TAKEN FROM AERIAL PHOTOGRAPHS.	
			ENEMY'S SEARCH LIGHTS. WERE SEEN, APPARENTLY GUIDING THE MOVEMENTS OF AN AEROPLANE.	
			THE NOISE OF THE PROPELLER WAS HEARD AT M.G. EMPLACEMENTS. IN THE LEFT SECTOR. FRONT LINE	

2449 Wt. W14957/M90 750,000 1/16 J.B.C. & A. Forms/C.2118/12.

61

SECRET

Vol ~~III~~ 2

CONFIDENTIAL.

W A R D I A R Y.

of the

184th Machine Gun Company.

from July 1st to July 31st 1916 .

VOLUME 3.

Army Form C. 2118.

Instructions regarding War Diaries and Intelligence Summaries are contained in F. S. Regs., Part II. and the Staff Manual respectively. Title Pages will be prepared in manuscript.

WAR DIARY
or
INTELLIGENCE SUMMARY
(Erase heading not required.)

Place	Date	Hour	Summary of Events and Information	Remarks and references to Appendices
~~RICHEBOURG ST VAAST~~ LAVENTIE	JULY 1ST	10 P.M. 2.45 A.M.	VICKERS FIRED INDIRECT ON N19 B 39.9. FORT NISAYS. AREA AROUND RUE D'ENFER AND DISTILLERY. AND C.T. NEAR N.19 A 5.0. AN AVERAGE OF 4000 ROUNDS PER GUN WAS EXPENDED ENEMY STILL CONTINUES TO BRING M.G. FIRE TO BEAR ON ROADS BY JOCKS POST. ROANTIN AVE. AND ALSO ACROSS THE MASSELOT POST SECTOR LOOPHOLE AT No 4A WAS ALTERED AND THE WHOLE STRENGTHENED AN EMPLACEMENT WAS BUILT IN THE BOUGHS OF A TREE BEHIND ARTILLERY OBSERVATION POST IN THE RUE TILLELOY. A ROPE PAINTED GREEN, AND TACKLE WAS ALSO BEEN ERECTED. AT THIS POSITION.	Eam.
	JULY 2ND	12 M.N. 4 A.M.	VICKERS GUNS FIRED AT GAP POINT 36 AND F.6. SUCCESSFULLY BETWEEN 12 MIDNIGHT AND 4 A.M.	
		9 P.M. 10 P.M.	INDIRECT FIRE WAS BROUGHT TO BEAR ON RUE D'ENFER. TRACK FROM RUE DEBAVEL TO AUBERS WAS SEARCHED. HOSTILE M.G.s VERY ACTIVE ON RIGHT. CONTINUALLY SWEEPING THE PARAPET. OUR ARTILLERY FIRED AT GAPS F29. F28. ENEMY FIRED OFF A BOUQUET OF GREEN FLARES. THIS WAS A SIGNAL FOR RETALIATION OF SHRAPNEL	
		12 NOON	O.C. 183 M.G. COY MADE A TOUR OF THE TRENCHES AND POSTS WITH O.C. 184 M.G. COY. PRIOR TO RELIEVING THIS COY 3-7-16.	Eam.
	JULY 3RD		GUNS FIRED FROM NEW GUN POSITION AT SUDDEN DEATH TREE ON THE RUE TILLELOY. GUN WAS PLACED IN POSITION AT DAWN. WEATHER BEING MISTY NO TARGETS WERE AVAILABLE UNTIL 5 A.M. ENEMY'S FRONT LINE WAS ENFILADED. A LITTLE LATER PART OF ENEMY WAS SEEN COMING OUT OF RED TILE HOUSE. FIRE WAS BROUGHT TO BEAR ON THEM. HOSTILE PARTY DISPERSED. AND THERE IS GOOD REASON TO BELIEVE THAT ENEMY SUFFERED CASUALTIES FROM No 1. LEP. ON RUE PETRIE TO ASSIST IN MASKING GUN POSITION IN TREE RETALIATION TO ALL MACHINE GUN FIRE DURING THE LAST TWO DAYS HAS INCREASED.	
		4 P.M.	No 183 M.G. COY TOOK OVER OUR TRENCHES AND POSTS. CONSIDERABLE DELAY WAS CAUSED OWING TO O.C. 183 M.G. COY HAVING 6. GUNS IN FRONT LINE. COY MARCHED IN COLUMN OF ROUTE TO LESTREM. AND SETTLED DOWN IN THERE BILLETS VERY QUICKLY	Eam.

Instructions regarding War Diaries and Intelligence Summaries are contained in F. S. Regs., Part II. and the Staff Manual respectively. Title Pages will be prepared in manuscript.

WAR DIARY
or
INTELLIGENCE SUMMARY
(Erase heading not required.)

Army Form C. 2118.

Place	Date	Hour	Summary of Events and Information	Remarks and references to Appendices
LESTREM	JULY 4TH	10.30 A.M.	COY ATTENDED BATHS. 1/HALF PONT RIQUEL. HALF LA GORGUE	
		2.30 P.M.	GUNS + EQUIPMENT WERE INSPECTED. AND DEFICIENCES NOTED.	
		4.3. P.M.	COY WERE PAID 14 DAYS IN ADVANCE	Eaw.
	JULY 5TH	9.30 A.M.	TWO VICKERS GUNS WERE TAKEN TO BRIGADE ARMOURERS SHOP FOR REPAIRS.	
		10.30 A.M.	MEN WERE TRAINED IN INFANTRY DRILL AND SIGNALLING. 5 MEN REPORTED SICK. MEDICAL OFFICER ATTENDED NEXT MORNING. 9.A.M. 6.7.16.	Eaw.
	JULY 6TH	10 A.M.	COY TAKEN FOR ROUTE MARCH TO MERVILLE ARRIVING THERE AT 11 A.M. DIFFICULTY WAS EXPERIENCED IN GETTING MULES OVER BRIDGES.	
		11. A.M.	COY ARRIVED AT MERVILLE. COY WERE DISMISSED FOR 1 HOUR	
		3. P.M.	COY ARRIVED BACK AT BILLETTS AT LESTREM. 2 MEN REPORTED SICK WITH SCABIES. WERE TAKEN IN AN AMBULANCE TO LA GORGUE FOR TREATMENT	
		4. P.M.	ORDERS WERE RECEIVED FOR COY TO PROCEED TO VIELLE CHAPELLE.	
		6. P.M.	COMPANY WERE READY TO MOVE OFF. COMPANY HALTED AT VIELLE CHAPELLE. O.C. & 2ND IN COMMAND PROCEEDED TO 115 BDE HD QTRS. THE BDE MJR ORDERED 2ND COMMAND TO BRING COMPANY ON TO RICHEBOURG ST VAAST. ARRIVING THERE AT 8.40 P.M.	
		8.40 P.M.	NOS 1.2 + 3 SECTIONS WENT STRAIGHT INTO THE TRENCHES: NO 1 TAKING RIGHT SECTOR FRONT. NO 2 TAKING OVER LEFT SECTOR FRONT. NO 3. 2ND RES POST.	
RICHEBOURG ST VAAST	JULY 7TH	6. A.M.	RELIEF COMPLETED. DELAY WAS CAUSED OWING TO DIFFICULTY OF TRANSPORTING AMMUNITION IN FRONT LINE	Eaw.
		2.30 P.M.	O C + 2ND IN COMMAND MADE A TOUR OF THE TRENCHES. BREASTWORK OF FRONT LINE IS IN VERY BAD STATE OF REPAIR OWING TO RECENT BOMBARDMENTS. DISTRIBUTION OF GUNS AS FOLLOWS:- 5 GUNS FRONT LINE; 4 " 2ND RESERVE LINE; 4 " 3RD do.	
	JULY 9TH	10.30 – 12 MIDNIGHT	GUN FIRED INDIRECT FROM PORT ARTHUR 1.F.D OVER BAY S.41. GROUND ROUND HALPEGARBE ROAD 12.A.3.3. AND ENGINEERS DUMPING GROUND WAS SEARCHED. GUN AT S9.A.1.4. FIRED ON ENEMY'S FRONT LINE FROM S16.B.3 TO S.14 C.0.5. 1000 Rounds were FIRED. GUN AT FACTORY KEEP FIRED ON FRONT LINE FROM S16.C.5.8 TO S16.D.0.2.	Eaw.
		12 MIDNIGHT – DAWN	GUNS MOUNTED AT S10 B 9 4. FIRED DIRECT ON GAPS FROM S10 D 4.4 TO S11.A.2.2. 2000 ROUNDS WERE FIRED. ENEMY M.G.S. WERE VERY ACTIVE ON OUR EMPLACEMENTS AT PORT ARTHUR	Eaw.

2449 Wt. W14957/M90 750,000 1/16 J.B.C. & A. Forms/C.2118/12.

Army Form C. 2118.

Instructions regarding War Diaries and Intelligence Summaries are contained in F. S. Regs., Part II. and the Staff Manual respectively. Title Pages will be prepared in manuscript.

WAR DIARY
or
INTELLIGENCE SUMMARY
(Erase heading not required.)

Place	Date	Hour	Summary of Events and Information	Remarks and references to Appendices
RICHEBOURG ST. VAAST	9.4.16	10.30–11.30 P.M.	GUN AT FACTORY KEEP FIRED ON ENEMYS FRONT LINE FROM S.16.C.10.0. 1000 ROUNDS WERE FIRED.	
		10–11.30 P.M.	GUN AT PORT ARTHUR FIRED ON VILLAGE OF HALPEGARBE.	
		12.30–2.30 A.M.	GUN AT WINDY CORNER FIRED ON C.T. AT S.16.B.0.4 to S.11.C.6.0	
		12 Midnight – 2 A.M.	2 GUNS IN RIGHT SUB SECTOR KEPT GAP OPEN AT A.3.	
		10–11.30 P.M. 1.30–3.30 A.M.	1 GUN AT BAY S11.1. FIRED AT GAP A.2. 450 ROUNDS WERE FIRED	
			ENEMY M.G.S VERY ACTIVE NEAR BAY S11.1	
		11.50 P.M.	HOSTILE AEROPLANE PASSED OVER PORT ARTHUR.	Sam:
	10.4.16	Dusk–Dawn	GAP AT A5 WAS KEPT OPEN. ALSO GAP AT A3. 1950 ROUNDS WERE FIRED	
			GAP AT A2 WAS KEPT OPEN BY GUN S11.1.	
		12–10 A.M.	GUN AT S.16.C.3.4. FIRED ON HOSTILE WORKING PARTY HEARD NEAR THIS GUN POSITION. CRIES WERE HEARD, WORKING PARTY DISPERSED.	
			AT FACTORY KEEP I.F.P. SWEPT ENEMYS C.T'S + ROADS S.16.C.10.0 2250 ROUNDS WERE FIRED.	
			WINDY I.F.P. S.9.A.1.4. SEARCHED ENEMYS C.T.S FROM S.16.C.0.3 TO S.11.C.6.0. THIS GUN WAS TEMPORARY OUT OF ACTION OWING TO PROLONGED STOPPAGE.	
			ENEMY SHELLED PORT ARTHUR I.F.P WITH SHRAPNEL M.G.S WERE ALSO VERY ACTIVE IN THIS SECTOR AND AREA ROUND WINDY CORNER.	
			ENEMY SNIPING POST HALF RIGHT FROM No 1 POSITION. SNIPER WAS SILENCED	
		11.30 P.M.	ENEMY AEROPLANE WAS HEARD OVER WINDY POST AND SEEN TO DROP A GREEN LIGHT.	Sam:
			GUN EMPLACEMENT AT S11.1. REBUILT. FRONT OF B.E. No1. CLEARED OF RUBBISH. BAY 40 IMPROVED AND BUILT UP WITH SAND BAGS.	
	July 11th	Dusk–12.30 A.M.	GAPS IN ENEMYS WIRE AT A.2. 3. + 5. KEPT OPEN BY DIRECT FIRE. FIRE WAS SUSPENDED AT 12.30 FOR ONE OF OUR WORKING PARTIES TO GO OUT.	
			ORCHARD POST GUN. SWEPT C.T. FROM A3. TO LA BASSEE ROAD. FRONT OF BOIS du BIEZ SEARCHED INCESSANTLY DURING THE NIGHT.	
			HOSTILE C.T. S.16.B.4.1. SEARCHED FROM I.F.P. S.9.A.2.4. ALSO RUE de BOIS EACH SIDE OF DISTILLERY FROM S.11.C.5.3. TO S.11.B.1.0.	
			EDWARDS POST GUN FIRED ON GIRLISH LAUGHTER S11.A.9.6. 3000 RDS WERE FIRED BY ALL THESE GUNS.	
		10–10.30 P.M.	PORT ARTHUR SHELLED WITH SHRAPNEL. CONSIDERABLE M.G. FIRE ALSO BROUGHT TO BEAR ON THIS POST.	Sam:
		11.45 P.M.	AEROPLANE HEARD OVER LANSDOWNE POST. WAS SEEN TO DROP GREEN LIGHT	
			NEW GUN EMPLACEMENT BUILT ON FACTORY.	

2449 Wt. W14957/M90 750,000 1/16 J.B.C. & A. Forms/C.2118/12.

Army Form C. 2118.

Instructions regarding War Diaries and Intelligence Summaries are contained in F. S. Regs., Part II. and the Staff Manual respectively. Title Pages will be prepared in manuscript.

WAR DIARY
or
INTELLIGENCE SUMMARY

(Erase heading not required.)

Place	Date	Hour	Summary of Events and Information	Remarks and references to Appendices
Richebourg St Vaast	July 12th	9-10-30 PM.	From Orchard Post I.F.P. heavy I.F. brought to bear host C.T. between Gap A3 and La Bassee Road	
			Lansdowne Post Gun. Traversed road in front of Bois de Biez.	
			Covered Post searched La Bassee Road up to Distillery	
			Windy Corner Gun traversed C.T. at S16	
			Factory Keep. Fire was brought to bear on bend in Road n.e. Ferme Toulette	
			Cats Post I.F.P. searched buildings at Ligny le Petit.	
			Edwards Post fired on enemy stronghold at Girlish Laughter.	
			Guns in front line kept up an intermittent fire on gaps in enemys wire.	
			Heavy retaliation fbn M.G. on our left sector.	
			Covered way emplacements improved.	S.Cam
	July 13th		Guns in front line fired on enemys wire	
			Indirect fire was brought to bear on the following hostile positions:-	
			Bois de Biez. Buildings at Ligny le Petit. Hostile C.T. at S16 + earthwork at S11.A.9.6.	
			A very good M.G.E. constructed at Chocolate.	
			Sector cards made for I.F.P.	S.Cam.
	July 14th	11 P.M.	Raid was made by the 4th Royal Berks. Owing to heavy shell + M.G. fire only a few men reached the parapet. No prisoners were taken.	
			Vickers supported this raid. By placing heavy barrage on roads + C.Ts. between S.W. of Bois de Biez to La Tourelle Cross Roads	
			" in front line supported the advance by firing direct on C.Ts. on either flank. 4000 Rds per Gun was expended	
			We were informed that M.G. fire was a valuable assistance to raiders.	S.Cam.
	July 15th	9-30-11-30 P.M.	6 Guns fired indirect on following hostile positions:-	
			Front of Bois de Biez. Cross Roads at Ligny le Petit + Ferme du Bois. La Bassee Road from La Tourelle to Distillery and hostile earthwork at S11.A.9.6.	
			Gaps in front line kept open gaps in enemy's wire.	S.Cam.

2449 Wt. W14957/M90 750,000 1/16 J.B.C. & A. Forms/C.2118/12.

Instructions regarding War Diaries and Intelligence Summaries are contained in F. S. Regs., Part II. and the Staff Manual respectively. Title Pages will be prepared in manuscript.

WAR DIARY
or
INTELLIGENCE SUMMARY
(Erase heading not required.)

Army Form C. 2118.

Place	Date	Hour	Summary of Events and Information	Remarks and references to Appendices
Richebourg St Vaast	July 6th	12 noon 3 PM	Coy was relieved by 114 M.G. Coy Commanded by Capt Hall.	
		4.30 PM	Transport was ready to move off.	
			Coy proceeded to LES HUIT MAISONS where billets for the night were to have been taken over.	
			arriving here we found that incoming Engineers had taken possession.	
			Coy proceeded towards LAVENTIE	
		5.30 PM	a Cycle orderly handed a message TO O.C. That we were to take over Left Position of FAUQUISSART SECTION. and have our guns in position by 8. P.M.	
			Coy arrived at LAVENTIE at 4. P.M.	
			Guns were placed in the following Positions:-	
			2 Guns in Front Line 1 AT A.1. POST 1 at Flank Post. 2 Guns at TOCKS POST.	Sam.
	July 7th		An attack on German Front Line was arranged opposite BOND ST – SUTHERLAND AVE.	
			The following Regts were to take part:-	
			4th Royal BERKS on the RIGHT 2ND BUCKS ON THE LEFT. 4th OXFORDS & 5 GLOSTERS to be general Reserve.	
			advance to be made in four waves by each REGT Concerned.	
			M.G.s in 1.F.Ps. round TOCKS POST were to direct a heavy Barrage on area in rear of Positions attacked.	
			Two Guns to follow behind 4th Wave of Infantry.	Sam
	July 18th		Guns fired indirect at Road used by 16TH BAVARIAN REGT	
			No 1 GUN FORMED BARRAGE between N 16. B.9.3 and Park N15. C.9.5	
			2 " " " N 14 D 8.5 & PATH N 15 C 3.1.	
			3. Searched Wood & C.T. at N 15. C.9.3.	
			4. Traversed Road at North End AT N 14 B.	
			5. Searched Bottom of Road at N 14 B.	
			6. fired at Stronghold at ROAD BEND N 14. B. 6. 1.	Sam
			Gun Emplacements in Front Line & 1.F.Ps were Strengthened	

2449 Wt. W14957/M90 750,000 1/16 J.B.C. & A. Forms/C.2118/12.

Instructions regarding War Diaries and Intelligence Summaries are contained in F. S. Regs., Part II. and the Staff Manual respectively. Title Pages will be prepared in manuscript.

WAR DIARY
or
INTELLIGENCE SUMMARY

(Erase heading not required.)

Army Form C. 2118.

Place	Date	Hour	Summary of Events and Information	Remarks and references to Appendices
Laventie	July 19th	Dusk – Dawn	Guns in Front Line fired at Enemy's wire. Guns in New 1.F.Ps at Jocks Post fired a few Rounds at [illegible] emplacement	
	July 20th		Guns were placed in Front Line at the following Positions to support ~~Enemy~~ Batt's Attack. 4 Guns to support advance of Bucks 4 " " " " Berks 1 " in Reserve held by Bucks 1 " " " " Berks to repel Hostile Counter attack in event of Raid failing 6 Guns placed in 1.F.Ps at Jocks Post. 6 P.M. Heavy Barrage of Fire was directed on Hostile C.Ts fire was kept up until 11 P.M. Information was received that attack was a failure. Our Front Line was heavily shelled by the Enemy between 11 AM & 6 P.M. doing Great Damage to our Parapets. On application for Reinforcements 2 Sgts + 6 Men were Dispatched from H.Q. Section. Only two Gun teams were sent over owing to other two teams being out of action. We brought all our Guns out of action 3 being struck by [illegible] Bullets & Completely Disabled Our Casualties were: 1 Officer 2/Lt [illegible] severely wounded 16 O.Rs wounded.	[illegible]
	July 21st	12 MN – Dawn	Guns in Front Line fired at Enemy's Parapet. " in 1.F.Ps at Jocks Post formed a Barrage of Roads at N.21.A.9.8½.	[illegible]
	July 22	12 MN – Dawn	Guns in Front Line fired at Enemy's Wire. " " Jocks Post formed Barrage on Road at N.21.A.9.8½.	[illegible]

2449 Wt. W14957/M90 750,000 1/16 J.B.C. & A. Forms/C.2118/12.

Army Form C. 2118.

Instructions regarding War Diaries and Intelligence Summaries are contained in F. S. Regs., Part II. and the Staff Manual respectively. Title Pages will be prepared in manuscript.

WAR DIARY
or
INTELLIGENCE SUMMARY
(Erase heading not required.)

Place	Date	Hour	Summary of Events and Information	Remarks and references to Appendices
Laventie	July 23		Guns in Front Line fired at Gaps in Enemy's Wire " also enfiladed SUGAR LOAF SALIENT From Bond St. to Devon Ave. I.F. brought to bear from JOCKS POST I.F.P. between N21 A 9 4 and C.T. N21 A 5 4½. RHONDA SAP was also searched. Hostile M.G.s replied to our fire at Jocks Post.	[illegible]
LE DRUMEZ	July 24		This Coy relieved No 97 & 91 M.G. Coys on 23rd inst. Relief started at 8.30 pm. completed by 12 MN. Position of Guns as under: 4 Front Line 4 Second Line 4 3rd Line 4 at Hd Qtrs Le Drumez Vickers at Winchester Post. Searched Cross Roads at Rue d'Enfer	
	July 25		Guns in Front Line kept open the following Gaps N.C 6 & 8. Indirect fire was brought to bear on following positions RUE D'ENFER. LA PETRIE CROSS ROADS and Road from MOULIN DU PIETRE to N25 C. 4 3. A Draft of ten men arrived from Grantham. All were taken from Welsh Regiments Their surnames all being Jones.	[illegible]
	July 26		Guns in Front Line placed as follows. 1 at M 24 C 4.1. M30 A 1.5. M30 C. 1 2½ M/35 B. 4 1. " Second " EARTH PLACE. 2 AT MOATED GRANGE. 1 EBENEZER FARM " Third " LONELY POST 1 AT WINCHESTER POST 1 AT MIN POST 1 AT ROUGE CROIX. " Reserve " 4 Guns at Hd Qtrs at Le Drumez. Gaps No 4 5 8 12 were kept open. The following ~~Continued~~ hostile C.Ts & Road were fired on. RUE D'ENFER to DISTILLERY N19 D 8½. " " N25 C 6 2 " " N25 C 5 2 - PIETRE	[illegible] [illegible]

2449 Wt. W14957/M90 750,000 1/16 J.B.C. & A. Forms/C.2118/12.

Instructions regarding War Diaries and Intelligence Summaries are contained in F. S. Regs., Part II. and the Staff Manual respectively. Title Pages will be prepared in manuscript.

WAR DIARY
or
INTELLIGENCE SUMMARY
(Erase heading not required.)

Army Form C. 2118.

Place	Date	Hour	Summary of Events and Information	Remarks and references to Appendices
LE DRUMEZ	July 24		Gaps in Enemys Wire was kept open.	
			From Cinema Post searched Rue d'Enfer	
			" Winchester " searched Railway at Moulin du Pietre and traversed Road S.E.	
			" Min Post " Road & Railway to Cross Roads at Pietre	
			" Moated Grange traversed Rue d'Enfer to Cross Roads at Pietre	
			Indirect fire was brought to bear from Baluchi Road enfilading German trenches from Bird Cage to Trivelet House.	
			Guns at C.R.A. enfiladed the German Front & Second Line from Bird Cage to Ducks Bill	
			a great number of Scabies have arisen during the last 2 weeks no doubt this is due to long period that Coy have been in the Trenches.	[illegible]
	July 28		Guns in Front Line fired at usual Gaps in Enemys wire.	
			Indirect fire was brought to bear on the usual C.Ts & Road used by Enemy from Reserve Post to the Trenches.	
			Guns at C.R.A. & Baluchi Road again enfiladed German Front & Second Line trenches	
			I.F.Ps at Cinema Post have been strengthened.	[illegible]
	July 29.		Guns in the Front Line fired at the usual Gaps N.C. 4. 5. 8. 12.	
		2 P.M.	Guns at C.R.A. & Duck Hall enfiladed German Front & Second Line working in conjunction with F.A. Btty. this was carried out in the hope of making enemy retire into the Salient at Bird Cage.	
			Our I.F.Ps at Min Post were shelled no damage being done.	[illegible]

2449 Wt. W14957/M90 750,000 1/16 J.B.C. & A. Forms/C.2118/12.

Army Form C. 2118.

Instructions regarding War Diaries and Intelligence Summaries are contained in F. S. Regs., Part II. and the Staff Manual respectively. Title Pages will be prepared in manuscript.

WAR DIARY
or
INTELLIGENCE SUMMARY

(Erase heading not required.)

Place	Date	Hour	Summary of Events and Information	Remarks and references to Appendices
LE DRUMEZ	July 30th		Vickers in Front Line Fired at Gaps in Enemy's Wire on withdrawal of Infantry Patrols. Infantry sent out a patrol who ensconced itself in a Shell Hole near a Gap in Enemy's Wire. They were to signal our Front Line Guns by means of Flashlight Should any attempt to repair the Gap. Patrol went out & signalled repeatedly to our Guns to fire but were unable to do so owing to reasons stated. Enemy Fired a few shells round Wimbeck Post.	[signature]
	July 31.		Guns in Front Line fired at Usual Gaps in Enemy's Wire. Hostile Working Party at Work on HC5. was fired on. Working Party immediately dispersed. Indirect Fire was brought to bear on open Country behind Enemy's Line. I.F.P. have been improved and Strengthened.	[signature]

[signature] Capt

O.C. 154 McGleay

2449 Wt. W14957/M90 750,000 1/16 J.B.C. & A. Forms/C.2118/12.

Confidential

Vol 3

WAR DIARY

OF

184 COMPANY

MACHINE GUN CORPS.

FROM AUG 1ST

TO AUG 31ST 1916

Army Form C. 2118.

Instructions regarding War Diaries and Intelligence Summaries are contained in F. S. Regs., Part II. and the Staff Manual respectively. Title Pages will be prepared in manuscript.

WAR DIARY

~~or~~

~~INTELLIGENCE SUMMARY~~

(Erase heading not required.)

Place	Date	Hour	Summary of Events and Information	Remarks and references to Appendices
LE DRUMEZ	1/8/16	5/15. P.M.	184. M.G. Coy were relieved by the 182 M.G. Coy. Coy were then marched to rest Billets at. LESTREM. R.2.C.8.4.	Eaus
LESTREM	2/8/16	8. AM.	Section Officers held at. Kit Inspection, followed by 2. Hours Infantry Drill.	
		11. AM.	Company were paraded and marched to La GORGUE, where they Bathed.	Eaus
		3 P.M.	do were paid up till the 31st. July.	
	3/8/16.	11/AM.	Company fell in for Route March. and marched to MERVILLE where the men broke off for 1 Hour.	
		9 A.M.	Company fell in at. 9AM. and marched back to Billets. arriving there about 10 A.M. in the afternoon. Company practiced GUARD. MOUNTING and INFANTRY DRILL. and also constructed a small revolver Range alongside the Farm.	Eaus
	4/8/16	6/30 AM.	PHYSICAL DRILL. INFANTRY DRILL, were practiced. Gas Masks & Box Respirators were inspected.	Eaus
	5/8/16.	9 AM.	work was started on a Range Sited at. R.2.B.5.6. and continued until mid-day. In the afternoon part of the Company went to the Sports held by the 184th Bde. in the Grounds of No 4 Coy. A.S.C.	Eaus
	6/8/16.	5.30 P.M.	Divisional Gas Officer Inspected the Gas Helmets of the Coy. The Helmets with one exception proved satisfactory After Inspection, Limbers were packed. ready for G.O.C.s. Inspection next day.	Eaus

2449 Wt. W14957/M90 750,000 1/16 J.B.C. & A. Forms/C.2118/12.

Instructions regarding War Diaries and Intelligence Summaries are contained in F. S. Regs., Part II. and the Staff Manual respectively. Title Pages will be prepared in manuscript.

Army Form C. 2118.

WAR DIARY
or
INTELLIGENCE SUMMARY

(Erase heading not required.)

Place	Date	Hour	Summary of Events and Information	Remarks and references to Appendices
Lestrem	2/8/16.	6 A.M.	Coy paraded for G.O.C's inspection and marched to the Parade Ground of the 2/4 Ox & Bucks L.I. situated near MERVILLE. The General Inspected the men & Limbers and did not express Satisfaction at what he saw. He remarked that the mens clothing was filthy, Equipment not correctly worn. Harness did not fit the Mules and that the Limbers were dirty. The Company then marched off the Parade Ground and formed up on the Main MERVILLE Road behind the Parade Ground. Guns were then Drawn from the Limbers and a Tactical Scheme was arranged. The Objective chosen was a wood 1500 yards away. The Tactical exercise was to show the General how M.G's advanced over the open. Four Guns were Placed so as to bring Indirect Fire to bear on a Selected Target and thus give cover to the advancing Guns. The remaining 12 Guns advanced to a Hedge, where they divided and Split up into batteries of 4. 8. Gun Teams at a given signal advanced across the open as rapidly as Possible and took up positions affording the best cover for the best field of fire against objective. The General expressed his dissatisfaction with the scheme. He remarked that the positions taken up by the Guns were bad, in that they were too near to Prominent objects, Guns having been placed near Trees. The Coy then marched back to billets In the afternoon, a Horse Show was held by the 184th Bde. The G.O.C. 61st Division remarked upon the good turn out of the Mules & Limbers	E.A.W.

2449 Wt. W14957/M90 750,000 1/16 J.B.C. & A. Forms/C.2118/12.

Army Form C. 2118.

Instructions regarding War Diaries and Intelligence Summaries are contained in F. S. Regs., Part II. and the Staff Manual respectively. Title Pages will be prepared in manuscript.

WAR DIARY

~~or~~

~~INTELLIGENCE SUMMARY~~

(Erase heading not required.)

Place	Date	Hour	Summary of Events and Information	Remarks and references to Appendices
LESTEM.	9/8/16	6 AM.	Coy paraded for a Route March. Route chosen was to CALLONNE SUR LYS. across country route was chosen.	
			On arriving at CALLONNE SUR LYS. the Coy were dismissed for an Hour.	
			Coy were fallen in again at. 8. A.M. and arrived back at Billets at. 9 A.M.	Eaw:
		10 AM.	Coy paraded for Physical Drill.	
		2 Pm	Coy were marched to Divisional Baths at LA GORGUE	
	9/8/16.	12 AM Days	Coy. relieved No 183. M.G. Coy. and took over M.G. Positions in the Line, between BOND STREET and ERITH St. inclusive. to M24 C.6.1.	
			Machine Guns were placed in the following Positions. in the Front Line:-	
			FRONT LINE	
			M.24 C 4.1. M 24. B. 5. 1. N.13 D.4 9.3. N.14. A. 2.3. N.8 D. 1. 8. = 5 Guns.	
			FRONT LINE POSTS.	
			FAUQUISSART POST FLANK POST = 2 Guns.	
			SECOND LINE RESERVE	
			CINEMA HOUSE (1G) C.R.A.(1G) MASSELOT HOUSE (2G) COPSE POST (1G) JOCKS LODGE (2 G) . 4 Guns.	Eaw.
			IN RESERVE . AT HEADQUARTERS.	
			2 Guns at G.33.c.9.6. 2 Guns.	
	10/8/16.		RELIEF Completed our Transport returned to No 4 Coy A.S.C at LE DRUMEZ	
			Vickers Guns in conjunction with Patrols. covered Gaps in Enemys Wire.	
			Hostile patrols were dispersed by Vickers Guns N8.d.1.9.	
			Enemy shelled C.R.A. House very heavily. Gun Emplacement was not hit.	
			Posts taken over from No 183 M.G. Coy were in a filthy condition	Eaw.

2449 Wt. W14957/M90 750,000 1/16 J.B.C. & A. Forms/C.2118/12.

Instructions regarding War Diaries and Intelligence Summaries are contained in F. S. Regs., Part II. and the Staff Manual respectively. Title Pages will be prepared in manuscript.

WAR DIARY

~~or~~

~~INTELLIGENCE SUMMARY~~

(Erase heading not required.)

Army Form C. 2118.

Place	Date	Hour	Summary of Events and Information	Remarks and references to Appendices
Laventie	11/8/16		Guns in Front Line Left Sector. traversed Enemys parapet with good Effect. Two Guns from Jocks Lodge were brought up into Reserve, for any front Line Guns being put out of action. Enemy M.G.s Traversed the RUE MASSELOT. fire opening at 9. 30 P.M. Dug Outs at C.R.A. House. were Strengthened	[illegible]
	12.8.16		Guns mounted in Front Line fired at Gaps in Enemys wire. " near SALLY PORT found a Working Party beside Crater opposite WICK SALIENT. Party Dispersed rapidly. Indirect Fire was brought to bear on the RUE d. ENFER. FERME de la PORTE & Cross Roads at PIETRE A few. I.F.P. has been constructed at M.18 B. 6½. 1. Enemy. Shelled C.R.A. at 5. P.M. and Continued for 15 minutes. ONE Section Officer reports. observing 10 Carrier Pigeons flying towards German Lines.	[illegible]
	13/8/16.	8. 20P.M.	Working Party observed to jump over their Parapet evidently to repair their wire. They were fired on and Dispersed Quickly.	[illegible]
	14.8.16.		Vickers Guns in conjunction with Patrols fired on Gaps in Enemys wire. German. M.G. was noticed in Ditch in No MANS LAND, our Gun at. N.8.d.1.8. fired at this Gun and Silenced it. Indirect Fire on Enemy's back area.	[illegible]
	15.8.16.		Guns in Front Line covered Gaps in Enemys wire. Intense Fire was brought to Bear on Front Line at N13. d. 9.6. Indirect fire was also brought to bear on Enemy's back. areas. Roads & C.T.s.	[illegible]

2449 Wt. W14957/M90 750,000 1/16 J.B.C. & A. Forms/C.2118/12.

Instructions regarding War Diaries and Intelligence Summaries are contained in F. S. Regs., Part II. and the Staff Manual respectively. Title Pages will be prepared in manuscript.

WAR DIARY

or

~~INTELLIGENCE SUMMARY~~

(Erase heading not required.)

Army Form C. 2118.

Place	Date	Hour	Summary of Events and Information	Remarks and references to Appendices
Laventie	16/8/16		Guns in Front Line, brought intense fire to bear on Enemys Wire from 10 P.m until 10.10 P.m. Fire then lifted on to Enemys Parapet. Six Guns were brought to bear on Selected area. Hostile C.T.s were swept by Indirect fire. Enemy M.G. Fire was very heavy for about half an hour after our Enterprise commenced	[illegible]
	17/8/16.		Guns in Front Line kept open the usual Gaps in Enemys Wire. Between 2 & 3 A.M. at special Intervals. Heavy M.G. Fire was directed on Enemy's Wire an Parapet. according to Programme. Indirect Fire was brought to bear on Enemys C.T.s in rear of area selected.	[illegible]
	18/8/16		Between 10-45 P.M. & 11.9 P.M. Guns in Front Line swept Enemy's parapet. across the SUGAR LOAF at 11.49 P.M. Parapet was also swept. SUGAR LOAF SALIENT was Enfiladed from 10 P.m until 2 A.M. Indirect Fire was brought to bear on Distillery.	[illegible]
	19/8/16		Our Guns in conjunction with Lewis Guns. fired at Enemy's Wire and Parapet. during the night. at stated Intervals. Special attention was paid to Gaps in Enemys. Wire. C.T.s in area of Rue d' Enfer were swept by Indirect fire. Range Cards have been constructed for. Post occupied & unoccupied by our Guns.	[illegible]

WAR DIARY

~~or~~

~~INTELLIGENCE SUMMARY~~

(Erase heading not required.)

Army Form C. 2118.

Instructions regarding War Diaries and Intelligence Summaries are contained in F. S. Regs., Part II. and the Staff Manual respectively. Title Pages will be prepared in manuscript.

Place	Date	Hour	Summary of Events and Information	Remarks and references to Appendices
Laventie	Aug 20th		Vickers Guns in the Front Line. assisted the raid of the Ox & Bucks by bringing Direct fire to bear on Enemy's Parapet from the following Positions	
			At 10-40 P.M. enfiladed until 10-43. P.m. the German Front Line from N8.d.4.3. to N14.c 2.5.	
			at 10.43. P.m. direction of Fire was changed on to Hostile C.T.s in rear of Position raided	
			No 2 Gun fired from N8.1. traversing German Front Line from N14.b.8.4. to N14a.5.0.	
			at 10.43 this Gun changed direction of Fire by enfilading SUGAR LOAF	
			No 3 Gun opened Fire at 10.40. and traversed area about to be raided.	
			at 10.43. Hostile C.Ts were swept with Fire from this Gun.	
			No 4 Gun Enfiladed with Salient, switching off at 10-43 on to Roads running South from TRIVELET to the RUE D'ENFER.	
			No 5 Gun at M24.4 left. opened Fire. Enfilading Hostile Trenches from N19a4.4. to N14.a.9.2. at 10.43 P.m. changed direction of Fire on to C.Ts in rear of area selected for the raid. assisting the Barrage of Indirect Fire.	
			Vickers Guns Indirect from 4 Positions. Placing a Barrage of Fire on C.Ts. in rear of area Raided.	
			The First Raid was made at 10.40 P.m by the 4th Oxfords. The Leading Party got on the Enemy's parapet, where they found them in considerable numbers. Company after Bombing them withdrew Our Casualties were Eight wounded.	
			At 1.15. Vickers Guns Supported a raid by the 5th Glosters. by firing the same barrage as in the case of the Oxfords. An average of 4000 Rds per Gun were expended 2nd Raiding Party of the Glosters entered German Trenches at 1.15 am. Succeeding in Bombing & Bayonetting considerable of the Enemy.	
			Enemy were reinforced and party withdrew. The Brig. General congratulated M.G.Coy for its Good work	Gray

2449 Wt. W14957/M90 750,000 1/16 J.B.C. & A. Forms/C.2118/12.

Instructions regarding War Diaries and Intelligence Summaries are contained in F. S. Regs., Part II. and the Staff Manual respectively. Title Pages will be prepared in manuscript.

WAR DIARY
or
INTELLIGENCE SUMMARY
(Erase heading not required.)

Army Form C. 2118.

Place	Date	Hour	Summary of Events and Information	Remarks and references to Appendices
Laventie	Aug 21st		Our Guns kept open usual Gaps in Enemy's wire The Sugar Loaf was Enfiladed from COPSE POST. RUE DELAVEL was traversed, also road running from Distillery to the RUE d'ENFER.	Evans.
	Aug 22nd		Front Line Guns fired at usual Gaps. Gun at N13. B. 3. 9. fired on WICK SALIENT, was then moved to new Emplacement near DRURY LANE. Rue d'Enfer and Sugar Loaf was searched with Indirect Fire. Enemy M.G. fire was fairly active, and our wiring Parties had to cease work. Enemy Concentrated Searchlights on our Front Line Constantly during the night.	Evans.
	Aug 23rd		Our Gun at Bay 48 fired at Enemy working Party at 2.45 am. who immediately stopped work. being very Dark at the time result is not known. C.R.A House was shelled in the Early Morning.	Evans.
	Aug 24		Enemy's wire was fired at during the night from Front Line. Gun a Bay 104 fired at a working party in front of Sugar Loaf Salient, and dispersed them. Enemy made several attempts to repair their wire at different Points, but had to cease work every time owing to our M.G. Fire. Hostile Cross at M 24 d. 23. 1. was heavily fired on at 10.52 pm.	APPENDIX "A" Evans.

2449 Wt. W14957/M90 750,000 1/16 J.B.C. & A. Forms/C.2118/12.

Instructions regarding War Diaries and Intelligence Summaries are contained in F. S. Regs., Part II. and the Staff Manual respectively. Title Pages will be prepared in manuscript.

WAR DIARY
or
INTELLIGENCE SUMMARY

(Erase heading not required.)

Army Form C. 2118.

Place	Date	Hour	Summary of Events and Information	Remarks and references to Appendices
Laventie	25/8/16.		Gun mounted at Bay 48 fired on Gap at N14.B.5.2. Groans were heard & working Party Dispersed. Intermittent Traversing fire was brought to bear between FERME DELAVAL & FERME DELAPORTE, from Dusk - Dawn. Enemy opened intense bombardment from ELGIN St. to the South. 3 Bays between smashed completely.	[illegible]
	26/8/16		Guns in front line kept open the usual Gaps. The area between Ferme Delaval & Ferme Delaporte was traversed between 10 & 1.0 'clock. The Sugar Loaf was Enfiladed from Jocks LODGE.	[illegible]
	27/8/16.		Gun at Bay 109 Enfiladed Sugar Loaf & also from Copse Post I.F.P. Gun at Hun... I.F.P. Enfiladed German Front Line from M.30 A.5.0 to M.36.A.5.9. Indirect Fire was brought to bear on Road from Distillery to the RUE d'ENFER. Rue Tilleloy was shelled from Picantin to Masselot. Enemy M.G. direct & Indirect fire was fairly heavy. At 4AM a mine went up close to German Wire. about M30A.6.6.	[illegible]
	28/8/16.		Vickers Guns in conjunction with Patrols kept open usual Gaps in Enemys Wire. Sugar Loaf was Enfiladed by Indirect Fire from Copse Post I.F.P. Gun at Hunnery Enfiladed German Front Line from M/30 A 6.0. to M 36. a. 5.9. Enemy Shelled Picantin Trench, Res Line & Rue Tilleloy, between 8 Pm & 11.30 Pm. Our Patrol came in touch with Enemy Patrol opposite DRURY Lane. bombs were Exchanged, but no casualties on our Side.	APPENDIX "B" [illegible]
	29/8/16		Gun at Hunnery I.F.P. received message that Germans were on RUE d'ENFER at 5.55 Pm. Gun opened Fire at 6.10 Pm. on New Target and Continued in intermittent Bursts throughout the night. Sugar Loaf was Enfiladed from COPSE POST Enemy C.T.s & Light Railway at N21B 43 93 was searched. Enemys Searchlights were very active during the night.	[illegible]

2449 Wt. W14957/M90 750,000 1/16 J.B.C. & A. Forms/C.2118/12.

Instructions regarding War Diaries and Intelligence Summaries are contained in F. S. Regs., Part II. and the Staff Manual respectively. Title Pages will be prepared in manuscript.

WAR DIARY
or
INTELLIGENCE SUMMARY
(Erase heading not required.)

Army Form C. 2118.

Place	Date	Hour	Summary of Events and Information	Remarks and references to Appendices
Laventie	30/8/16.		Guns in Front Line kept open usual Gaps in Enemy's Wire. Guns in Left Sub Section fired direct at Gaps H.1.2.3.4 & 8. Right Sub Section H11 & 14. CORDITE I.F.P. searched Road from N15.C.30. COPSE I.F.P. searched Road from N20A 9.8. to N20.B.3.0. ROAD BEND I.F.P. searched Road from N20.c.2.6. to N20.C 9.0. Hummery I.F.P. " Rue d'Enfer from N19.c 6.0 to N25.B.4.3. Enemy shelled MASSELOT House with H.E. also Road Bend Post. " M.G.s were very active	Gary:
	31/8/16		Guns in Front Line in conjunction with Patrols fired at Gaps in Enemy's Wire and kept open Gaps as yesterday. Gun at Bay 38. observed German working Party at work on their Wire. Gun immediately opened fire on them and they were dispersed. An average of 2000 Rds per Gun was expended. Indirect Fire was brought to bear from Hummery I.F.P. ROAD BEND I.F.P. CORDITE I.F.P. & COPSE I.F.P. on usual Targets. Enemy M.G.s were very quiet. Heavy shelling was reported on the Left.	Gary:
			[illegible signature] Capt OC 184 Coy Machine Gun Corps	

2449 Wt. W14957/M90 750,000 1/16 J.B.C. & A. Forms/C.2118/12.

APPENDIX .A.

Aug 26th 1916.

The General Officer Commanding, FIRST ARMY. presented on the 24th inst, on Parade, the ribands of the MILITARY MEDAL to Q162 SGT. L. DOGGETT for Gallantry and Devotion to Duty.

[illegible] Capt.
OC 184 Coy. Machine Gun Corps.

APPENDIX 'B'

Aug 28th

2/Lt R. J. C. Oxley-Boyle. awarded

Military Cross. For Courage, and

Devotion to Duty

[illegible] Capt
OC 184 Coy Machine Gun Corps.

Vol 4

WAR DIARY

OF

184 COMPANY.

MACHINE GUN CORPS

SEPT. 1916.

184 COMPANY MACHINE GUN CORPS

Instructions regarding War Diaries and Intelligence Summaries are contained in F. S. Regs., Part II. and the Staff Manual respectively. Title pages will be prepared in manuscript.

WAR DIARY
or
INTELLIGENCE SUMMARY.
(*Erase heading not required.*)

Army Form C. 2118.

Place	Date	Hour	Summary of Events and Information	Remarks and references to Appendices
Laventie	Sept 1st		Vickers Guns in the front line, fired at Gaps in Enemy wire during the night. Vickers Gun at COPSE IFP enfiladed the SUGAR LOAF during the day + night. From CORDITE IFP, the RUE DELAVRÉ was searched. From NUNNERY IFP the MAUQUISSART SALIENT was enfiladed, one belt being fired every two hours. In reply to our Artillery + TM fire, enemy sent over a number of TM shells of a medium calibre. Several of these dropped near Gun Emplacement in Bay 26 but did not damage it.	E.J. 2 M.
do	Sept 2nd		At 6.10 PM Guns mounted at NUNNERY IFP opened intense fire on CTs and Roads at M 24 D. 4½. ½, which runs SW. from the MOULIN DU PIETRE. The SUGAR LOAF was enfiladed from COPSE IFP throughout the day + night. At 4.30 AM Vickers Guns opened heavy overhead, Indirect fire, working in conjunction with observation from SNAWDEN OP, it scattered a party of the enemy who were proceeding up the Road that leads from PIETRE. Section Officer reported that our TM fire was very accurate on the Enemy's Parapet.	E.J. 2 M.

Instructions regarding War Diaries and Intelligence Summaries are contained in F. S. Regs., Part II. and the Staff Manual respectively. Title pages will be prepared in manuscript.

WAR DIARY
or
INTELLIGENCE SUMMARY.
(Erase heading not required.)

Army Form C. 2118.

Place	Date	Hour	Summary of Events and Information	Remarks and references to Appendices
Laventie	Sept 3rd		This Company was relieved by No. 152 MG Coy.	E.J. 2nd Lt
			Company marched to Reserve Billets at LESTREM.	
			Scale of work was drawn up & approved by the Brig^r General.	
Lestrem	Sept 4th	6 AM	Company Officer inspected Company, Equipment, Gas Helmets, & Respirators	E.J. 2nd Lt
		9.30-10.30.	Infantry Drill	
		10.30-11.30	Gun Drill	
		11.30-12.30	Gun Cleaning.	
		2-5 PM	Backward & New Men were given extra drill under Section Officers	
Lestrem	Sept 5th	6 AM-7.30	Physical Drill & Inspection by Company Officers.	E.J. 2nd Lt
		10.30-11.30	Company Drill.	
		11.30-12.30	Immediate Action on Guns.	
			Afternoon Parades were as yesterday.	
Lestrem	Sept 6th	6 AM-7.30	Infantry Drill & Physical training.	E.J. 2nd Lt
		9.30-10.30	Training for Sports	
		11.30-12.30	Guard Mounting.	

2353 Wt. W2544/1454 700,000 5/15 D. D. & L. A.D.S.S./Forms/C. 2118.

Army Form C. 2118.

Instructions regarding War Diaries and Intelligence Summaries are contained in F. S. Regs., Part II. and the Staff Manual respectively. Title pages will be prepared in manuscript.

WAR DIARY
or
INTELLIGENCE SUMMARY.
(Erase heading not required.)

Place	Date	Hour	Summary of Events and Information	Remarks and references to Appendices
Lurton	Sept 7th	6AM 7.30	Infantry Drill + Physical Drill	EJ 2nd Lt
		9.30-11.30	Men were Bathed.	
			Training + cleaning up ready for Sports.	
do	Sept 8th	6.30 AM To 7.30	Constructing Range.	EJ 2nd Lt
			Company Sports took place in the afternoon	
do	Sept 9th	6AM	Company Paraded for Route March. Company halted at No 4 ASC Ground to practise going into Action with Limbers.	EJ 2nd Lt
do	do	3.15pm	The Corps Commander inspected the Company + Transport on the Sports Ground + was pleased with their smart appearance + turnout.	
do	Sept 10th	12.45 noon	Company paraded + marched to Sports Ground. An Inter Section Competition was held. Sections going into Action. Points were given for time, Setting of Gun + General Smartness. No 2 Section under 2nd Lieut ACL Thomas were the winners.	EJ 2nd Lt

2353 Wt. W2544/1454 700,000 5/15 D. D. & L. A.D.S.S./Forms/C. 2118.

Army Form C. 2118.

Instructions regarding War Diaries and Intelligence Summaries are contained in F. S. Regs., Part II. and the Staff Manual respectively. Title pages will be prepared in manuscript.

WAR DIARY
or
INTELLIGENCE SUMMARY.
(Erase heading not required.)

Place	Date	Hour	Summary of Events and Information	Remarks and references to Appendices
Lestrem	Sept 11		Company paraded at 8 AM ready to march to relieve No 183 M Gun Coy in the MOATED GRANGE Sector.	[illegible]
			Relief was completed by 11.30 A.M.	
			Guns were placed as follows:—	
			4 Guns in the front line	
			6 Guns in Reserve	
			NUNNERY 1 Gun SIGNPOST KEEP – 1 Gun WINCHESTER – 1 Gun	[illegible]
			MOATED GRANGE – 2 Guns SURPRISE – 1 Gun	

2353 Wt. W2544/1454 700,000 5/15 D. D. & L. A.D.S.S./Forms/C. 2118.

Army Form C. 2118.

WAR DIARY
or
INTELLIGENCE SUMMARY.
(Erase heading not required.)

Instructions regarding War Diaries and Intelligence Summaries are contained in F. S. Regs., Part II. and the Staff Manual respectively. Title pages will be prepared in manuscript.

Place	Date	Hour	Summary of Events and Information	Remarks and references to Appendices
Le Drumme[illegible]	11/9/16		also 6 guns at Hd Qtrs packed in limbers ready for any emergency	[initials]
do	12-9-16		Guns in front line fired intermittently at Enemys wire and parapet at 8.45 PM gun at Bay 60 fired at hostile working party and dispersed them. Retaliation to our M.G. fire was very slight	[initials]
do	13-9-16		Gun at NUNNERY fired at German front line from M30-a-5-2 to M30-c-5-0 Indirect fire was brought to bear by gun at SIGNPOST enfilading MAUQUISSART SALIENT Dug outs were cleared and improved	[initials]
do	14-9-16		Guns in front line fired at enemys parapet and wire when patrols and working parties permitted Guns at NUNNERY, MOATED GRANGE, SIGN POST and WINCHESTER fired intermittently on CTs, and roads in rear. These guns also fired during the day	[initials]

2353 Wt. W2544/1454 700,000 5/15 D. D. & L. A.D.S.S./Forms/C. 2118.

Army Form C. 2118.

Instructions regarding War Diaries and Intelligence Summaries are contained in F. S. Regs., Part II. and the Staff Manual respectively. Title pages will be prepared in manuscript.

WAR DIARY
or
INTELLIGENCE SUMMARY.

(Erase heading not required.)

Place	Date	Hour	Summary of Events and Information	Remarks and references to Appendices
Le Drummy	15-9-16		Guns in front line fired at enemys parapet and wire. Vickers Guns in rear fired as yesterday	[illegible]
"	16-9-16		Between 5 & 5.15 PM guns in conjunction with M T Ms and artillery fired indirect on enemys roads and CTs in rear Between 8.15 & 9 PM Vickers Guns fired at same targets Guns in front line fired at enemys parapet and wire when patrols were not out	[illegible]
"	17-9-16		Guns in front line fired at enemys wire and parapet also hostile working parties Between 6 and 6.20 PM Vickers Guns in conjunction with TMs fired at enemys roads and CTs in rear from WINCHESTER and MOATED GRANGE. Gun at SIGN POST enfiladed the MAUQUISSART SALIENT and trenches running N from same	[illegible]

2353 Wt. W2544/1454 700,000 5/15 D. D. & L. A.D.S.S. Forms/C. 2118.

Instructions regarding War Diaries and Intelligence Summaries are contained in F. S. Regs., Part II. and the Staff Manual respectively. Title pages will be prepared in manuscript.

WAR DIARY
or
INTELLIGENCE SUMMARY.
(Erase heading not required.)

Army Form C. 2118.

Place	Date	Hour	Summary of Events and Information	Remarks and references to Appendices
[illegible] Nunnery	18-9-16		Vickers Gun at NUNNERY traversed the road running from N31A02 to N25 C 5-2, the volume of fire being very heavy between 5 & 5-20PM. Guns at WINCHESTER and MOATED GRANGE fired at roads and CTs in rear. Guns in front line fired at enemys parapet and wire. Fire from these guns was much hindered owing to patrols being out. M G. Retaliation was very slight	[signature]
"	19-9-16		Our TM's did considerable damage to parapet opposite Bay 21. Gun at Bay 98 fired at a hostile working party dispersing them. Gun at MOATED GRANGE fired during the night searching the cross roads at PIETRE and traversing road running to M25-C-5-2, other guns in rear fired at enemys roads and CT's	[signature]
"	20-9-16		Two guns in the front line kept open gaps in enemys wire made by our TM's. Guns in rear fired as usual.	[signature]

2353 Wt. W2544/1454 700,000 5/15 D. D. & L. A.D.S.S./Forms/C. 2118.

Instructions regarding War Diaries and Intelligence Summaries are contained in F. S. Regs., Part II. and the Staff Manual respectively. Title pages will be prepared in manuscript.

WAR DIARY
or
INTELLIGENCE SUMMARY.
(Erase heading not required.)

Army Form C. 2118.

Place	Date	Hour	Summary of Events and Information	Remarks and references to Appendices
	Sept			
LE DRUMNEY	21st		Gun in front line kept open gaps in the Enemys Wire Gun in Rear fired on Enemys Roads and CTs in rear	W/P L[t]
do	22nd		Gun in front line fired on Gaps in Enemys wire in conjunction with Pickets Gun at Winchester fired at M.30 a 8.8. Gun at SIGNPOST fired on CTs & Roads in area around the MOULIN DU PIETRE fire being registered between 4-40 + 5-10 pm Gun at Moated Grange fired at Enemys Back areas during the night	W/P
do	23		All guns fired as on the 22nd inst, there was considerable MG & rifle fire on Bay 66 whenever our gun fired, enemy retaliated with MG & rifle fire	W/P L[t]
do	24		Between 6 + 6-30 pm Gun at Winchester fired on hostile HTM position at M.36 a 7¼. 8¾, during the rest of the night gun fired at Enemys road in neighborhood of this position.	W/P L[t]

2353 Wt. W2544/1454 700,000 5/15 D. D. & L. A.D.S.S. Forms/C. 2118.

Army Form C. 2118.

Instructions regarding War Diaries and Intelligence Summaries are contained in F. S. Regs., Part II. and the Staff Manual respectively. Title pages will be prepared in manuscript.

WAR DIARY
or
INTELLIGENCE SUMMARY.

(Erase heading not required.)

Place	Date	Hour	Summary of Events and Information	Remarks and references to Appendices
	Sept.			
LE DRONMY	25th		From Winchester Guns searched Roads & CTs from M 36 a 7¾ 9½ to X Cross Roads at PIETRE between the hours of 6 AM & 4 pm this gun also fired from 6 pm to 10 pm on CTs. Gun in the front line swept Enemy Parapet throughout the night. Gun at MOATED GRANGE fired during the night at X Roads at PIETRE. Enemy MG was fairly busy at MOATED GRANGE	W.P.L.
"	26th		Guns in the front line fired at gaps in Enemy wire & also swept Enemy parapet. The Enemy blew up a small mine during the night. Two M.G. were placed on the left of the crater. About 4 am we fired two [illegible] & our raiding party went across & bombed Enemy front line. In reply German M.G. & rifle fire [illegible] heavy. M.G. fired for a few minutes which silenced their M.Gs.	W.P.L.

Instructions regarding War Diaries and Intelligence Summaries are contained in F. S. Regs., Part II. and the Staff Manual respectively. Title pages will be prepared in manuscript.

WAR DIARY
or
INTELLIGENCE SUMMARY.
(Erase heading not required.)

Army Form C. 2118.

Place	Date	Hour	Summary of Events and Information	Remarks and references to Appendices
	26th			
LE DRUMMEY	27th		Guns fired intermittently during the night at gaps in enemy wire. Guns at SIGNPOST, WINCHESTER & MOATED GRANGE fired at targets in back areas. About 5pm enemy shelled area around MOATED GRANGE	[illegible]
"	28th		Guns in front line fired at usual gaps in enemy wire. Other guns fired at CT's & Roads during the day & night	[illegible]
"	29		Guns [illegible] fire in front line at night owing to working parties being out repairing wire. Guns in rear [illegible] during the day & night on enemy CT's & Roads	[illegible]

2353 Wt. W2544/1454 700,000 5/15 D. D. & L. A.D.S.S./Forms/C. 2118.

Instructions regarding War Diaries and Intelligence Summaries are contained in F. S. Regs., Part II. and the Staff Manual respectively. Title pages will be prepared in manuscript.

WAR DIARY
or
INTELLIGENCE SUMMARY.
(Erase heading not required.)

Army Form C. 2118.

Place	Date	Hour	Summary of Events and Information	Remarks and references to Appendices
LE DRUMMEY	Sept 30th		Guns in front line kept open gaps in enemy's wire during the night. Other guns fired indirect during the day & night on enemy CTs & roads.	WJPL
		10AM	The GOC Infantry Brigade inspected the Company and Transport. He expressed extreme satisfaction with the general smartness and appearance of the Company.	WJPL

W J Pratten Lieut
OC 184 Coy MGC

2353 Wt. W2544/1454 700,000 5/15 D. D. & L. A.D.S.S./Forms/C. 2118.

CONFIDENTIAL

Vol 5

WAR DIARY

OF THE

184 COMPANY MACHINE GUN CORPS

FROM 1ST OCTOBER 1916. TO 31ST OCTOBER 1916

VOLUME V

Instructions regarding War Diaries and Intelligence Summaries are contained in F. S. Regs., Part II. and the Staff Manual respectively. Title Pages will be prepared in manuscript.

WAR DIARY

or

~~INTELLIGENCE SUMMARY~~

(Erase heading not required.)

Page 1

Army Form C. 2118.

184 Machine Gun Company
October 1916

Place	Date	Hour	Summary of Events and Information	Remarks and references to Appendices
LAVENTIE	Oct 1st		Gun at ~~Sig~~ SIGN POST LANE I.F.P fired from 7.15 pm to 10.45 pm at Road running S.W from X roads at PIETRE. Gun at Winchester IPP fired from 7 pm to 9.30 pm at roads & C.Ts running from N.25.b.2-2½ towards AUBERS, and from 10.30 to 10.50 pm at suspected M.G. emp.t at MOULIN de PIETRE. Guns in front line fired at the usual Gaps & also at a new one at M30 b 1.0. The enemy replied immediately to our fire from MOATED GRANGE. E. sweeping the ground immediately in rear of this post.	G.G.G.
	2nd		Vickers Gun at Sign post fired indirect fire between 6.30 pm & 10.20 pm at Road running S.W. from X roads at PIETRE. Gun at Moated Grange fired between ~~8.30~~ 8 pm & 8.30 pm at road running between Pietre & Marquinart. Guns in front line fired at Gaps in enemy's wire, this fire was very much restricted owing to patrols being out. Enemy M.G. retaliation was fairly active around Sign post between 6.30 & 7.30 pm. Enemy shelled the vicinity ~~of~~ around Moated Grange between 7.30 & 7.45 pm.	G.G.G. / G.G.G.
	3rd		V. Gs in front line fired at usual targets. V. Gs at Moated Grange & Sign post Lane searched CTs & roads in rear. Two enemy patrols was reported; one on our right was fired on effect not ascertained. Enemy retaliated with artillery & M.G fire the night left of TILLELOY STREET. No damage was done.	G.G.G.

2449 Wt. W14957/M90 750,000 1/16 J.B.C. & A. Forms/C.2118/12.

Army Form C. 2118.

Page 2

Instructions regarding War Diaries and Intelligence Summaries are contained in F. S. Regs., Part II. and the Staff Manual respectively. Title Pages will be prepared in manuscript.

WAR DIARY
or
~~INTELLIGENCE SUMMARY~~
(Erase heading not required.)

October 1916 — 184th Machine Gun Company

Place	Date	Hour	Summary of Events and Information	Remarks and references to Appendices
LAVENTIE (MOATED GRANGE SECTOR)	Oct 4th		1 Gun in front line at M.24.c.7½.1. fired intermittently on new gap in wire.	GGG
			Gun at junction of M.29.1 & M.35.5 fired between 6.45 pm & 11.30 pm at enemy's parapet & wire.	GGG
			Guns in rear fired on hostile roads, Railway & C.Ts.	
			at 3 pm Enemy sent about 10 4.2 cm's on area around MOATED GRANGE.	GGG
			Enemy replied to our M.G. fire with 77 cm & minenwerfer on S. TILLELOY.	GGG
	5th		M.Gs fired as usual from our front line ~~&~~ reserve posts. The enemy was very quiet.	GGG
			Enemy working party dispersed by night M.G.	
	6th		Guns in front line fired on enemy's parapet & wire throughout the night: fire restricted owing to friendly patrols. Guns in reserve searched back areas.	GGG
	7th		Fire from front line restricted owing to wiring patrols being out.	
			About 7 p.m. enemy enfiladed our line with a light gun firing from direction of BOIS de BIEZ. A new I.F.P. constructed at ~~[illegible]~~ M.30.9.	GGG
	8th		Enemy very quiet. Guns in our front line fired on enemy's parapet & wire.	GGG
	9th		New I.F.P. at M.29.c.6.6. under construction; & shelter for men at SURPRISE POST.	GGG
	10th		Guns in front line fired on usual targets. Moated Grange gun dispersed ~~[illegible]~~ enemy working party about M.36.d.5.5.	GGG
			Same gun fired during afternoon at roads & C.Ts running from X roads at Pietre. There was no hostile retaliation.	GGG

2449 Wt. W14957/M90 750,000 1/16 J.B.C. & A. Forms/C.2118/12.

Army Form C. 2118.

Instructions regarding War Diaries and Intelligence Summaries are contained in F. S. Regs., Part II. and the Staff Manual respectively. Title Pages will be prepared in manuscript.

WAR DIARY
or
~~INTELLIGENCE SUMMARY~~
(Erase heading not required.)

October 1916 — 184th M G Company

Place	Date	Hour	Summary of Events and Information	Remarks and references to Appendices
Laventie.	October			
(MOATED			Guns fired as usual from the front line.	GGG
GRANGE	11th		Guns in in Reserve Posts fired on Roads & Railway in vicinity of BAS POMMEREAU.	GGG
SECTOR)	12th		2 V Guns at Moated Grange fired from 6pm to 7.30pm at roads & railways in vicinity of BAS POMMEREAU.	GGG
			V Gun at Signpost fired from 6pm to 8.30pm at C.Ts & road around MOULIN DU PIETRE.	GGG
	13th		2 V Guns at Moated Grange again fired on targets near BAS POMMEREAU.	GGG
			Guns in front line fired on enemy's wire – Gun at M30.1 dispersed enemy working party.	GGG
	14th		Front line guns again fired on Gaps.	GGG
	15th		A party of 2/4th R. Berks raided enemy trench opposite WINCHESTER TRENCH.	GGG
			Raid was supported by M G fire & was very successful in killing the enemy according to the report.	GGG
	16th		Guns fired as usual in front & Reserve lines.	
	17th		Patrols prevented fire from our front line except opposite M.30a.8½.5 where gaps were fired on.	GGG
			Hostile M G fire fell near WINCHESTER POST & RUE BACQUEROT.	GGG
	18th		Nothing to report	
	19th		Fire again restricted owing to patrols.	GGG

2449 Wt. W14957/M90 750,000 1/16 J.B.C. & A. Forms/C.2118/12.

Instructions regarding War Diaries and Intelligence Summaries are contained in F. S. Regs., Part II. and the Staff Manual respectively. Title Pages will be prepared in manuscript.

WAR DIARY
or
~~INTELLIGENCE SUMMARY~~
(Erase heading not required.)

Army Form C. 2118.

October 1916 — 184th M. G. Company.

Place	Date	Hour	Summary of Events and Information	Remarks and references to Appendices
LAVENTIE (Moated Grange Sector)	1916 October 20th		Front line guns fired as usual. Gun at WINCHESTER fired on back areas	GEG
	21st		Guns in front line fired as usual, but were restricted by patrols being out. L T M fell among gun team but failed to explode	GEG
	22nd		Night very quiet. M. Gs in front line fired on usual targets. A patrol of the Ox & Bucks captured a German officer.	GEG
	23rd		Guns in front line fired until patrols went out on usual targets. 1. Gun at Winchester fired on back areas. Captain G.E. GOTT. 2nd Bedf. R. – Machine Gun Corps assumed command of 184 Company. Captain Pialtenton to 183 Company to command.	GEG
	24th		Brig. Gen. Hon R. White comdg 184 Brigade inspected the transport of the company & complimented the men on their turn out. Guns at Moated Grange & Signpost fired on enemy's C.Ts & roads in rear in conjunction with 2/1st Bucks firing rapid.	GEG GEG
			Front line guns fired as usual. 2/Lts J.M. DEAN & F. W. CASWELL joined the company [illegible]	GEG
	25th		1. Gun fired on back areas, 2 Guns on Right cooperated with 2/1st BUCKS in rapid firing scheme	GEG
	26th		Guns fired on back areas during a dummy raid.	GEG
	27th		1. Gun in Front Line & Bob fired on usual targets. 2Lt HARCOURT from 93 Company arrived as 2nd in Command.	GEG
	~~28th~~		Front line guns fired as usual during night of 27/28th. Half teams of 167 Company came with their guns into the line on ~~night~~ 27th	GEG

2449 Wt. W14957/M90 750,000 1/16 J.B.C. & A. Forms/C.2118/12.

Army Form C. 2118.

WAR DIARY
or
~~INTELLIGENCE SUMMARY~~

(Erase heading not required.)

Instructions regarding War Diaries and Intelligence Summaries are contained in F. S. Regs., Part II. and the Staff Manual respectively. Title Pages will be prepared in manuscript.

October 1916. 184th Machine Gun Company.

Place	Date	Hour	Summary of Events and Information	Remarks and references to Appendices
LAVENTIE (Moated Grange Sector)	Oct 28th		The company was relieved by 167th Company and marched to PACAUD for the night.	GEG APPENDIX I
	29th		Company moved to ROBECQ (P.29.c.7.9.) and billetted there.	GEG. APPENDIX II
	30th		Company refitting, cleaning up etc.	GEG.

G. E. Gott Captain.
Comdg 184 M.G. Company.
1. XI. 16

2449 Wt. W14957/M90 750,000 1/16 J.B.C. & A. Forms/C.2118/12.

APPENDIX I

Extract from Company Orders. 184 M.G. Coy.
27. X. 16.

2\. The Company will be relieved tomorrow by 167 Company.
20 men will be marched up to WINCHESTER DUMP by Cpl Davies & will then split up – 2 to each gun in the line.
They will report to each team commander & will assist in "carrying" down to the head of WINCHESTER C.T.
March off from Coy H.Q 10.30 A.M.

The Transport Officer will send 5 complete limbers to be at WINCHESTER DUMP at 12 noon.
These limbers will be loaded in turn as teams arrive – when the gear of 2 teams has been placed in a limber it will return with the 2 teams to Coy H.Qrs.

No teams will start to move out until 12 noon – & only when the team commander or officer are satisfied that they incoming team has taken over properly – & knows all that it should know about the position.

The company will parade ready to move off at 3.30 p.m. at Coy H Qrs.

Sd G.H. Mapleton Capt

APPENDIX VI

Extract from
Company Orders by Capt G. E. Gott
Comdg 184 M G Coy. 28. X. 16.

Breakfast 8 am

1. Parades.
Sections will parade under S.O. at 9.am to clean up billets.

- - - - - - - - - -

Section parade 9.50 am. ready to move off.
dress full marching order.
Transport will be ready & hooked in by that hour.

CONFIDENTIAL

Vol 6

WAR DIARY

OF THE

184 COMPANY.

MACHINE GUN CORPS.

FROM 1. 11. 16

TO 30. 11. 16

VOLUME 6.

Instructions regarding War Diaries and Intelligence Summaries are contained in F. S. Regs., Part II. and the Staff Manual respectively. Title pages will be prepared in manuscript.

WAR DIARY

~~or~~

~~INTELLIGENCE SUMMARY.~~

(Erase heading not required.)

PAGE I

Army Form C. 2118.

NOVEMBER. 1916

184th MACHINE GUN COMPANY

Place	Date	Hour	Summary of Events and Information	Remarks and references to Appendices
ROBECQ.	Nov: 1st		Day spent in drill & further refitting. Six picquetting poles were made by a local blacksmith – 5ft long with an iron tipped point, iron ring & collar at the top – and taken on by the transport.	[illegible]
ROBECQ. to AUCHEL	2nd		The company marched out of ROBECQ at 8am, marching in fours with the transport in rear. Officers in front & in rear of the ~~[illegible]~~ fours – but not among them. The company marched into AUCHEL at 12.30pm; one man attached from the infantry fell out.	[illegible]
AUCHEL to HOUVELIN	3rd.		The company marched off at 9.15am and arrived at HOUVELIN at 2.30. 3 men fell out.	[illegible]
HOUVELIN to TINQUETTE.	4th		Company ~~[illegible]~~ marched off at 11am & arrived at TINQUETTE at 1pm. ~~[illegible]~~ Two men fell out on the line of march: all the men who fell out up to this date had bad feet & were suffering from having been so long on trench warfare.	[illegible]
TINQUETTE to ROZIÈRE	5th.		Company marched off at 7.30am & arrived at ROZIERE at 1.35pm. The Brigadier congratulated the company on its turn out, & requested that his appreciation be communicated to all ranks.	[illegible]
ROZIÈRE to RANSART.	6th		The company marched off at 9.10am & arrived at RANSART. (2 miles NE of DOULLENS) at 12.30pm. Three men returned from Fd Amb.	[illegible]

2353 Wt. W2544/1454 700,000 5/15 D. D. & L. A.D.S.S. Forms/C 2118.

Instructions regarding War Diaries and Intelligence Summaries are contained in F. S. Regs., Part II. and the Staff Manual respectively. Title pages will be prepared in manuscript.

WAR DIARY

~~or~~

~~INTELLIGENCE SUMMARY.~~

(Erase heading not required.)

Army Form C. 2118.

PAGE 2

184th MACHINE GUN COMPANY.

Place	Date	Hour	Summary of Events and Information	Remarks and references to Appendices
	1916 Nov			
RANSART.	7th		Close order drill before breakfast. A very wet day: all sections cleaning & overhauling guns & equipment etc - oiling ammunition in belts. Pte MONKS tried before F.G.C.M. & acquitted.	G.S.G. G.S.G.
RANSART	8th		Again very wet. A 30 yds range was found & used. Half the company was bathed under Company arrangements. 2/Lt WORTH took a class of N.C.Os in map reading. Four men admitted to hospital.	G.S.G. G.S.G.
RANSART	9th		One section on 30 yds range: others under section arrangements. More of the company bathed during the day. This was the first opportunity they had had since being at ROBECQ on Oct 31st.	G.S.G. G.S.G.
RANSART	10th		Company carrying on training. N.C.Os under 2/Lt Worth	G.S.G.
RANSART	11th		Company carrying on training	G.S.G.
RANSART	12th		Company carrying on training	G.S.G.
RANSART	13th		Company carrying on training	G.S.G.
RANSART	14th		Company carrying on training	G.S.G.
RANSART	15th		A scheme was carried out for the Brigadier in the neighbourhood of billets	G.S.G.

2353 Wt. W2544/1454 700,000 5/15 D. D. & L. A.D.S.S. Forms/C. 2118.

184th Company MACHINE GUN CORPS

Instructions regarding War Diaries and Intelligence Summaries are contained in F. S. Regs., Part II. and the Staff Manual respectively. Title pages will be prepared in manuscript.

WAR DIARY
or
~~INTELLIGENCE SUMMARY.~~
(Erase heading not required.)

Army Form C. 2118.

PAGE 3

NOVEMBER 1916

Place	Date	Hour	Summary of Events and Information	Remarks and references to Appendices
	1916 Nov			
RANSART to CANAPLES	16th		The Company marched from RANSART to billets in CANAPLES.	G.E.G.
CANAPLES to CONTAY	17th		The company marched from CANAPLES to CONTAY.	G.E.G.
CONTAY.	18th		The day was spent in cleaning guns + oiling ammunition.	G.E.G.
CONTAY to ALBERT	19th		The Company marched to ALBERT ~~&~~ went into billets there.	G.E.G.
ALBERT.	20th		The day was spent cleaning up + oiling up - preparing to go into the line.	G.E.G.
			The Commanding Officer went up to view the ~~front~~ the brigade was	G.E.G.
			to take over from the 55th Bgde in the MOUQUET FARM Sector	G.E.G.
ALBERT to the Trenches	21st		The Company moved up through POZIERES to the trenches in the	G.E.G.
			MOUQUET FARM SECTOR	G.E.G.
			FOUR GUNS under 2/Lt PARSONS No 2 Section went up to the Front Line "DESIRE	G.E.G.
			TRENCH". ~~[illegible]~~ & EIGHT guns - No 3 + 4 Section (with 8	G.E.G.
			guns altogether) were posted in REGINA & HESSIAN TRENCHES.	G.E.G.

A.C.R.

184th COMPANY MACHINE GUN CORPS.

Instructions regarding War Diaries and Intelligence Summaries are contained in F. S. Regs., Part II. and the Staff Manual respectively. Title pages will be prepared in manuscript.

WAR DIARY or ~~INTELLIGENCE SUMMARY~~.

(Erase heading not required.)

PAGE 4

Army Form C. 2118.

November 1916

Place	Date	Hour	Summary of Events and Information	Remarks and references to Appendices
MOUQUET FARM Sector	22nd		FIRE was brought to bear during night 21/22nd on Back areas GUNS at HESSIAN DUG OUT were found by the enemy who shelled lightly with whizz bangs. Desultory shelling otherwise.	[illegible]
" "	22nd		Fire again brought to bear on Back Areas during 22/23rd. nothing else to report except fairly heavy shelling on various parts of front	[illegible]
" "	23rd		Two of the guns in DESIRE trench ~~tonight~~ ordered back. One gun placed in REGINA Trench under 2Lt CASWELL the other in near of ZOLLERN REDOUBT. DESULTORY shelling by enemy	[illegible]
" "	24th		Guns in HESSIAN & two in REGINA again fired on Back areas during night 23/24th. Gun at HESSIAN DUG OUT holed in barrel casing by shrapnel. Considerable trouble experienced owing to cold weather & thick oil clogging the guns.	[illegible]
	25th		Fire again brought to bear on back areas during 24/25th night. Otherwise nothing to report except desultory enemy shelling	[illegible]
" "	26th			

2353 Wt. W2544/1454 700,000 5/15 D. D. & L. A.D.S.S./Forms/C. 2118.

184 Company MACHINE GUN CORPS.

Instructions regarding War Diaries and Intelligence Summaries are contained in F. S. Regs., Part II. and the Staff Manual respectively. Title pages will be prepared in manuscript.

WAR DIARY or ~~INTELLIGENCE~~ SUMMARY.

(Erase heading not required.)

PAGE 5

Army Form C. 2118.

NOVEMBER 1916

Place	Date	Hour	Summary of Events and Information	Remarks and references to Appendices
	1916 Nov			
MOUQUET FARM TRENCHES	26th		Guns in REGINA TRENCH trench drew during night 25th/26th but no damage was caused, except that emplacement which had been started was blown in by a 5.9 shell. There were no other events of importance to us during the day	GGG
"	27th		GUNS firing during 26th/27th on back areas again drew hostile 5.9 fire. A new emplacement was made in ~~16th Street~~ SIXTEEN STREET as that near HESSIAN DUG OUT was made too hot to use by hostile shell fire as soon as guns started to fire.	GGG

184th COMPANY MACHINE GUN CORPS.

Instructions regarding War Diaries and Intelligence Summaries are contained in F. S. Regs., Part II. and the Staff Manual respectively. Title pages will be prepared in manuscript.

WAR DIARY
or
~~INTELLIGENCE SUMMARY.~~
(Erase heading not required.)

NOVEMBER 1916

Army Form C. 2118.

PAGE 6

Place	Date	Hour	Summary of Events and Information	Remarks and references to Appendices
MOUQUET FARM SECTOR	1916 NOV 28th		GUNS in HESSIAN & REGINA TRENCHES again fired on back areas during night 27/28th. Otherwise no events of any importance occurred to affect the company.	GGG GGG GGG
"	29th		The COMPANY was ordered that it would be relieved during night ~~30th~~ GGG 30th Nov/1st Dec. The O.C. incoming company (183 M.G Coy) was shown round the company post. Guns in HESSIAN & REGINA TRENCHES again fired on back areas.	GGG GGG GGG
	30th		The Company was relieved by 183 M.G. Coy. Guides from 184th company met the incoming gun teams at MOUQUET FARM at 1.30 pm. The guides took the incoming teams straight to their gun positions. & Relief was reported complete at 4.20 pm	GGG GGG GGG GGG

G.E. G[illegible] Captain
Comdg 184 Machine Gun Company

2353 Wt. W2544/1454 700,000 5/15 D. D. & L. A.D.S.S./Forms/C. 2118.

CONFIDENTIAL

Vol 7

WAR DIARY

OF THE

184. COMPANY

MACHINE GUN CORPS.

FROM. 1. 12. 1916 TO 31 - 12 - 1916

VOLUME No 7.

184th Company. Machine Gun Corps.

Instructions regarding War Diaries and Intelligence Summaries are contained in F. S. Regs., Part II. and the Staff Manual respectively. Title Pages will be prepared in manuscript.

WAR DIARY
or
~~INTELLIGENCE~~ SUMMARY
(Erase heading not required.)

Page 1

Army Form C. 2118.

DECEMBER 1916.

Place	Date 1916	Hour	Summary of Events and Information	Remarks and references to Appendices
MARTINSART	Dec 1st		The Company in billets near MARTINSART: day occupied in cleaning guns which came out of the line on the previous day. There was one casualty during ~~[illegible]~~ the previous day Pte CHEGWIDDEN being wounded. 2/Lt Mills reported for duty on 24.XI.16 – Lt North & 2/Lt Urquhart on ~~X~~30.XI.16 reported for duty.	G.C.G. G.C.G. G.C.G.
To HEDAUVILLE	Dec 2nd		The company marched to huts at HEDAUVILLE; the Brigade going into RESERVE.	G.C.G.
HEDAUVILLE	Dec 3rd		Day spent cleaning guns, & equipment & Bathing.	G.C.G.
HEDAUVILLE	Dec 4th		Day spent checking & issuing ~~[illegible]~~ clothing etc: stores having at last arrived.	G.C.G.
HEDAUVILLE	Dec 5th		Parades. Physical training & Gun drill. Men at baths.	G.C.G.
HEDAUVILLE	Dec 6th		Company on a route march.	G.C.G.
HEDAUVILLE	Dec 7th		Parades during morning. Afternoon washing clothes.	G.C.G.
HEDAUVILLE	Dec 8th		Company on Brigade & Coy fatigue: cleaning roads & lines.	G.C.G.
HEDAUVILLE	Dec 9th		RAIN ~~[illegible]~~ hindered parades. Sections on mechanism cleaning guns etc.	G.C.G.
HEDAUVILLE	Dec 10th		Sunday. Company has use of baths & Thresh Machine.	G.C.G.
HEDAUVILLE	Dec 11th		Cleaning & Inspection of guns, rifles equipment etc: washing limbers: checking Section rolls.	G.C.G.
To MARTINSART.	Dec 12th		Company marched to support billets at ~~[illegible]~~ MARTINSART.	G.C.G.
MARTINSART.	Dec 13th		Cleaning guns – cleaning & draining billets.	G.C.G.
MARTINSART	Dec 14th		Company on fatigue behind the trenches.	G.C.G.
MARTINSART	Dec 15		Company on fatigues behind the trenches.	G.C.G.
MARTINSART	Dec 16		Company on fatigue behind the trenches.	G.C.G.
MARTINSART	Dec 17th		Majority of company on fatigue behind the trenches.	G.C.G.
MARTINSART	Dec 18th		Majority of company on fatigue behind the trenches.	G.C.G.
MARTINSART	Dec 19th		50% of Coy on fatigue behind the trenches: remainder preparing guns to go into the line.	G.C.G.

2449 Wt. W14957/M90 750,000 1/16 J.B.C. & A. Forms/C.2118/12.

184th Company. Machine Gun Corps.

WAR DIARY or INTELLIGENCE SUMMARY

(Erase heading not required.)

Page IV

Army Form C. 2118.

Instructions regarding War Diaries and Intelligence Summaries are contained in F. S. Regs., Part II. and the Staff Manual respectively. Title Pages will be prepared in manuscript.

December 1916

Place	Date 1916	Hour	Summary of Events and Information	Remarks and references to Appendices
To the Trenches in MOUQUET FARM SECTOR	DEC 20th		The Company relieved 182 Company M.G. Corps in the trenches. The Guns go into the line taking up positions as shown on attached map. Appendix I. 2/Lt MacKay reports sick – To C.C.S.	GEG Appendix I GEG
In the Trenches	21st		Work done; cleaning out dug outs which were handed over in a very dirty condition. Gun emplacements built & improved. Lt Kay taken very ill & has to be carried from his dugout.	GEG GEG GEG
In the Trenches	DEC 22nd		Work done. cleaning & improving dug outs & emplacements. Dugout at R22. b. 4½. 5½. had door blown in by 5.9s ammunition boxes buried or destroyed – no one injured. One gun fired on GRANDCOURT – MIRAUMONT ROAD. Ptes Bissel & George wounded carrying up RUM. Lt Kay to Officers hospital GEZAINCOURT.	GEG GEG GEG
In the Trenches	DEC 23rd		No events of importance – improvements carried on especially at MOUQUET FARM (Coy H.Qrs) where cellar chambers are cleared & dead Germans removed. Same target & GRANDCOURT fired on.	GEG
In the Trenches	DEC 24th		No events of importance.	GEG GEG
In the Trenches	DEC 25th		During night of 24th/25th fire brought to bear on dense tracks about R10.b.3.7. & R.28.b.5½.7. This did not draw artillery fire. Improved entrances & emplacements.	GEG GEG
In the Trenches	DEC 26th		Tracks at R10.b.3.7. again fired on.	GEG
In the Trenches	DEC 27		Two Royal Engineer Officers came round the majority of the gun positions with the C.O. with a view to improving dug outs. A most welcome prospect as some teams were in very poor shelters indeed.	GEG GEG

2449 Wt. W14957/M90 750,000 1/16 J.B.C. & A. Forms/C.2118/12.

184th Machine Gun Company

Instructions regarding War Diaries and Intelligence Summaries are contained in F. S. Regs., Part II. and the Staff Manual respectively. Title Pages will be prepared in manuscript.

WAR DIARY
or
~~INTELLIGENCE SUMMARY~~
(Erase heading not required.)

Page III

Army Form C. 2118.

December 1916

Place	Date 1916	Hour	Summary of Events and Information	Remarks and references to Appendices
MOUQUET FARM Sector	Dec 28th		The Company was relieved by 183rd Company M. G. Corps.	G.E.G.
			The Company proceeded to HOTS at MARTINSART.	G.E.G.
to MARTINSART				
MARTINSART	Dec 29th		The day occupied in cleaning up, all men bathed & issued with clean clothing.	G.E.G.
to HEDAUVILLE	Dec 30th		The company proceeded to Reserve Billets at HEDAUVILLE	G.E.G.
			~~A~~ G.E.G. Two officers went by Lorry to AMIENS with other parties from the brigade	G.E.G.
			to purchase goods for men's Xmas DINNER.	G.E.G.

G. E. Gott Captain
Comdg 184th Company
Machine Gun Corps.

2449 Wt. W14957/M90 750,000 1/16 J.B.C. & A. Forms/C.2118/12.

for War Diary

APPENDIX V

ENEMY

GRANDCOURT

BRITISH FRONT LINE

WIGAN LANE

COURCELETTE

Cav. H.Q.

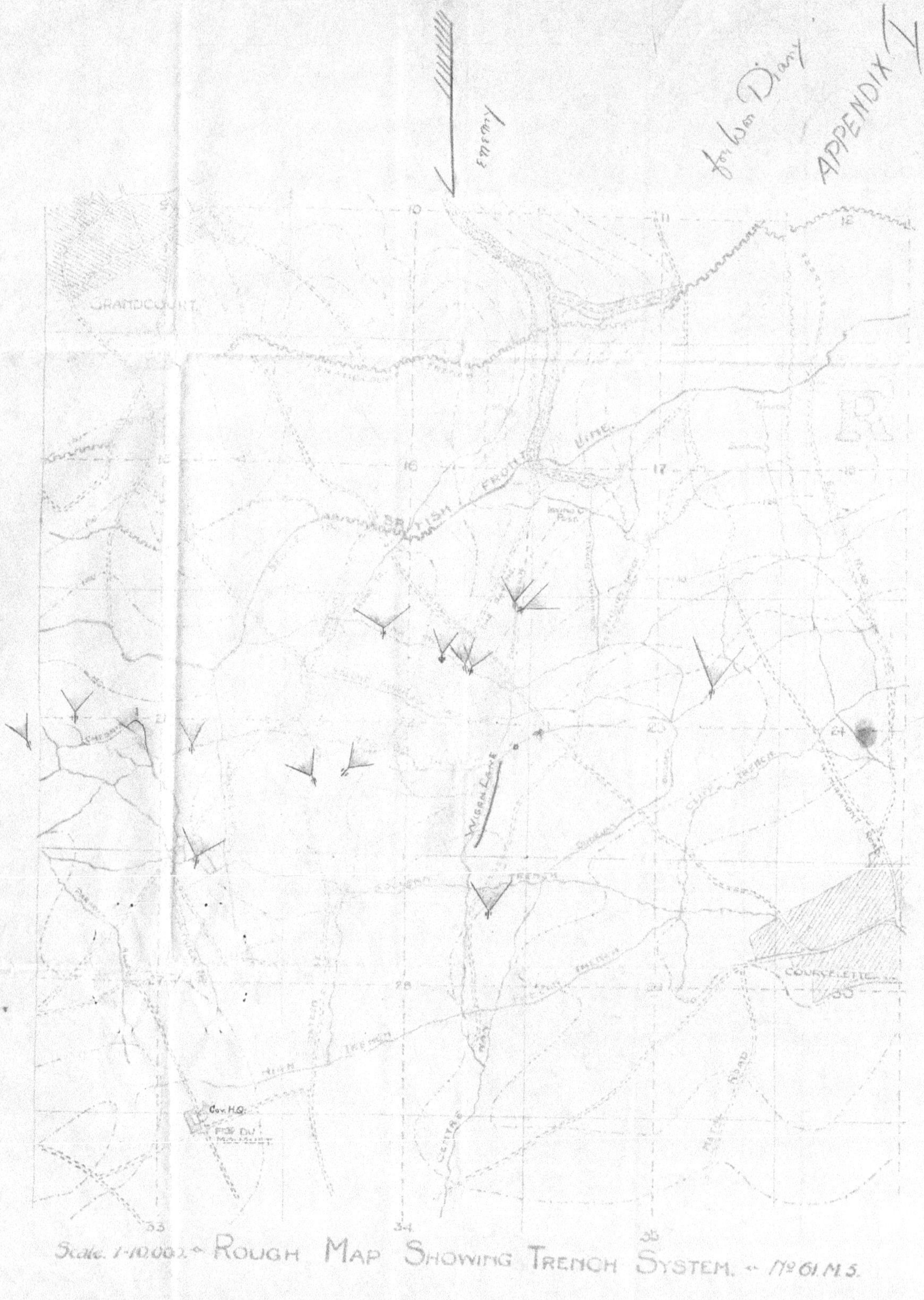

Scale. 1-10,000. ROUGH MAP SHOWING TRENCH SYSTEM. No 61. M.S.

MACHINE GUN POSITIONS

184 Machine Gun Company

December 20th 1916.

G.E. Gotts Captain
Comdg 184 Coy
M.G.C.

Vol 8

CONFIDENTIAL.

WAR DAIRY.

OF

184 COMPANY MACHINE GUN CORPS.

FROM 1ST TO 31ST JANUARY 1917.

VOLUME 8

184 Coy., M. G. C.

Instructions regarding War Diaries and Intelligence Summaries are contained in F. S. Regs., Part II. and the Staff Manual respectively. Title Pages will be prepared in manuscript.

WAR DIARY
~~or~~
~~INTELLIGENCE~~ SUMMARY

(Erase heading not required.)

Army Form C. 2118.

Place	Date	Hour	Summary of Events ~~and Information~~	Remarks and references to Appendices
HEDAUVILLE	JANUARY 1916			
do.	1st		Physical Training, Gun Drill and improvement of billets carried out. Junior N.C.O. and Rangefinder Squads commenced.	[illegible]
do.	2.		Similar programme to above — Visit from G.O.C. Bde. during morning — satisfactory results.	[illegible]
do.	3.		Training carried on — [illegible] by all sections.	[illegible]
do.	4		Cleaning billets and [illegible] during morning, Afternoon reserved for sport.	[illegible]
do.	5.		Training continued — Inspection by G.O.C. Bde. during afternoon of Company in [illegible] Drill and Transport, results satisfactory.	[illegible]

2449 Wt. W14957/M90 750,000 1/16 J.B.C. & A. Forms/C.2118/12.

184 Coy. M.G.C.

Instructions regarding War Diaries and Intelligence Summaries are contained in F. S. Regs., Part II. and the Staff Manual respectively. Title Pages will be prepared in manuscript.

WAR DIARY
or
INTELLIGENCE SUMMARY
(Erase heading not required.)

Army Form C. 2118.

Place	Date	Hour	Summary of Events and Information	Remarks and references to Appendices
	January 1916.			
HEDAUVILLE	6		Morning training carried out – everything cleaned up and packed for week end. Company Christmas dinner – successful – everybody very happy. –	[illegible]
	7		Church Parade complimented by G.O.C., Bde. for smartness.	[illegible]
	8.	10.30 am.	Company moved off and proceeded towards MARTINSART to relieve 183 M.G. Coy. in support (see Appendix I.)	[illegible]
MARTINSART			On arrival, company billeted in huts W.2.c.2.7. transport in the village. Working party programmes for week received. Parties for the 9th detailed.	
	9.		Working parties away – remainder of company bathed.	[illegible]
Map. LENS 11 1:100,000.				

2449 Wt. W14957/M90 750,000 1/16 J.B.C. & A. Forms/C.2118/12.

184 Coy. M. G. Corps

Instructions regarding War Diaries and Intelligence Summaries are contained in F. S. Regs., Part II. and the Staff Manual respectively. Title Pages will be prepared in manuscript.

WAR DIARY
or
~~INTELLIGENCE SUMMARY~~
(~~Erase heading not required.~~)

Army Form C. 2118.

Place	Date	Hour	Summary of Events and Information	Remarks and references to Appendices
MARTINSART	JAN. 1917 10		Working parties supplied – remainder engaged with improvement of billets (bedsteads) and cleaning limbers, guns & stores.	H.C.A.
— " —	11		Working parties supplied – cleaning up and issue of clothing to men available	H.C.A.
— " —	12		Working parties as usual – Limber stores thoroughly overhauled.	H.C.A.
— " —	13		Working parties supplied. – Clothing issued – Conference for Recreational Training during Rest Period.	H.C.A.
— " —	14		Packing for move to rest area commenced – limbers cleaned. Capt. Gatt returned from leave – proceeded to join 2/5 Bn. Gloucester Regt., per Brigade order. Visit from O.C. 53 M.G. Coy. who relieved us. All S.A.A. and tools handed over to 53 M.G. Coy.	H.C.A.
MAP. LENS 11 1:100,000				

2449 Wt. W14957/M90 750,000 1/16 J.B.C. & A. Forms/C.2118/12.

184 Coy. M. G. Corps.

Instructions regarding War Diaries and Intelligence Summaries are contained in F. S. Regs., Part II. and the Staff Manual respectively. Title Pages will be prepared in manuscript.

WAR DIARY
or
~~INTELLIGENCE SUMMARY~~

(~~Erase heading not required.~~)

Army Form C. 2118.

Place	Date	Hour	Summary of Events ~~and Information~~	Remarks and references to Appendices
MARTINSART	JAN. 1917 15	7.30	Company paraded to march to PUCHVILLERS (Appendix II) Marching of men excellent – very few men fell out [illegible]. Arrived at destination without mishap of any description. Company billeted in huts – very	
PUCHVILLERS		(AFTER NOON)	comfortable – Transport lines fair – Following day to be a rest. Letter of commendation on good march discipline of the company received from G.O.C. Bde.	H.C.T.
— " —	16.		Cleaning up during forenoon – Parade for inspection at noon – Football during afternoon	
			Orders received for move to LONGUEVILLETTE.	H.C.T.
— " —	17	10.20 am	Company moved off and proceeded to march to	
			LONGUEVILLETTE (see appendix III)	H.C.T.
			Marching again good – no mishaps –	
			Coy. arrived destination – comfortable billets for	
LONGUEVILLETTE		5.0 pm	all – Lieut. Hills most successful billeting officer	H.C.T.
MAP LENS 11. 1/100,000.		12 NN.	Orders received to move to DOMQUEUR.	

2449 Wt. W14957/M90 750,000 1/16 J.B.C. & A. Forms/C.2118/12.

184 Coy. M.G. Corps

Instructions regarding War Diaries and Intelligence Summaries are contained in F. S. Regs., Part II. and the Staff Manual respectively. Title Pages will be prepared in manuscript.

WAR DIARY
or
~~INTELLIGENCE SUMMARY~~
(Erase heading not required.)

Army Form C. 2118.

Place	Date	Hour	Summary of Events and Information	Remarks and references to Appendices
	Jan. 1917			
LONGUE-VILLETTE	18	9.5	Parade to march to DOMQUEUR (appendix IV) – Marching again good – Mistake in route made at LONGVILLERS but soon rectified. G.O.C. 'Box' very pleased with turnout.	H.C.A.
DOMQUEUR		3.15pm	Arrived DOMQUEUR – Coy. billeted very comfortably. Transport lines not good. Limbers at roadside.	
		9.0pm	Orders received for move to MAISON PONTHIEU the final destination.	
DOMQUEUR	19	11.20 am	Coy. Paraded to march to MAISON PONTHIEU (appendix V) Marching again good – men in excellent spirits.	H.C.A.
MAISON PONTHIEU		3.0pm	Arrived about 3.0pm. Company complete – Billets fair – Transport lines also fair.	
			The company ~~to~~ marched excellently every kilometre – no man falling out on any day and none ever badly fatigued.	H.C.A.
MAP. LENS 11. 1:100,000			The lead animals which were lent to units to assist their transport were missed on occasional hills – the position is not good.	

2449 Wt. W14957/M90 750,000 1/16 J.B.C. & A. Forms/C.2118/12.

184 Cov. M.G. Corps

Instructions regarding War Diaries and Intelligence Summaries are contained in F. S. Regs., Part II. and the Staff Manual respectively. Title Pages will be prepared in manuscript.

WAR DIARY
or
~~INTELLIGENCE SUMMARY~~
(Erase heading not required.)

Army Form C. 2118.

Place	Date	Hour	Summary of Events ~~and Information~~	Remarks and references to Appendices
MAISON-PONTHIEU	JAN. 1917 19.		The men soon settled down and commenced improvement of billets.	H.C.A.
— " —	20		Cleaning up of area – improvement of billets carried on – palliasses filled. Programme of work for coming week completed (Appendix VI)	H.C.A.
— " —	21		Church Parade – 83 men joined the company from units in B.E.F. re 1st Army Letter O.B.181 d 3.10.16.	
	22		Work carried out as Training Programme – new men from units started. The men from [illegible] and [illegible] Lt. [illegible] R. Berks very good material – 1 Berks very fair [illegible] on [illegible]. Company canteen commenced and much appreciated by men – large stock soon cleared. Billets now very comfortable.	H.C.A.
MAP LENS 11. 1:100,000	23.		Work carried out as per Training Programme above. Football team started in Regimental Training.	H.C.A.

2449 Wt. W14957/M90 750,000 1/16 J.B.C. & A. Forms/C.2118/12.

184 Coy M.G. Corps

Instructions regarding War Diaries and Intelligence Summaries are contained in F. S. Regs., Part II. and the Staff Manual respectively. Title Pages will be prepared in manuscript.

WAR DIARY

or

~~INTELLIGENCE SUMMARY~~

(Erase heading not required.)

Army Form C. 2118.

Place	Date	Hour	Summary of Events ~~and Information~~	Remarks and references to Appendices
MAISON PONTHIEU	JAN 1917. 24		Work and Training carried on – hindered rather by snow.	H.G.H.
			Men working very well	H.G.H.
	25		– ditto	H.G.H.
	26		Training Programme for following week compiled (Appendix VII)	H.G.H.
	27			
	28	–	Church Parade	H.G.H.
	29	–	Work re Training Programme – Instructions received	
			re keeping on Programme	H.G.H.
	30	–	Warning Order for move to new area on 4th received.	
			Work going well and all O.K.	H.G.H.
	31	–	Training carried on re Training Programme and instructions from Brigade Hqts.,	H.G.H.

H.G. Howard Lieut.
Comdt. 184 Coy. M.G. Corps

2449 Wt. W14957/M90 750,000 1/16 J.B.C. & A. Forms/C.2118/12.

(APPENDIX I)

Company Movement Order 6/1/17

No 7

MAP SHEET LENS 11 1:100.000

The 184 M G Coy will relieve 183 M G Coy in support on the 18th Jan 17

The Coy will pass the starting point P34.c.8.3 at 10.40 am and march via BOUZINCOURT – NORTHUMBERLAND AVENUE to huts at W10.c.2.7

The Coy follows the 5/GLOSTERS at 500 yds interval.

Transport and QM Stores will take over those occupied by 183 Coy – Ord. Room will be at the latter billet if possible.

Lieut Mills will proceed to take over billets at 9.15 am on the 18th – 2 Signallers will accompany him.

2 Lieut Urquhart will arrange for one NCO to proceed with any sick animals to take ~~over~~ charge of transport lines at 9.15 am. The above NCO will report to Lt Mills at MARTINSART.

2 Lieut MacKay will, in event of 183 not sending an officer to take over, remain behind to hand over billets, transport lines and S.A.A – He will also ascertain that no claims are to be lodged by any billetees. Forms will be supplied by O.R.

The Coy. will parade on Coy. parade ground at 10.25 – full marching order – Section officers will hold an inspection previous to this to see that all clothes, equipment and arms are clean, steel helmets washed mess tins secured correctly, and boots dubbined. A report to the above effect to be handed to O.R by 10 am

The transport will join on to the rear of the company at the Crucifix P34.c.3.7 by 10.40 am.

2 Lieut Urquhart will arrange that the leading limber arrives at such time as to cause no check.

Two G.S. wagons will report at 8 am. – 2 Lt Urquhart will arrange for their distribution.

Blankets rolled and tied securely in bundles of 10 to be at QM Stores by 7.45 am.

Officers' kits to be at QM Stores by 9.15 am sharp.

The Guard will march 20 yds in rear of the last vehicle and act as a stragglers party.

No 1&2 Copy O.R.
3&4 " War Diary
5 " Bde.
6 " Lt Mills
7 " " North.
8 " 2/Lt Parsons.
9 " " Martin
10 " " Urquhart
11 " C.S.M.

H C Harcourt Lieut.
O.C. 184 Coy M.G.C.

(APPENDIX II)

COPY.1&2

Company orders by Lt. H G. Harcourt
Commanding 184 Coy. M.G.C.
14.1.17.

MAP
LENS 11
1:100.000.

The Company will move into billets at PUCHEVILLERS 15.1.17.
REVEILLE 4.45 am.
BREAKFAST 5.45 am.
Parade for inspection of billets & Equipment 6.45 am.
Each section must have its hut perfectly clear – with the exception of billets stores – for this inspection.
Mens packs must be as for march.
Sections are responsible for ground around their huts.
End huts will clear for 30x on open side, unless a boundary is within that distance.
Time for Parade to move off 7.40 am.
Order of march 2.3.4.1
Company will pass starting point – ROAD JUNCTION W 3.d.4 2. – at 8.16 am and move by route NORTUMBERLAND AVE – BOUZINCOURT HEDAUVILLE – VARENNES – HARPONVILLE – PUCHEVILLERS.
2/Lieut URQUHART will arrange that the transport joins the rear of the company at this point, at such a time as to cause no check.
Company will march 500x behind 2/4 OX & BUCKS 4.1.
Halts will be made 15' to clock hour and march resumed at clock hour.
A whistle will be blown 1' before halt to warn all drivers to get well into the right of the road.
A second whistle will be blown 2' before march is resumed.
All men will adjust their packs at this signal.
Blankets will be securely rolled & tied in bundles of 10 by 6.30 am and loaded on LTMB lorry under orders from OC 184 LTMB.
After the blankets have been placed near the lorry, two men will be left in charge – in full marching order – these men will ride on lorry with blankets and be responsible for unloading at destination.
Every pair of Gum Boots at present in possession of men of Company will be handed in to QM Stores by 6 pm this evening.
It is strictly forbidden to take Gum Boots out of the area and any man found wearing them after this will be subject to severe disciplinary action.
All SAA, tools & Stores will be deposited at the QM Stores for handing over.
Section Officers are responsible that the above – as far as it applies to their section – is carried out.
(Where an article is a billet store it will be left and handed over with billet)
Billeting instructions will be issued to those concerned later.
Limbers will be packed by night of 14th inst.
Overcoats will be rolled by Gun Teams and put in limbers.
The unexpended portion of the days rations will be carried by the men and a halt will be made for the midday meal.

Copy 1 & 2 Coy HQ.
3 & 4 War Diary
5 Bde.
6 Lt. Mills
7 " North.
8 2/Lt Parsons.
9 " Martin
10 " Urquhart
11 Coy S.M.

H.G. Harcourt Lieut,
O.C. 184 Coy. M.G.C.

(APPENDIX III)

Company Orders
by Lieut H.G. Harcourt
Commanding No 184 M.G. Coy
Copy No 3

Date
16-1-17

The Company will march to LONGUEVILLETTE tomorrow 17inst.

Reveille 6-30 AM.

Breakfast 7-15 AM.

Parade at 9-0 AM for inspection of huts and billets by O.C. All equipment to be adjusted as for the march. Billets to be clear and clean, limbers packed.

Parade at 10-0 AM in full marching order.

The Coy will move off from the huts at 10-20 sharp.

2/Lieut Urquhart will arrange that the transport joins onto the rear of the Coy as it passes X roads 300x below the huts. No check is to be caused.

Officers' horses to be at the huts at 10-15 a.m.

Jerkins or jerkins will not be worn.

2/Lt Parsons with sigs. Brooks and Newton will report to Bde Hqs at 7 AM to proceed to new area for billeting.

2/Lt Parsons will be mounted.

One signaller will meet the supply wagon at 2-30 PM at X roads 500x NE of LONGUEVILLE CHURCH. The rations for LTMB will be on same wagon.

Blankets are to be rolled + securely tied in bundles of 10 by 7-15 AM. They will be loaded on LTMB lorry. Two men will ride with the blankets to unload same. They will also assist to unload LTMB stores.

G S wagon will report at No 55 billet at 8-30 am to load up officers' kits

[signature]

for O.C. 184 Coy M.G.C.

Copies 1-2 Coy Hqs.
3-4 War Diary
5 Brigade Hqs
6 Lieut Mills
7 " North
8 " Parsons

Copy 9 2/Lt Martin
10 " Urquhart
11 " Coy. S.M.

(APPENDIX IV.)

Copy 1&2

17.1.17

Company Orders

by Lieut H.G. Harcourt

Commanding 184 Coy M.G.C.

MAP
SHEET LENS 11
1:100.000

The Company will move tomorrow to the DOMQUEUR area.

REVEILLE 6.30 am.
BREAKFAST 7.15 am
PARADE 8.15 am for inspection of billets by C.O.

Equipment to be as for march, billets and vicinity clean and clear.

PARADE 9.5 am full marching order

The Coy will march 500ˣ in rear of 2/4 OXFORDS. The following route will be taken. X Roads 1100ˣ S of O in LONGUEVILLETTE FIENVILLERS - BERNAVILLE - LONGVILLERS - DOMQUEUR.

Haversack rations will be carried.

Halt for lunch 12.30 pm to 1.15 pm.

Lt Mills will proceed to billet the Coy in new area. Ptes Brook and Boden will accompany him - instructions will be issued to those concerned.

Blankets to be rolled and securely tied in bundles of 10 by 7.15. These will be loaded on LTMB lorry as previously. Two men will ride on lorry to unload.

G.S. wagon will be at QM Stores to load officers' Kits by 7.30 am.

All limbers to be packed and ready to move by 8.30 am

Water-cart will in future always travel filled

The C.O. was greatly pleased with the good marching under most trying conditions today and urges that this be maintained

Copies 1 & 2 Coy HQ.
3.4 War Diary
5 Bde.
6 Lt Mills
7 " North
8 2/Lt Parsons
9 " Martin
10 " Urquhart
11 " C.S.M.

H.G. Harcourt Lieut,
O.C. 184 Coy M.G.C.

(APPENDIX V)

18.1.17

Company Orders.
by Lieut H.G. Harcourt commanding
184 Coy. M.G.C.

MAP
SHEET LENS 11
1:100.000

The Company will march tomorrow to the MAISON PONTHIEU area.

REVEILLE 6.30 am.
BREAKFAST 7.15 am
PARADE 9.0 am in clean fatigue, for C.O's inspection of Billets, which must be clean & clear.
PARADE 10.0 am full marching order for inspection.
PARADE 11.20 am outside Orderly Room

Order of March. – Sections 1.2.3. & 4.

Blankets to be rolled in bundles of 10 & to be at Q.M. Stores at 8. am.

G.S. wagon to be at Orderly Room at 9.30 am for Officers' Kits.

Lieut Mills will proceed to billet the Coy in new area. Ptes Brook & Boden will accompany him.

Transport will be limbered up and ready to march off at 11.20 am

Copy 1 & 2 Coy HQ.
" 3 & 4 War Diary
" 5 Brigade HQ.
" 6 Lieut Mills
" 7 " North
" 8 2/Lt. Parsons
" 9 " Martin
" 10 " Urquhart
" 11 C.S.M.

H.G. Harcourt Lieut,
O.C. 184 Coy.
M.G.C.

APPENDIX 6.

PROGRAMME OF TRAINING

184 COMPANY MACHINE GUN CORPS

FOR WEEK → JAN 22 - 27 1917

	9·0AM TO 10·0AM	10·0AM TO 11·0AM	11·15AM TO 12·0	12·0 TO 1·0 PM.	
MONDAY	SECTIONS IN CLOSE ORDER DRILL	ELEMENTARY GUN DRILL	DESCRIPTION OF GUN	CARE AND CLEANING OF GUNS.	RECREATIONAL TRAINING
TUESDAY	GUN DRILL	MECHANISM	STRIPPING	SECTIONS IN CLOSE ORDER DRILL	
WEDNESDAY	COMPANY IN CLOSE ORDER DRILL	MECHANISM.	ACTION	POINTS B.D.A. FIRING AND CLEANING	
THURSDAY	ACTION AND SIGHTSETTING	I.A.	STRIPPING AND MINOR REPAIRS	POINTS B.D.A. FIRING	
FRIDAY	COMPANY IN CLOSE ORDER DRILL	GUN DRILL	MECHANISM	I. A.	
SATURDAY	ACTION	I.A.	CARE OF GUNS AND CLEANING TO 12.30.		

H.C. [illegible] Lieut
M.C. 184 Coy.
[illegible]

APPENDIX 7

PROGRAMME OF TRAINING.

184 COMPANY MACHINE GUN CORPS

FOR WEEK → JAN 29TH – FEB 3RD 1917.

	9 AM – 10.0 AM	10.0 AM – 11.0 AM	11.15 AM – 12.0	12.0 – 1.0 PM.	AFTERNOON	EVENING 5.0 TO 6.0 PM.
MONDAY	COY IN CLOSE ORDER DRILL	JUDGING DISTANCE	ACTION	STRIPPING AND CLEANING GUNS	RECREATIONAL TRAINING.	LECTURE – VISUAL TRAINING
TUESDAY	USE OF GROUND AND COVER ADVANCE IN OPEN COUNTRY		VISUAL TRAINING	I.A		
WEDNESDAY	ADVANCE IN OPEN COUNTRY	USE OF GROUND AND COVER	MARCHING WITH COMPASS	ACTION.		LECTURE – M.GUNS IN ATTACK
THURSDAY	SIGHT SETTING AND LAYING AND FIRE ORDERS	J.D. AND RANGE FINDING	MECHANISM	USE OF GROUND AND COVER.		
FRIDAY	COY IN COMBINED DRILL	I.A.	J.D. AND RANGE CARDS	MAP READING		LECTURE – MAP READING.
SATURDAY	ACTION	FORMATION IN ATTACK WITH GUNS	ADVANCED DRILL	CLEANING GUNS AND BELTS TO 12.30		

A C Harcourt Lieut,
O.C. 184 Coy M.G.C.

CONFIDENTIAL

ORIGINAL.

Vol 9

WAR DIARY
OF THE
184 COMPANY
MACHINE GUN CORPS.

FROM 1ST. 2. 1917 TO 28th. 2. 1917

VOLUME 9.

184 Coy. M.G.C. **WAR DIARY** ~~or~~

~~**INTELLIGENCE SUMMARY**~~

~~(Erase heading not required.)~~

Army Form C. 2118.

Instructions regarding War Diaries and Intelligence Summaries are contained in F. S. Regs., Part II. and the Staff Manual respectively. Title Pages will be prepared in manuscript.

Place	Date	Hour	Summary of Events ~~and Information~~	Remarks and references to Appendices
MAISON PONTHIEU.	FEB 1917 1		Training continued and hastened – Attack schemes – tactical use of ground	
	2.		System of Attack work. – advancing under cover, simulating barrages. The company was inspected while at work by the Corps Commander (Lieut-Gen. Sir C.L. Woollcombe, K.C.B.) – everything went satisfactory. The Corps Comdr. expressed, in writing through the G.O.C. Bde, "his satisfaction at the smart turn out and good practical work of the M.G. Coy. Officers, N.C.O's and men." The G.O.C. Bde also made a mark of appreciation "of the good spirit shown by all ranks during trying times this Winter".	
	3.		Work commenced – party set out to practise advance with 2/5 GLOSTERS at GAPENNES others at work on training ground – but had to be suspended owing to move orders being received. Limbers packed ready for move. Advance party of 154 M.G. Coy. arrived & took over billets.	
MAP. LENS.11 1:100000				

2449 Wt. W14957/M90 750,000 1/16 J.B.C. & A. Forms/C.2118/12.

184 Coy. M.G.C. **WAR DIARY** ~~or~~ ~~**INTELLIGENCE SUMMARY**~~

(~~Erase heading not required.~~)

Army Form C. 2118.

Instructions regarding War Diaries and Intelligence Summaries are contained in F. S. Regs., Part II. and the Staff Manual respectively. Title Pages will be prepared in manuscript.

Place	Date	Hour	Summary of Events ~~and Information~~	Remarks and references to Appendices
MAISON-PONTHIEU.	FEB. 1917. 4.		Coy. ordered to march to ARGENVILLERS & moved off 12.45 pm. Arrived at 4 pm. No mishap. G.S. Wagon from Bde. did not turn up & therefore double journey had to be made for some stores.	APPENDIX I
ARGENVILLERS. (ABBEVILLE 14)			Orders issued for move to LE CROTOY on 5th.	
do.	5.		Coy. moved off to march to LE CROTOY - no extra transport wagons overloaded. - Longest march yet made by coy. about 19 miles march good - no men fell out although some showed signs of fatigue towards end of day.	
ST. FIRMIN.			Guides picked up at RUE & coy. taken to billets at ST. FIRMIN. arriving about 5 pm. - Billets comfortable.	
			Orders received for range firing at BOUT DES CROCS on 6th.	
ST. FIRMIN.	6.		Sections away to range for Part II Table C. - firing very fair. Corps M.G.O. present.	
			Rations insufficient for the prepared day.	
			Attached men fired on 30 yds. range. - Weather cold but good.	
	7.		Firing continued - ~~[illegible]~~ Service Targets - Ranging and application - Boots issued.	
MAP. LENS. 11. ABBEVILLE 14. 1:100,000.	8.		Firing continued - Service application	

2449 Wt. W14957/M90 750,000 1/16 J.B.C. & A. Forms/C.2118/12.

184 Coy, M.G.C. **WAR DIARY** or ~~INTELLIGENCE SUMMARY~~

Army Form C. 2118.

Instructions regarding War Diaries and Intelligence Summaries are contained in F. S. Regs., Part II. and the Staff Manual respectively. Title Pages will be prepared in manuscript.

(Erase heading not required.)

Place	Date	Hour	Summary of Events ~~and Information~~	Remarks and references to Appendices
ST. FIRMIN	FEB., 1917 9.		Demonstrations carried out on sands showing effects of barrage – combined fire – traversing etc. 184 Coy's teams complimented by C.M.G.O. on good firing when giving demonstrations as all targets were hit with the first bursts in each case. Guns cleaned & limbers packed ready for move to BUIGNY.	Appendix II.
BUIGNY.	10.		Coy. paraded and moved off at 9.0. Arrived at billets about 3.0 pm. Billeting carried out on our own – very comfortable.	
MOUFFLERS (LENS .11)	11.		Coy paraded to march to ~~[illegible]~~ GORENFLOS ~~[illegible]~~ ~~[illegible]~~. Lorries picked up or billet arrangements made – no orders received. Lieut Mills went on in advance to GORENFLOS & found that we were to go to MOUFFLERS. Route altered on his return, making an extra 4½ miles on march. – Arrived about 4.30 pm & billeted ourselves – quite comfortable. Orders received for entraining on 13th at LONGPRÉ.	Appendix III.
MOUFFLERS	12.		Parade for packing & cleaning – Transport moved off at 11.30 am under 2 Lieut. MARTIN to ST SAVIOUR (where one night was spent) in route for WEINCOURT.	
MAP. ABBEVILLE 14 1:100,000				

2449 Wt. W14957/M90 750,000 1/16 J.B.C. & A. Forms/C.2118/12.

184 Coy. M.G.C. **WAR DIARY**

or

~~INTELLIGENCE SUMMARY~~

(Erase heading not required.)

Army Form C. 2118.

Instructions regarding War Diaries and Intelligence Summaries are contained in F. S. Regs., Part II. and the Staff Manual respectively. Title Pages will be prepared in manuscript.

Place	Date	Hour	Summary of Events ~~and Information~~	Remarks and references to Appendices
MOUFFLERS.	FEB 1917 12	(Contd)	Remainder of Coy. rested.	
			The following received from G.O.C. Bde.,	
			"The Brigadier General has heard with much pleasure of the smartness, good conduct and cleanliness of this company during their stay at LE CROTOY."	
			This is most creditable to all ranks.	
	13.		The transport moved from ST SAVIOUR to proceed to WEINCOURT arriving there at 8.30 pm. – Everything satisfactory.	
			The men of company marched to LONGPRÉ Railhead via BOURDON and entrained at 11.30 am. Detrained at MARCELCAVE at 8.30 pm and marched to billets at WEINCOURT. Huts comfortable & no mistake – arrangements good.	
WEINCOURT				
do.	14.		Coy. cleaned guns, belts and equipment preparatory to going into the line.	
			Line sector reconnoitred by Lieut. Worth from T 8 d to T 13 c.	ROSIERS. COMB. SHEET 1:40,000.
TRENCH REFS ROSIERS (COMB) 1:40,000. SHEET LENS 11 1:100,000	15.		When it was decided to place two sections on the 15th and one section on 16th.	

Army Form C. 2118.

Instructions regarding War Diaries and Intelligence Summaries are contained in F. S. Regs., Part II. and the Staff Manual respectively. Title Pages will be prepared in manuscript.

WAR DIARY
or
INTELLIGENCE SUMMARY
(Erase heading not required.)

Place	Date	Hour	Summary of Events and Information	Remarks and references to Appendices
	FEB 1917 15		Nos 1 and 3 Sections paraded at 8 am and proceeded to Motor Lorries at WEINCOURT CHURCH. Sections arrived at DENIECOURT at 11-30 AM where they were met by french guides and carrying party and all guns were in position by 4 pm without mishap or casualties. Enemy very quiet all this day.	
			The remainder of the Company with transport, paraded at 10-45 AM to proceed to billets at FRAMERVILLE which was reached about 2 pm. Quite comfortable	
	16		No 2 Section paraded at 9 am to proceed to the trenches as previously arranged. Arrived at DENIECOURT about noon and were met by french guides and carrying party. The whole of this relief was carried out very successfully and without any casualties. Position of Guns notified to Bde.	
			The remainder of the Company with transport paraded at 12 noon to take over new billets at RAINECOURT. Not very comfortable here.	
			No firing was carried out on this night	
	17		General trench routine was carried out; the enemy was very quiet during the day but between 7 & 8 pm, trench C5 was shelled with HE & Lachrymatory	
	18		Lieut W.L. Napier joined the Company to take over Command. Company HQs came into the line at DENIECOURT, arriving there about 4.30 pm	

2449 Wt. W14957/M90 750,000 1/16 J.B.C. & A. Forms/C.2118/12.

184 Coy. M.G.C. WAR DIARY
or
~~INTELLIGENCE SUMMARY.~~
(~~Erase heading not required.~~)

Instructions regarding War Diaries and Intelligence Summaries are contained in F. S. Regs., Part II. and the Staff Manual respectively. Title pages will be prepared in manuscript.

Army Form C. 2118.

Place	Date	Hour	Summary of Events ~~and Information~~	Remarks and references to Appendices
IN THE LINE DENIECOURT SECTOR.	FEB 1917			
	18		Company Headquarters near to DENIECOURT CHATEAU very comfortable	
	19		General Trench routine – enemy not active.	
	20	11 am	The Ravine gun position shelled during the morning – no hits on any actual position.	
		–	General repair work carried out.	
	21		Day fairly quiet – snipers active –	
			No. 2 section at "SPUD" relieved by No. 4 section.	
	22		Those sectors are made trenches in very bad condition	
			Enemy quiet	
	23		2/LT. GRIFFITHS reported for duty from Base Depot – posted to No. 4 section temporarily went into the line tonight.	
		pm 7.0	Day quiet – artillery duel between 7.0pm and 9 pm.	
		7.45	S.O.S. signal given – No. 1 section putting a barrage	
		8.45	until 8.45 – nearly 4000 rds. fired –	
		9.0	Artillery died down – remainder of night quiet	
	24.		Enemy shelled communications heavily during day.	
		8.0 pm	Line heavily bombarded by enemy for about 20 minutes – remainder of night quiet.	

2353 Wt. W2544/1454 700,000 5/15 D. D. & L. A.D.S.S./Forms/C. 2118.

Instructions regarding War Diaries and Intelligence Summaries are contained in F. S. Regs., Part II. and the Staff Manual respectively. Title pages will be prepared in manuscript.

184 Coy., M.G.C., WAR DIARY ~~or~~ ~~INTELLIGENCE SUMMARY.~~

(*Erase heading not required.*)

Army Form C. 2118.

Place	Date	Hour	Summary of Events ~~and Information~~	Remarks and references to Appendices
LINE	1917 FEB	24th	One sergeant killed by sniper in ELEPHANT TRENCH.	
DENIECOURT SECTOR	25		Fairly quiet day – our artillery active – little reply. trenches very bad.	
	26.		Intermittent shelling during day – our aircraft active	
		9.0pm.	Dummy raid carried on right Bn., centre coy. front. Our guns co-operated by firing on following targets from positions shewn	
			No. 1. Gun at ~~D~~ B 24 b. 6560 fired on communicator at T 19 b. 2'6.	
			" 3 " " T 13 c 3050 " " New German communicator at T 13 d 4.3.	
			No. 4 " " T 13 a. 50.95 " " GERMAINS' TRENCH.	
			5 " " T 13 b. 05.30 " in enfilade on SODA ALLEY.	
			No retaliation by enemy. – night otherwise quiet.	
	27.		Morning misty – able to wire front of positions – day quiet. Our artillery shelled throughout the night – no reply by enemy.	
	28.		General trench routine – arrangements for relief of No. 1. section by No. 2/ ~~[illegible]~~ and of ½ No 3 by 2nd ½ of No 3 made.	
			Enemy artillery active on whole of our front intermittently during day.	

2353 Wt. W2544/1454 700,000 5/15 D. D. & L. A.D.S.S./Forms/C. 2118.

Instructions regarding War Diaries and Intelligence Summaries are contained in F. S. Regs., Part II. and the Staff Manual respectively. Title pages will be prepared in manuscript.

184 Coy. M.G.C. WAR DIARY or ~~INTELLIGENCE SUMMARY~~.

(Erase heading not required.)

Army Form C. 2118.

Place	Date	Hour	Summary of Events ~~and Information~~	Remarks and references to Appendices
LINE. DENIECOURT SECTOR.	28.	p.m. 4.30	About 4.30 pm. enemy shelling increased considerably. Minenwerfer 8" - 5.9" + 4.2" mostly used - bombardment becomes intense	
		4.45	about 4.45 pm particularly on front of centre company - left battn. O/c section in VALET SECTOR (No. 1.) reported that "Enemy raided and	
		7.30.	entered our line about 7.30 pm. - He bombed numerable dugouts but was eventually driven out. This seemed to be confined to centre and right coy. sectors" A large number of gas shells fell in the vicinity of Battn. H.Q. Shelling on left of my position continued throughout the night.	
			There was no S.O.S. signal sent up from outpost or front line and these guns did not fire.	
			O/c Nos. 5 + 6 guns reported similarly to above adding "my No. 6 gun position was hit by a heavy shell about 6.30 pm also dugout. The gun and men about it were buried but were eventually dug out. One man of reserve numbers was buried in debris of dugout - it was impossible to dig him out - believed killed - digging still in progress.	
			O/c No 1, 2, 3 + 4 guns reported same particulars of raid. Dugout entrances in his sector blown in.	

Instructions regarding War Diaries and Intelligence Summaries are contained in F. S. Regs., Part II. and the Staff Manual respectively. Title Pages will be prepared in manuscript.

184 Coy. M.G.C.

WAR DIARY

or

~~INTELLIGENCE SUMMARY~~

(Erase heading not required.)

Army Form C. 2118.

Place	Date	Hour	Summary of Events ~~and Information~~	Remarks and references to Appendices
LINE DENIECOURT SECTOR.	FEB 1917 28th contd		We suffered no other casualties than the one gunner buried by dugout fall. All section officers report that it was impossible for them to fire as they were not warned of the enemy's advance until he was in our lines. No. 1 section ~~was~~ not given a definite account until after he had reached our front trench. Had an S.O.S signal been sent up No. 1 sections guns could have effectively dealt with the raiders before they reached our outpost line, again had they been warned of his presence ~~[illegible]~~ ~~[illegible]~~ a heavy barrage, through which he would have had to pass, could have been put out. Guns No. 5 & 6 could also have brought a heavy cross fire to bear on the front raided with good results. Owing to weather conditions trenches and communications have been in a waterlogged condition for the past ten days and the supply of ammunition and rations was difficult. Satisfactory results have been obtained however by use of pack animals. Contrary to expectations, the French positions were very well sited ~~[illegible]~~, especially those on the left sub-sector. These emplacements are circular with a diameter of 6 feet and one would suppose ~~that~~ that they could be easily picked up from air photographs.	

2449 Wt. W14957/M90 750,000 1/16 J.B.C. & A. Forms/C.2118/12.

Army Form C. 2118.

Instructions regarding War Diaries and Intelligence Summaries are contained in F. S. Regs., Part II. and the Staff Manual respectively. Title Pages will be prepared in manuscript.

184 Coy. M.G.C. WAR DIARY
or
~~INTELLIGENCE SUMMARY~~

(Erase heading not required.)

Place	Date	Hour	Summary of Events ~~and Information~~	Remarks and references to Appendices
LINE DENIECOURT SECTOR.	Feb 1917 28 Contd.		all positions had ample dugout accommodation for teams The taking over was most satisfactory – the 'Entente' was greatly enhanced by the cordiality shown by both officers and men	
			W. Napier Lt Comdg., 184 Company, M.G. Corps	

2449 Wt. W14957/M90 750,000 1/16 J.B.C. & A. Forms/C.2118/12.

Copy No 3.
War Diary

MAP:-
LENS 11.
ABBEVILLE 14.
1:100.000

APPENDIX I

Company Orders by Lieut ~~[illegible]~~ H. G. Harcourt
Comdg 184 Coy. M. G. C.

3-2-1917

The Company will move to AGENVILLERS tomorrow 4th inst
Reveille 7 AM.
Breakfast 8. AM.
Dinners 12 Noon.

Parade to march off - full marching order - at 12.45 Pm
The Company will march by route :- YVRENCH.-
YVRENCHEUX- GAPENNES- AGENVILLERS.
Halts will be made 15 mins to clock hour and
march resumed at Clock Hour.
Lieut Mills will proceed to AGENVILLERS. and
report to Staff Captain for Billets, re
184 INF Brigade's G 24 d/3-2-1917. Ptes Brooks &
Boden will accompany him.
A Guide will be at Cross Roads 500 YDS N of
2nd L in AGENVILLERS at 3.45 Pm to guide the
Company.
Limbers will be packed ready to move off by
11. Am.
Billets clear and clean - Equipment complete as for
March.
Blankets securely rolled in Bundles of 10 to be at
Q.M. Stores by 9 A.M. they will be packed on
Limbers and G.S. Wagon.
Section Officers will hand "No Damage" certificate
in to Orderly Room at 11. Am
a/C.Q.M.S. PATON will draw Rations for the 5th
from refilling Point of the 182ND INF Brigade
CANCHY. at 10 AM tomorrow.
After Rations are Drawn the wagon will
return to AGENVILLERS CHURCH where a runner
will report as guide for it, to Company H.Q

Copy No 1 Company H.Q
2 do do
3 War Diary
4 184 Brigade
5 183 do
6 Lieut Mills
7 " Caswell
8 " Parsons
9 2Lieut McKay
10 " Martin
11 C. S. M.
12. C. Q. M. S.

Issued at. 8 P.M.

H.G. Harcourt Lieut
OC 184 Coy M.G.C.

Copy No 3
War Diary

APPENDIX II

Company Orders by Lieut S. S. Worth
Commanding 184 Coy M.G.C.

9-2-1917

The Company will move tomorrow to BUIGNY via:-
FAVIER. PONTHOILE. NOUVION.

Reveille 6. AM
Breakfast 7 AM
Parade 8.45 AM in full marching
order to move off 9 AM.

Blankets to be rolled and handed to QM Stores at 6.30 AM.

G.S. Wagon & Cooks Cart will be loaded by, and move off at 7.30 Am, as an advanced Party. They will proceed to the Church at BUIGNY, where they will meet 2/Lieut McKay.

All Limbers will be packed and transport ready to move off by 8.40 Am.

All Billets to be left clear & in a clean condition. Section Officers are responsible for obtaining "No Claim" Certificates.

Halts will be made 15 minutes to the clock hour, and march resumed at the clock hour. A Halt will be made for dinner at 12.45 Am, and march resumed at ~~Clock Hour~~ 1-30 P.M.

Haversack Rations will be carried.

Copy No 1 Company Office
2 do do
3 War Diary
4 Lt Parsons
5 " Caswell
6 " North
7 2/Lt McKay
8 " Urquhart
9 " Allen
10

S. S. Worth Lieut
O.C. 184 Coy M.G.C.

Issued at 10 P.M.

Copy No 3
War Diary.

APPENDIX III

Company Orders by Lieut. S.S. Worth
Comdg 184 Company M.G.C

10-2-1917

The Company will move to GOREFFLOS via :- ABBEVILLE. BELLANCOURT. FAILLY.

Reveille 6 am
Breakfast 7 am
Parade 9 am in full marching order to move off 9-10 am. to pass starting point at CROSS ROADS. BUIGNY Church at 9-30 am.

Order of march. No 182 M.G. Coy. 183 M.G. Coy 184 M.G. Coy. an Interval of 200 yds between each Company.

Blankets to be rolled in Bundles of 10 and handed in to Q-M Stores at 7.30 am.

Transport to be packed ready to move off at 8.30 am.

All Billets to be left clean & in a clean condition. Section Officers are responsible for obtaining "No Claim" certificates.

Halts will be made 15 mins to the clock hour & march resumed at clock hour.

A Halt will be made at 12.45 Pm for dinner, and march resumed at ~~clock hour~~ 1-30 Pm.

Haversack Rations will be carried.

Copy No 1 Company H.Q
2 do do
3 War Diary
4 Lieut Mills
5 " Caswell
6 " Parsons
7 " North
8 2/Lieut McKay
9 " Martin
10 " Allen
11 C. S. M
12. C. Q. M. S.

S. S. Worth.
Lieut
OC 184 Coy M.G.C.

Issued at 8 30 pm

CONFIDENTIAL

Vol. 10

W A R D I A R Y

---- of ----

184 COMPANY, MACHINE GUN CORPS

for period

1ST MARCH 1917 to 31ST MARCH 1917.

VOLUME X.

Instructions regarding War Diaries and Intelligence Summaries are contained in F. S. Regs., Part II. and the Staff Manual respectively. Title pages will be prepared in manuscript.

184 M. G. Coy, **WAR DIARY**
or
~~INTELLIGENCE SUMMARY.~~
(Erase heading not required.)

Army Form C. 2118.

Place	Date	Hour	Summary of Events ~~and Information~~	Remarks and references to Appendices
DENIECOURT	1917 MARCH 1st		A large amount of work carried out on positions damaged by enemy bombardment on night of 28th ult. No firing was carried out by our guns owing to our patrol activity	
	2.		General trench routine carried out. Positions repaired & improved.	
	3.		Work on trenches around positions. Ammunition was prepared for placing in position. Position in PEASANT COPSE reconnoitred for a gun to sweep front of right company left subsector. Position decided upon.	
	4.		Gun placed in PEASANT COPSE during hours of darkness. Rockets sent up from various positions to ascertain if all are visible in case of emergency. All lights visible to our guns.	
	5.		Refill of Nos 1. 2. 3 & 4 gun positions by reserve section. All [illegible] carried out.	

A5834 Wt. W4973 M687 750,000 8/16 D. D. & L. Ltd. Forms/C.2118/13.

Army Form C. 2118.

184 M.G Coy, ~~WAR DIARY~~ *or* INTELLIGENCE SUMMARY.

(Erase heading not required.)

Instructions regarding War Diaries and Intelligence Summaries are contained in F. S. Regs., Part II. and the Staff Manual respectively. Title pages will be prepared in manuscript.

Place	Date	Hour	Summary of Events and Information	Remarks and references to Appendices
DENIECOURT	1917 MARCH			
	6.		Enemy artillery caused a little damage near some of our positions. Repairs carried out. A new position near PRESSOIR taken over. Good field of fire. Position known as No. 1. A.	
	7.		Improvement of new positions & general trench routine. During night a scheme of visual signalling to M.G's & ART. was carried out. Certain posts were assumed to be raided by enemy & information sent back to M.G's by means of lamp or runner. Test carried out very satisfactory. Barrage placed in front of posts raided successfully in one minute after message sent out from front line.	
	8.		Owing to numbers of enemy seen in open on one or two previous days an open emplacement was built in left sub sector. General trench work & routine.	
	9.		Work carried on with trenches & emplacements.	
	10.		Barrage scheme reorganised in certain posts attacked by observation of fire. General improvement work.	

A5834 Wt. W4973 M687 750,000 8/16 D. D. & L. Ltd. Forms/C.2118/13.

Instructions regarding War Diaries and Intelligence Summaries are contained in F. S. Regs., Part II. and the Staff Manual respectively. Title pages will be prepared in manuscript.

Army Form C. 2118.

184 M.G. Coy. WAR DIARY
or
~~INTELLIGENCE SUMMARY~~.
(*Erase heading not required.*)

Place	Date	Hour	Summary of Events ~~and Information~~	Remarks and references to Appendices
	1917 March			
DENIECOURT	11		No target firing took place. ~~although~~ Patrol activity on all of our front. The enemy held a concert on the line near ST. GEORGE'S CHAPEL after which he fired a lot with M.G.s. Slight damage from shells on some positions.	
	12.		General Trench Routine – preparations for relief on 14th–15th by 182 M.G. Coy.	
	13.		O.C. 182 M.G. Coy. shown round the line – arrangements for relief made. General work of improvement.	
	14.		Relief preparations & general repair work etc. Transport lines at ~~DE~~ RAINCOURT moved to HARBONNIERES with gun teams in reserve who prepared billets for company.	
		8.0pm.	Relief commenced from DENIECOURT CHATEAU. Guides from teams in the line reporting heavy going.	
			Relief difficult owing to mud & darkness of night. All	

A5834 Wt. W4973 M687 750,000 8/16 D. D. & L. Ltd. Forms/C.2118/13.

184 M.G. Coy **WAR DIARY**

or

~~INTELLIGENCE SUMMARY~~.

(*Erase heading not required.*)

Instructions regarding War Diaries and Intelligence Summaries are contained in F. S. Regs., Part II. and the Staff Manual respectively. Title pages will be prepared in manuscript.

Army Form C. 2118.

Place	Date	Hour	Summary of Events ~~and Information~~	Remarks and references to Appendices
DENIECOURT	1917 MARCH 15.		Teams out by 4 a.m. 15th. Hot rum toddy & the march to HARBONNIERES.	
HARBONNIERES			On arrival all sections settled down in good billets. Latter part of day spent in cleaning up.	
— " —	16.		Company engaged in cleaning & overhauling guns, stores etc, — Baths & issues of clothing	
— " —	17		Overhauling carried on — News received that the Bdes. in the line were advancing & that we were to be prepared to follow up. Fighting kit prepared & coy. made ready to advance. All surplus gear stored. Orders received to move to HERLEVILLE on 18th.	
— " —	18.	10 a.m.	Coy. marched off and proceeded to HERLEVILLE. Men billeted in a hut – officers in an old dug out. One riding horse unfortunately broke its leg & was shot	

A5834 Wt. W4973 M687 750,000 8/16 D. D. & L. Ltd. Forms/C.2118/13.

Instructions regarding War Diaries and Intelligence Summaries are contained in F. S. Regs., Part II. and the Staff Manual respectively. Title pages will be prepared in manuscript.

WAR DIARY
or
~~INTELLIGENCE SUMMARY.~~
(Erase heading not required.)

Army Form C. 2118.

Place	Date	Hour	Summary of Events ~~and Information~~	Remarks and references to Appendices
	1917 MARCH.			
HERLEVILLE	19		Orders received to move to PERTAIN – Company moved off at 9.45 am. Blockage on LIHONS-CHAULNES road owing to bad condition of road – company did not arrive in billets at PERTAIN until 5 am. on 20th. Company rested & cleaned up.	
	20	21.	Road repairing carried out. – improvement of billets. overhauling guns.	
	22.		Positions for Defence Line on W. bank of R. SOMME reconnoitred. Gun positions sited to command bridgeheads. between EPANANCOURT and CIZANCOURT. Road repairs by company.	
	23.		Work commenced on positions on W of R. SOMME.	
	24		Work on emplacements and roads continued.	
	~~25~~.			
	25.		Lieut. S. S. Worth appointed to be 2nd in command of No. 14 M. G. Coy. –	

184 M.G. Coy. **WAR DIARY**

or

~~**INTELLIGENCE SUMMARY.**~~

(Erase heading not required.)

Army Form C. 2118.

Instructions regarding War Diaries and Intelligence Summaries are contained in F. S. Regs., Part II. and the Staff Manual respectively. Title pages will be prepared in manuscript.

Place	Date	Hour	Summary of Events ~~and Information~~	Remarks and references to Appendices
	1917 MARCH			
PERTAIN.	25.	(Contd) 8.30 am	Lieut Boswell with two guns complete proceeded to join 2/5 R BERKS; 2 Lieut Urquhart with two guns complete proceeded to join 2/4 O.B.L.I. On arrival at ENNEMAIN and ATHIES respectively positions to defend the villages were taken up and prospective emplacement sites chosen.	
	26		Company on work at roads and emplacements on W. of SOMME Defence Line. These latter were camouflaged & finished.	
	27		Road Repairing. Warning order received to move to ATHIES on 28th	
			2 Lieut D.H. RIDDELL joined the company from M.G.C. Base.	
	28	~~noon~~ 1 pm	Coy. Paraded and proceeded to ATHIES.	
ATHIES.			Billets found near the river and company settled.	
	29.		Overhauling Guns, stores etc. Improving billets.	
	30		Orders received to move to CAULAINCOURT	
		1.15 pm	Company moved off and marched to CAULAINCOURT arriving about 4.30 pm. Very few billets. Three small villas found. — remainder of company erected improvised shelters.	
CAULAINCOURT.				

A5834 Wt. W4973 M687 750,000 8/16 D. D. & L. Ltd. Forms/C.2118/13.

Army Form C. 2118.

Instructions regarding War Diaries and Intelligence Summaries are contained in F. S. Regs., Part II. and the Staff Manual respectively. Title pages will be prepared in manuscript.

184 M.G. Coy. WAR DIARY
or
~~INTELLIGENCE SUMMARY.~~

(*Erase heading not required.*)

Place	Date	Hour	Summary of Events ~~and Information~~	Remarks and references to Appendices
	1917 MARCH			
CAULAINCOURT	30.		Ground ~~[illegible]~~ in front of VERMAND reconnoitered with view to attack.	
			Four guns told off to accompany the infantry in the attack.	
— " —	31.	8.0 am.	Information received that R. BERKS had entered and occupied VERMAND during the hours of darkness.	
			VERMAND and ground on EAST reconnoitered.	
		12 NOON.	Lieut Parsons and 2 Lieut Allen with four teams complete proceeded to VERMAND and took up positions on EAST of village. One gun at R26 central firing E. – 3 on line R20 c 8.2 – R26.b. 0.5 (SHEET 62c S.E.)	
		6.15 pm.	Orders received from Bde that another two guns were required to report to O.C. 2/5 R. BERKS for use on L. flank of village.	
		7.0 pm.	2 Lieut Griffiths proceeded with two gun teams complete.	

W Napier CAPT.
COMDG. 184 COMPANY M.G. CORPS.

A5834 Wt. W4973 M687 750,000 8/16 D. D. & L. Ltd. Forms/C.2118/13.

Vol XI

<u>CONFIDENTIAL.</u>

W A R   D I A R Y

of

184TH COMPANY, MACHINE GUN CORPS.

from

April 1st, 1917 to April 30th, 1917.

VOLUME X1

****

184 M.G.Co.

WAR DIARY
or
INTELLIGENCE SUMMARY.
(Erase heading not required.)

Army Form C. 2118.

Instructions regarding War Diaries and Intelligence Summaries are contained in F. S. Regs., Part II. and the Staff Manual respectively. Title pages will be prepared in manuscript.

Place	Date	Hour	Summary of Events and Information	Remarks and references to Appendices
CAULAINCOURT	1.		no. 3 section [LIEUT. PARSONS, 2LT. ALLEN] in positions E. of VERMAND, one gun R.26. central firing E. Three guns on line R.20. C.8.2; R.26. B.0.5 (Sheet 62.C. SE)	
			no. 1. section [2LIEUT GRIFFITHS] in position with 2 guns N.W. of VERMAND, R.25. D.8.8, R.25 B.8.3 (Sheet 62.C. SE). Orders received that brigade would attack BIHECOURT - R.15 central R.9.D.2.3 at dawn on 2ND. Operation orders issued. LIEUT McKAY and 2LIEUT RIDDELL + no. 4. section took up positions in accordance with operation orders	Appendix I
	2	5 am.	Brigade attacked in accordance with orders received 1.4.17 and carried objective. Machine Guns cooperated, 2ND LIEUT RIDDELL engaged party of hostile infantry with success and took 1 prisoner. He advanced with one gun and took up position in new line. 2LIEUT ALLEN also engaged hostile infantry, and got into positions as ordered. LIEUT McKAY advanced to reinforce in the new line. All guns were in position within one hour of the capture of the position. Casualties 1 O.R. wounded	
		1 pm.	Company Headquarters moved to VERMAND	
		9.30 pm.	no. 2 section [LT. CASWELL, 2LT URQUHART] relieved no. 3 section [LIEUT. PARSONS, 2LT. ALLEN]	
VERMAND	3.		Work carried out in consolidation of new line, emplacements & shelters built	
	4	6.45 pm.	Orders received that brigade would attack ridge R.5.A., R.5.C., R.11.b to R. OMIGNON and operation orders issued for attack [Sheet 62 C SE]	Appendix II
			Positions in line improved and consolidated. Sections in reserve at Company employed on work on roads in VERMAND.	
	5.		Attack ordered for 5th [Appendix II] postponed until night of 6th/7th.	
		10 pm.	no. 1 section [LT. MILLS and 2LT. GRIFFITHS] relieved no. 4 section [LT. McKAY and 2LT RIDDELL] new emplacements due E. of "no. 3 wood" [Sheet 62 C. S.E.] Casualties 1 O.R. Died of wounds.	

A5834 Wt. W4973 M687 750,000 8/16 D. D. & L. Ltd. Forms/C.2118/13.

Instructions regarding War Diaries and Intelligence Summaries are contained in F. S. Regs., Part II. and the Staff Manual respectively. Title pages will be prepared in manuscript.

WAR DIARY
or
INTELLIGENCE SUMMARY.
(Erase heading not required.)

Army Form C. 2118.

Place	Date	Hour	Summary of Events and Information	Remarks and references to Appendices
VERMAND	6	11.30 am.	Orders issued for attack on ridge R.5.a. R.5.c., R.11.b to R. OMIGNON (Sheet 62 C.S.E.)	Appendix II
		1.0 pm	no. 2 section [LT. CASWELL] engaged enemy working parties and dispersed them causing casualties.	
			New emplacements dug at R.16 C.4.6 (Sheet 62 C.S.E.) and to R. of no 2 wood (62. C.S.E.)	
			2Lt. URQUHART to F.A. (SICK) Draft of 2 O.R.	
	7	12.0 midnight	Brigade attacked in accordance with operation orders. The infantry were held up by wire and three unsuccessful attempts failed. Machine guns cooperated in accordance with orders. No. 2 section (LIEUT. CASWELL) on right engaged hostile M.G. which was impeding advance and silenced it. 1 gun of no. 2 section [LIEUT CASWELL] and one gun of no. 1 section effectively covered withdrawal of infantry. In accordance with special orders received no. 2 section [LIEUT. CASWELL] detailed two guns to cover L. flank of the brigade on the R. this brigade having obtained their objective. The remaining guns withdrew to positions previously occupied, and the reserve guns returned to Co. H.Q. Casualties 2 O.R. wounded	Appendix III. MAP A
			no. 3. section [LIEUT. PARSONS and 2LIEUT ALLEN] relieved no. 2 section [LIEUT CASWELL]	APPENDIX IV
	8th		Work on positions in the line continued. Reserve sections employed on improvement of roads in VERMAND	
		6.35 pm 9.15 pm 9.55 pm	Orders issued in regard to cooperation with advance of 182 Bde	APPENDIX V VI VII
	9th		no. 3 section [LIEUT. PARSONS] was unable to act in accordance with orders of 8th owing to advance of 184 Bde. into line attacked on night of 6/7th	
			Gun at R.16 B.2.4 (Sheet 62.C.S.E.) moved to R.11.A. to conform with advance of infantry.	
		2.30 pm	Guns engaged party of enemy near ASCENSION FARM which was being shelled by our artillery at the time. Casualties 1 O.R. wounded	
			Draft of 2 O.R. reported arrival	

A5834 Wt. W4973 M687 750,000 8/16 D. D. & L. Ltd. Forms/C.2118/13.

Instructions regarding War Diaries and Intelligence Summaries are contained in F. S. Regs., Part II. and the Staff Manual respectively. Title pages will be prepared in manuscript.

184 M.G. Co

WAR DIARY
or
~~INTELLIGENCE SUMMARY.~~

(Erase heading not required.)

Army Form C. 2118.

Place	Date	Hour	Summary of Events and Information	Remarks and references to Appendices
VERMAND	10	8.30am	Orders for relief of company by no. 106 Co. issued.	APPENDIX VIII
		11.30am	Company Headquarters moved to MARAUCOURT (Sheet 62.C. 1/40000)	
		3.0pm	Company relief complete	
MARAUCOURT	11.		Company occupied with cleaning guns equipment &c. Afternoon devoted to recreation	
- " -	12		Company moved to HOMBLEUX into billets. Sections in good billets in barns.	APPENDIX IX
HOMBLEUX	13.		Company employed on refitting limber deficiencies, gun equipment &c Draft of 9 OR.	
	14		Company paraded for training: morning parades including squad drill stripping, care & cleaning, gun drill, points to DIA, afternoon occupied with range work on 25 yards range.	
	15.		Company paraded in morning - physical training, squad drill, mechanism, stoppages, gun drill. Afternoon devoted to recreation	
	16		Inspection of company at training by G.O.C. 184 Bde. At the conclusion of the inspection the G.O.C. expressed his satisfaction with "the smart & soldierly appearance of the company" and his appreciation of "the excellent work carried out by them during the recent operations.	
	17		Training programme carried out included physical training, advanced drill, Pts. B.D.A and immediate action. Afternoon devoted to recreation	
	18.		Parades for physical training & limber packing & general preparations for move to reserve area at FORESTE	APPENDIX X

A5834 Wt. W4973 M687 750,000 8/16 D. D. & L. Ltd. Forms/C.2118/13.

184 M.G.Co. **WAR DIARY** *or* ~~INTELLIGENCE SUMMARY~~.

(*Erase heading not required.*)

Army Form C. 2118.

Instructions regarding War Diaries and Intelligence Summaries are contained in F. S. Regs., Part II. and the Staff Manual respectively. Title pages will be prepared in manuscript.

Place	Date	Hour	Summary of Events and Information	Remarks and references to Appendices
HOMBLEUX	19		Company relieved no. 97. M.G.Co in reserve area FORESTE (66D)	APPENDIX X
FORESTE	20		Company relieved no. 96 M.G.Co in the line Co. HQ at X.11 D. 2.0 (62B S.W.) Position of guns on relief as in map B. Casualties: nil	APPENDIX XI MAP B.
(RAIL' EMBT.) X.11 D 2.0	21		Considerable shelling of outpost line. New emplacements dug at M.36 C.20.75 M.20 B 4.7 and emplacements on left flank. Casualties nil	
	22		Two new emplacements dug one on crest of hill in front of sunken road to FAYET and one in front of FAYET guns in 'BROWN' line in new positions [The BROWN line consisted of a purely defensive position in view of possible counter attack, strong points were established and the line wired]. Position of guns as in MAP C. B, 15 D8 Casualties: nil	
	23		No. 2 Section [Lt CASWELL] carried out indirect fire on ST. QUENTIN and roads on the outskirts during the night. Work on emplacements continued. Draft of 1 O.R. reported Casualties nil	
	24		6 guns in outpost line relieved by 6 guns in BROWN line Two new emplacements and shelters completed in BROWN line and two emplacements built on left of outpost line Casualties nil	APPENDIX XII

A5834 Wt. W4973 M687 750,000 8/16 D. D. & L. Ltd. Forms/C.2118/13.

Instructions regarding War Diaries and Intelligence Summaries are contained in F. S. Regs., Part II. and the Staff Manual respectively. Title pages will be prepared in manuscript.

WAR DIARY
or
INTELLIGENCE SUMMARY.
(*Erase heading not required.*)

Army Form C. 2118.

Place	Date	Hour	Summary of Events and Information	Remarks and references to Appendices
RAILWAY EMBANKMENT	25	10.30pm	Two guns of no. 4 section relieved two guns of 182 Bde. in positions S6.D.5.7 and S.6.d.0.4 (MAP C). Guns in outpost line now as indicated O. 15 O 8. General routine work on emplacements etc. Casualties nil	APPENDIX XIII MAP C. APPENDIX XIV
	26.	6.45pm	Enemy attacked left of brigade. Attack repulsed by M.G. fire + rifle fire. no. 6. gun at S6D.5.7 got into action + did particularly good work inflicting many casualties on enemy. This gun of no. 4. section [2Lt. RIDDELL] was in charge of SGT. HAWKINS who handled his team with coolness + courage + in addition assisted materially in bringing in under heavy fire two badly wounded men. Casualties 2 OR wounded. 2nd Lieuts CRAIG + WOMERSLEY reported to the company + 6 O.R. Operation orders for raid issued	
	27.		In accordance with Bde. Order 93; (APPENDIX XV) (operation orders) M.G.s cooperated with infantry as follows. Two guns (at M.36 D.3.4.) located hostile M.G. at about N.31.A.9.2 which was impeding progress. This gun was engaged + silenced in two minutes. These guns continued to search ground in N.31. B, C + D. These M.G.s were located by the enemy and came under heavy fire from artillery and M.G. both emplacements being destroyed + some of the gun equipment damaged. The officer in charge of the guns 2Lt GRIFFITHS moved up the trench + got into action there. At 5.30 am a party of our infantry withdrawing from the crater in M.36 actual came under rifle + M.G. fire. The M.G. was located at M.36 B.0.5. 2Lt. GRIFFITHS at once opened fire with one gun of no1 section	APPENDIX XV

A5834 Wt. W4973 M687 750,000 8/16 D. D. & L. Ltd. Forms/C.2118/13.

Army Form C. 2118.

Instructions regarding War Diaries and Intelligence Summaries are contained in F. S. Regs., Part II. and the Staff Manual respectively. Title pages will be prepared in manuscript.

WAR DIARY
or
INTELLIGENCE SUMMARY.
(Erase heading not required.)

Place	Date	Hour	Summary of Events and Information	Remarks and references to Appendices
RAILY. EMBANKT.	night of 27/(28)	5.30am	The M.G. was silenced + casualties inflicted on enemy. At 6.30 am (28th) the guns withdrew to their original positions. No. 3 section [LT. PARSONS] came into action at M.29. C 9.2 with 4 guns + fired in accordance with Bde. orders. Casualties	
	28.		Machine guns fired in accordance with orders in cooperation with artillery on CUT DOWN COPSE M.36 [illegible] to M.36. a 9.5 at the following times 5.5 pm, 7.40 pm 28.4.17 and 6.15 am 29.4.17. 8 guns in outpost line relieved by 8 guns in BROWN LINE - relief complete at 1 am 29.4.17. 2LT. RIDDELL wounded in wrist. Casualties 1 O.R. killed 16 O.R. wounded. Shelters improved in OUTPOST line. Positions selected + emplacements dug from which section on left fired in accordance with operations above. Shelter made for gun team in BROWN LINE on left. 2Lt. ROWE reported arrival.	APPENDIX XV
	29		M.G.s cooperated with artillery as on 28th inst. Enemy artillery active on outpost line, one gun position being blown in and dugout wrecked. Shelters + emplacement on R. of BROWN line constructed. 2Lt ROWE reported arrival. Casualties 1 O.R. wounded	
	30		Guns cooperated with artillery as on previous day. Quiet day with little shelling: emplacements + shelters improved, bench sites overhauled + general routine work.	

A. S. Walker CAPT.
COMDG. 184 COMPANY M. G. CORPS.

A5834 Wt. W4973 M687 750,000 8/16 D. D. & L. Ltd. Forms/C.2118/13.

APPENDIX I

[illegible]

[illegible] the [illegible] Berks [illegible] and [illegible] Bucks [illegible] [illegible] [illegible] [illegible] [illegible] [illegible] [illegible] [illegible] [illegible] Guns [illegible] [illegible]

[illegible] [illegible] [illegible] [illegible] [illegible] [illegible] [illegible]

2. OBJECTIVE: [illegible] [illegible] Ry. Line [illegible]
The [illegible] from Cross Roads at [illegible] to R.10 central.
2/4th Bucks from R.5 central to [illegible]
On reaching the objectives patrols will be pushed to the Front at once and [illegible] 2 posts with Lewis Guns established to [illegible] [illegible] of the position.

3. [illegible] will be carried out along the [illegible] the Railway Line running through [illegible] Eastwards.
One Company [illegible] along the line on each side of STATION.
2/4 Berks from R.20 a.9.2. to R.15 a.4.3.
2/4 Bucks from R.15 a.4.3. to R.4 b.9.4.

4. The 59th Division will cooperate on the [illegible] of the 2/4 Bucks Objective R.4 central to [illegible], and the 183 Brigade on the left [illegible] of the OPERATION.

5. 2nd [illegible] with 1 Gun & Team will advance with Infantry along the N side of Road from STATION to [illegible]COURT and will take up a position [illegible]
If situation demands he will come into action [illegible] any Enemy Guns or Infantry that are holding advance.

6. [illegible] with 1 Gun & Team will advance [illegible] left flank of 2/4 Bucks. He will [illegible] and take up a position [illegible]

[illegible] remaining [illegible] Guns 183 M.G. Coy [illegible] 2 [illegible] [illegible] [illegible] [illegible] will [illegible] [illegible] [illegible] [illegible] [illegible]

[illegible] [illegible] [illegible] [illegible] [illegible] [illegible] on [illegible]COURT [illegible] [illegible]

Sheet 2.

inclusive to [illegible] Copse inclusive.
The 2 teams of No. 4 Section will take on from [illegible] Copse exclusive to [illegible] Wood exclusive.

8. Section Officers will watch situation closely and must keep themselves well informed of progress of our Infantry in front.
If the attack is held up anywhere steps must be taken immediately to break the resistance of the Enemy.
Section Officers must be prepared to send guns forward to consolidate the position as soon as possible after it is taken.

9. Zero will be [illegible].
Infantry begin advance from line of [illegible].
Artillery barrage commences on objective.
All Machine Guns will open fire at the [illegible].

10. [illegible] [illegible] T.O.d. [illegible]
[illegible] and [illegible] must [illegible] at this [illegible].

[signature] CAPT.
COMDG. 184 COMPANY M. G. CORPS.

[illegible] Operation Orders [illegible]

II. Appendix II

[illegible]

1 The [illegible] Lancashires will [illegible] the wire [illegible] of the CHATEAU Road.
[illegible] Oxfords [illegible] of Chateau Road.

2 If trench running [illegible] is occupied an attack by the above two Batts will be made with Artillery support.
Boundary between 2 Batts will be [illegible] Road

3. M.G. Action as follows

(a) O.C. No 1 Section will arrange to take 2 Guns on N edge of No 3 wood and on attack commencing will bring fire to bear on ridge R 4 b. & R 5 a.

(b) [illegible] Griffiths will advance with left flank of the Oxfords and will pay particular attention to valley in R 4 d.

(c) [illegible] Urquhart will advance with the Right Flank Lancashires, and act as situation demands.

(d) O.C. No 2 Section will detail 1 Gun Team to advance under [illegible] Allen [illegible] ~~Flank of [illegible] Oxfords.~~
[illegible] Allen will endeavour to [illegible] position at R 5 a from which enfilade [illegible]

be taken from R12a & R6.c.

4. O.C. No 3 Section will keep closely in touch with the situation and as the objectives being attained will move forward ~~[illegible]~~ one Gun to consolidate position ~~[illegible]~~.

5. Report centre will be at R6c 6.4. Road running between Nos 4 & 5 woods.

6. Artillery Programme as ~~[illegible]~~ follows.

Zero 5 AM 0 to +15

Bombard ~~[illegible]~~ ~~[illegible]~~ ~~Intensely~~

INTENSE +15 to +20.

Creep 100 yds every 2 minutes +20 to +30

Objective R5d 2.0 to R12a 2.0 from thence to S end of [illegible] Copse

7. ACKNOWLEDGE.

Issued at 6.45 pm

H.C. Harcourt Lieut
for Capt.
[illegible] M.G.

Q.N.Q. [illegible] Operation Orders. SECRET

SECRET NOT TO BE TAKEN INTO ACTION. 6. 4. 1917.

Ref Map 62c S.E. 1/20,000. [illegible]

APPENDIX III

1 Enemy holds line [illegible] trenches on approx line R5c 3.6 through R5b 0.4. S.E. of MAREVAL COPSE through R4b 4.5 and thence N.W. up the [illegible] in R5.

2 The OXFORDS and GLOUCESTERS will attack this line on the night of the 6th April. The 182nd Bde will cooperate on the S flank of the GLOUCESTERS, its objective being from about [illegible] [illegible] S. towards the S.E.

3 OBJECTIVES.

1. GLOUCESTERS from R4b 4.5 to R5c 4.2 exclusive.

OXFORDS from R5c 4.2 inclusive to R5c 6.9.

2. GLOUCESTERS from MAREVAL COPSE inclusive to [illegible].

OXFORDS from MAREVAL COPSE exclusive to about R5a 0.5.

4 (a) GLOUCESTERS will send a strong patrol to [illegible] which must be occupied if possible and to [illegible] [illegible].

(b) O.C. OXFORDS will establish strong points at R5c 8.6. R5c 5.8. & R5c 0.4 which must be behind the crest.

5 M.G. Company will cooperate as follows:-

(a) O.C. No1 Section will place 2 Guns in position near No2 Wood which will bring intermittent fire to bear on high ground comprised in Square R4. right limit of [illegible] R4 b 9.7 left limit [illegible] R3 b 8.9.

(b) [illegible] with 1 Gun will advance with left flank OXFORDS and take up a position about R5.a.5.3 to protect the flank

(c) 1 Gun will be in immediate support in No3 Wood and will be at the disposal of O.C. OXFORDS - [illegible].

6. (a) O.C. No2 Section will place 1 Gun in position about R17 a 8.2. This Gun will bring into action against any Enemy [illegible] enfilading Right flank Gloucesters and prevent counter attack on 1st Objective.

(b) [illegible] with 1 Gun will advance with Right Flank Gloucesters and act as situation demands.

(c) O.C. No2 Section will detail 1 Gun to be in immediate support in [illegible] opposite CHATEAU. This Gun will be ready to reinforce the line at any moment.

(d) O.C. No3 Section will detail 1 Gun & Team to report to & be at disposal of O.C. No1 Section at R10 c 6.5.

7. No 4 Section will be in reserve behind No 5 Coy. This section may be required to bring additional fire to bear on high ground in R3 b + R4.

8. No 3 Section will be in reserve at Cross Roads BIHECOURT.

9. No M.G. will come into action before ZERO.

10. ZERO + hours of artillery bombardment will be notified later.

11. Advanced Bgy H.Q. R.2.b.5. to which all reports should be sent.

ACKNOWLEDGE.

Issued at 11.30 am.

H.C. [illegible] Lt.
for

Addenda to QNA Operation orders dated [illegible]/4/17

12. 59 Bn. will co-operate on left flank, advancing from Cross Roads in R9 b central to left Objective R5c6.9 along spur NW.

13. OC No1 Section will cease fire on ridge at ZERO + 30

SGT Froggatt with 1 gun will report to OC No1 Section at 8pm

ZERO will be at midnight 6/7th at which hour the artillery bombardment will commence.

The lines of bombardment will be:–

ZERO – 0.25	– Moderate rate	On line of trench from R11.b.5.5 toward LEVERGUIER along the frontage to be attacked and from R11.b.5.5 along trench in a SE direction.
0.25 – 0.35	– Quicker rate	
0.35 – 0.40	Intense.	
0.40 – 0.60	Creep 100yds every 4 mins. to road running through M7a, R6c, R5b.	
0.60 – 1.30	Remain on this line.	
1.30	Fire will cease except for SOS which will produce fire in that locality from which SOS is sent up, on final line of bombardment.	

Artillery will also fire from ROAD JUNCTION R18 c.8.3 to ROAD JUNCTION R11.C.8.8. at ZERO and creep by lifts of 100yds every ~~4~~ 4 mins. till 0.50.

0.[illegible] – 0.60 on trench S.E. of ROAD.
0.60 – 1.30 on final barrage line
1.30 Fire will cease as above described

Heavies will fire on selected points about PONTRU and TUMULUS

ACKNOWLEDGE

A.C. Harcourt Lieut

for.

MAPA. Ref Sheet 62C. SE

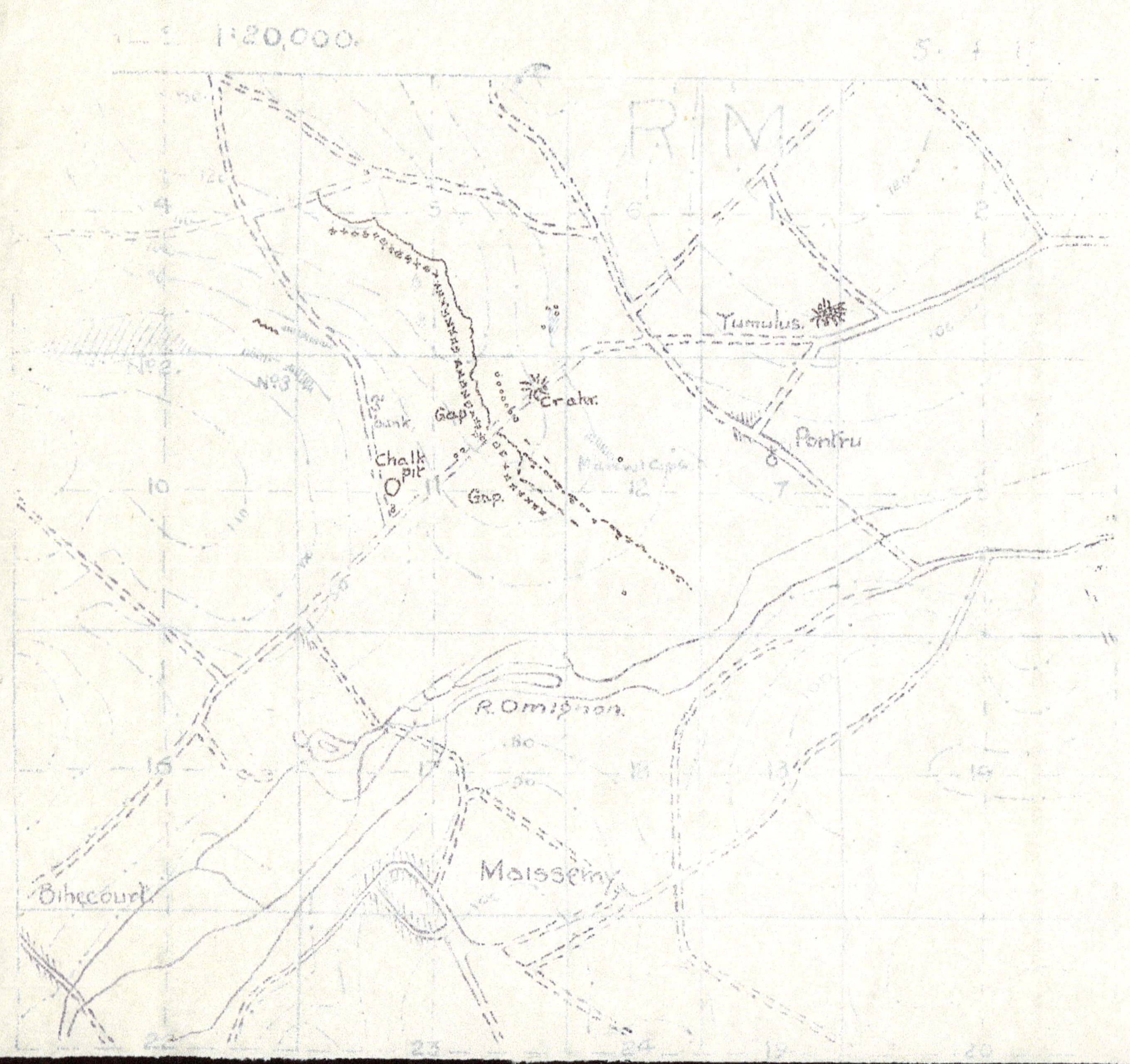

Q H A Operation Orders No 1

APPENDIX IV

7 4 1917

1 No 3 Section will relieve No 2 Section night of 8th in positions at present occupied by No. 2 Section

2 Guides of No 2 Section will be at CROSS ROADS BIHECOURT 7 30 Pm

3. Tripods will be handed over on relief. Guns, Spare Parts & Belt Boxes will be taken in by relieving Section.

4 No 3 Section will take in rations for 8th inst.

5 Handing over certificates to be made out in duplicate and signed by both Section Officers. Copy to Coy H.Q.

6 Batt H.Q. 2/4 BERKS in railway Cutting R20 d 9.5

7 ACKNOWLEDGE.

[signature] Capt.
COMDG. 184 COMPANY M.G. CORPS

Copies to O.C. No 2
" 3
" 1 for Information
War Diary File

Issued at 4 30 Pm

III APPENDIX V

Lt PARSONS 8/[illegible]/17
OC QNA 3

1. Orders given you this afternoon are cancelled

2. You will arrange to have 3 guns on road R.11.C.20 and will bring fire to bear on ground between MAREVAL COPSE + RIVER. 2 guns will be detailed for this

3. 1 gun will search ground in M.7 a, S. of TUMULUS

4. 182 Inf Bde are attacking on our right tomorrow morning 9th inst.

5. Time fire is to be opened will be notified you later

6. Aiming marks should be got out before dark

7. ACKNOWLEDGE.

6.55 pm [illegible]

APPENDIX VI

Lt. PARSONS
O C QMA 3 8/4/17

Artillery have cut a gap in enemys wire 30x wide. This gap is 30 yards to N. of BIHECOURT-BEAUMETZ-BLISE Road.

I enclose a map showing exactly where gap is, marked with a cross.

You will arrange to fire at this gap intermittently during night. The Emplacement[s] just in front of CHATEAU Road would be suitable.

You will not fire between 11 pm & 11 AM. at which time patrols will be out.

No of rounds fired at gap to be reported in T.P.R

[signature]

7.15 pm

VI

To O.C. 3 Q.H.A.

APPENDIX VII

8. 4. 1917

Ref to my note to you this evening regarding cooperation with 182 Bde attack, Artillery Bombardment commences 5.15 am. Infantry assaults 5.30 am. Artillery ceases 6 am.

Your 3 Guns will sweep prescribed areas, opening fire at 5.30 am, and closing fire at 6 am.

You should be careful not to fire S. side of river.

In the event of the 182 Bde gaining their objectives, it is probable that Enemy will have to withdraw from his position in front of our Sector. A careful lookout should be kept on Enemy's line, and any parties seen should be immediately fired on.

W Napier

9.45 pm

[illegible] Operation Orders [illegible]

APPENDIX VIII

[illegible]

1 [illegible]

2 [illegible]

3 [illegible]

4 [illegible] Cross Roads [illegible]

5 Sections [illegible]

6 [illegible] Cross Roads at 3 [illegible]

7 [illegible]

[illegible]

[illegible]

CAPT.

COMDG. 184 COMPANY M. G. CORPS.

1st A M.G. Coy. Operation Orders No 5
12.4.[illegible]

APPENDIX IX

1 The Company will march to Mon Fleur today 12-4-18 via
[illegible] - [illegible] - [illegible] - [illegible] - L'ECUMEE
DOULLY - TOULLE - [illegible] - MON FLEUX.
Company to pass starting point [illegible] at 11-50 am.

2 Company to parade 10.55 am outside Officers Quarters ready to move off at 11-5 am.
Order of march 3. 4. 1. 2. [illegible] full marching order.

3 Limbers and Cooks Wagon to be packed by 10.45 am.

4 Company Cooks will proceed at 10 am ~~[illegible]~~ & prepare dinners for the Coy at Mon Fleur.

5 Section Officers will inspect their Sections & details [illegible] before the 10.55 am parade.

Sheet 62C & 66D 1/40,000.

Operation ~~Company~~ Orders No 6

APPENDIX 184 Coy M.G. Corps 18.4.18

I The 184 MG Coy will relieve the 97 MG Coy in Reserve Area FORESTE 19.4.18

2 Lieut Caswell T3 Signaller will move from Coy HQ at 4.30am to take over new Billets

3 Company Parade 7.45 Am move off at 8 Am ROUTE:-
Main HORBLEUX. HAM Road to CANIZY-OFFOY BRIDGE - TOULLE. DOUILLY - FORESTE.
Order of march:-
H.Q. Nos 1. 2. 3. 4 Sections - Transport.

4 Billets will be thoroughly cleaned by 7 Am. Orderly Officer will inspect.

Copies to all S.O.s
1 Copy - War DIARY.
1 " 184 Inf Bde
1 " FILE.

Issued at 11 P.M.

W Napier CAPT.
COMDG. 184 COMPANY M. G. CORPS.

APPENDIX XI

184 Coy M. G. Corps 19.4.1917

Ref sheet 62.c SW

SECRET OPERATION ORDER No 4

NOT TO BE TAKEN INTO THE LINE.

1) The 184 M.G. Coy will relieve the 96th M.G. Coy in the line 20.4.17

2 1) No 1 Section will relieve Left Forward Guns in outpost line N of FAYET

2) No 2 Section will relieve Right Forward Guns in outpost line S of FAYET

3) No 3 Section will relieve Left BROWN Group N of SALENCY.

4) No 4 Section will relieve Right BROWN Group S of SALENCY.

3 No 3 & 4 Sections will move off at 2.30 Pm. Guides will be met at X Roads HOLNON at 5 Pm.

ROUTE:- GERMAINE - ETREILLERS - SAVY.

4 Nos 1 & 2 Sections will move off at 4 45 Pm, Guides will be met at X Roads HOLNON at 7.15 Pm.

ROUTE as for Nos 3 & 4 SECTIONS.

5 One man per Gun Team per Forward Group and one man per Sub Section in BROWN LINE, will be left in by No 96 M.G. Coy for 12 hours after the Relief.

6 Completion of Relief to be reported to Coy H.Q by out-going Teams. CODE:- "FAITHFUL FRITZ"

7 Coy H.Q RAILWAY EMB X 11 d.2.0.

QM Stores & Transport ATTILLY.

ACKNOWLEDGE.

Copy No 1 - Coy HQ
2
3 184 Inf Bde
4 WAR DIARY
5 FILE
6 O.C. No 1 Section
7 O.C. No 2 do

Copy No 8. O.C. No 3
9 - OC No 3 S. Sec.
10. OC No 4 Sect
11 - OC No 4 S. Sect
12 - Transport Officer
13 C.S.M
14 C Q M.S

No 15 - 96 M.G. Coy.

W Napier CAPT.
COMDG. 184 COMPANY M. G. CORPS.

MAP B. Sheet 62B S.W.

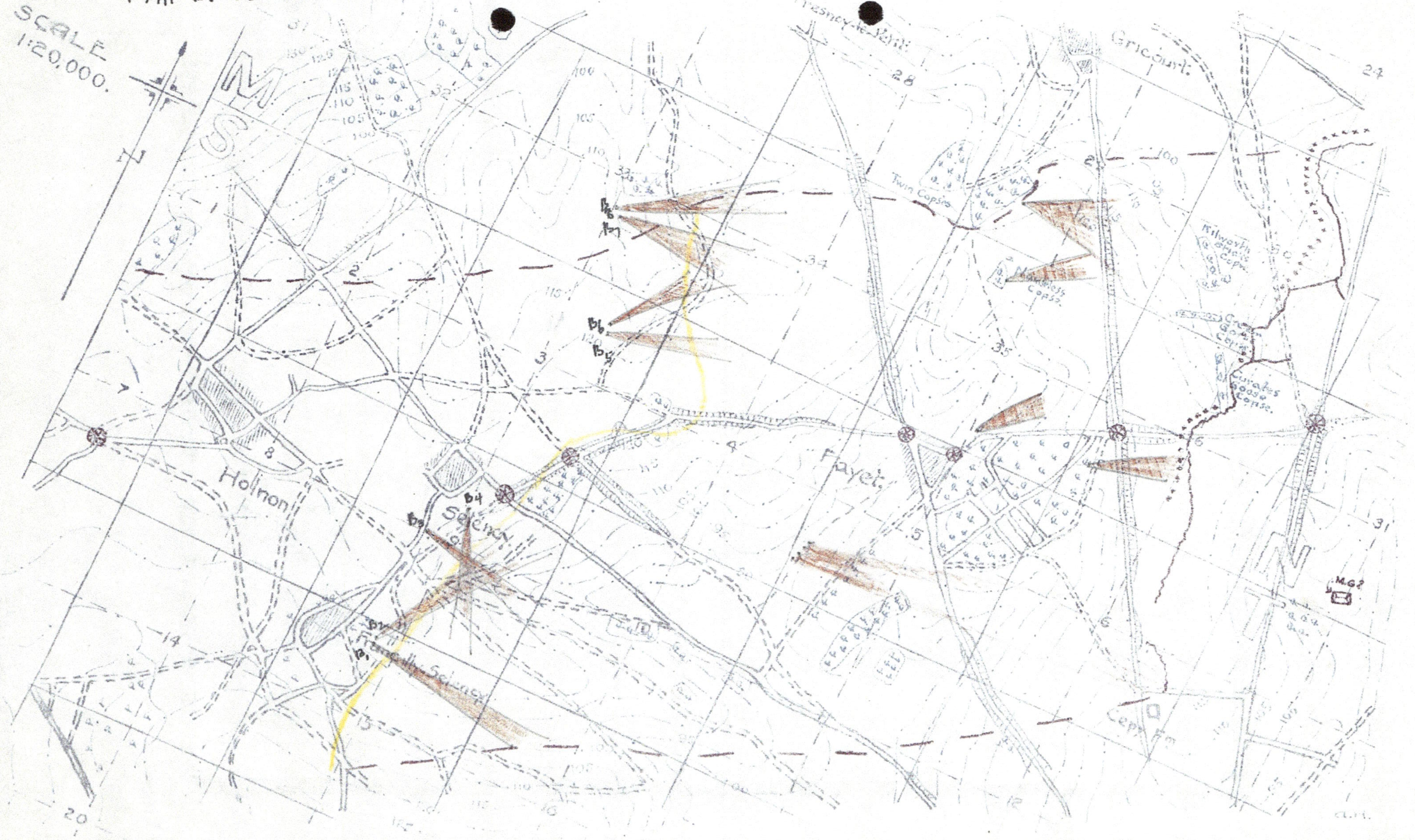

SCALE
1:20,000.
Fresnoy-le-Petit
Gricourt.
Twin Copses
Nameless Copse.
Kilworth Copse
Goose Copse.
Fayet.
Holnon
Selency
Francilly Selency
Cepy Fm.
M.G.?

Q.M.G. Operation Order No 1 / 24.4.17

APPENDIX XII

1 No 3 Section will relieve No 1 Section in OUTPOST line night of 24-25th

2 2 Guns No 4 Sec will relieve 2 Guns No 2 Sec in OUTPOST LINE night of 24-25th.

3. Guides from No 1 Sec will be at No 3 Sec HQ 9 pm

4 Guides from No 2 Sec will be at No 4 Sec HQ 9 pm.

5 1 Limber Gun team will stay in the line 12 hours after relief.

6 Trench & Belt Boxes will be taken over.

7. 2 Guns No 2 Sec will move up to Reserve near No 4 Sec HQ night of 24-25th.

Acknowledge

Issued at 11am

Copies to all Section Officers
1 copy War Diary
1 " File

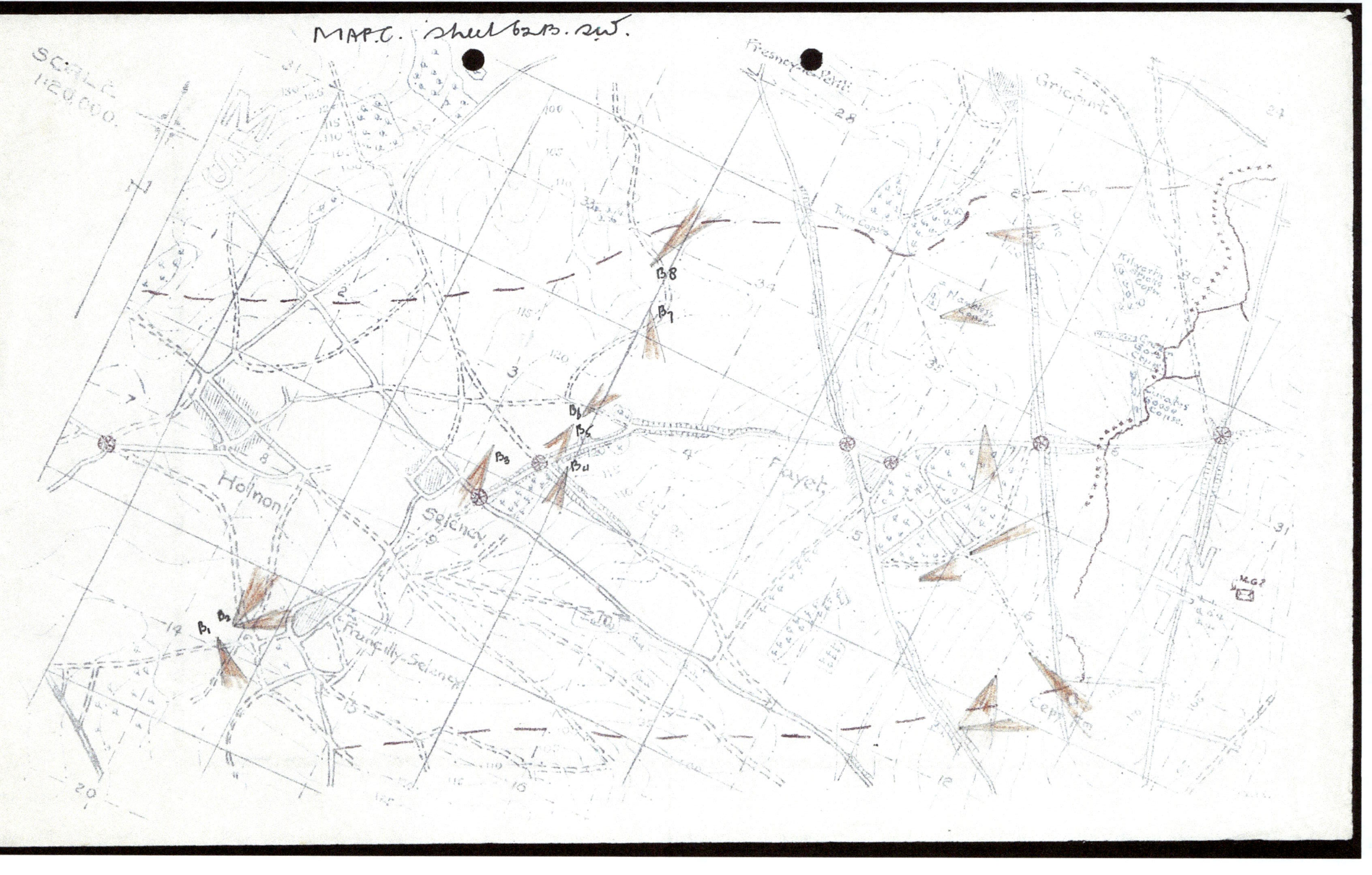

MAP C. shell bs. r.w.
SCALE 1:20,000.
Fresnoy-le-Petit
Gricourt
Twin Copse
Fayet
Holnon
Selency
Francilly-Selency
B1
B2
B3
B4
B5
B6
B7
B8

APPENDIX XIII

[illegible] A. Operation Orders No 8

[illegible].4.17

1 184 M.G. Coy will relieve 2 Guns of No 182 M.G. Coy. on night of 25/26th positions :- S6d.5.7
S6d.0.9.

2 1 Sub Section of No 4 Section at present in support, will be given a guide by O.C. No 2 Section and will be at Section H.Q. S5c.2.5. by 9 pm. night of 25th

3 182 M.G. Coy will supply guides. Time & place to be notified later.

4 182 M.G. Coy will leave 1 N.C.O. per Gun in the line for 12 hours after Relief.

5 Completion of relief to be reported to ~~this Office~~ by wire

Code for Completion:-
"SALLY IN OUR ALLEY"

ACKNOWLEDGE.

1 Copy - O.C. No 2 Sec
1 do - do No 4 "
1 do O.C. 182 M.G. Coy
1 do War Diary
1 do File.

[illegible] Capt
Comdg Q. M. A.

[illegible] Operation Order No 8

APPENDIX XIV

[illegible].4.17

1 184 M.G. Coy will relieve 2 Guns of No 182 M.G. Coy on night of 25/26th
positions: S6d.5.7
S6d.0.4.

2 [illegible] Section of the Section at present in support will be given a guide by O.C. No 2 Section and will be at Section HQ S5c.2.5 by 9 pm night of 25th

3 182 M.G. Coy will supply guides. Time & place to be notified later.

4 182 M.G. Coy will leave 1 N.C.O. per gun in the line for 12 hours after relief.

5 Completion of relief to be reported to ~~[illegible]~~ by wire

Code for completion:-
"[illegible]"

ACKNOWLEDGE.

1 Copy O.C. No 2 Sec
1 " " " No 4 "
1 " [illegible] M.G. Coy
1 do [illegible]
1 do File

[illegible] Capt
Comdg [illegible]

[SECRET]

APPENDIX XV

Reference: Q.N.A. Operation no. 11 of 27.4.17

Sheet 62 B. S.W.

1. The OXFORDS will raid the enemy's trench running from M.36 central as far as M.30 b.5.4 employing for the purpose not more than one company plus two platoons named in this order Y & Z

2. Deployment will be carried out by the company employed in normal attack formation on the line M.36.d.0.8 to about M.36.d.4.7

Y & Z platoons will deploy echeloned to the right rear of the company

The two special parties will deploy to the left rear of the company, the MOPPERS UP in front, WIRECUTTERS in the rear.

The utmost care will be exercised to make the Deployment as noiseless as possible

3. ZERO will be at 4.20 a.m. 28 April

4. The company will advance at ZERO

Y platoon will advance straight to crater at M.36.b.9.5. the remainder due N. the left flank resting on a trench running through M.36 central

↑N ↑N

5. M.G.s will cooperate as follows
(a) 2 guns of no1. section will be about M.36.d.3.2 and will fire on ground in M.31.c, M.31.d, & T.1.b. from ZERO onwards left limit of traverse 93° magnetic
(b) 4 guns of no.3 section will be in position about M.29.d.1.5 and will fire as per attached table

6. Report centre QUARRY M.34.d.9.6

7. ACKNOWLEDGE

Issued at noon
27.4.17

G. [illegible]
for
O.C. [illegible]

Copy
no.1 OXFORDS
no.2 GNA1
no.3 GNA3
no.4 B.M.
no.5 W.D.
no.6 file.

30

Ref. Operation Orders no. 10.
of 21.4.17

Herewith table of firing

1. no 3 section with fuse as follows:-

(a) ZERO to +5 on wood in M.36.c. central

Bearing 73° – 83° magnetic

Elevation { no 1 gun 0°43' to 1°2'
no. 2. gun 0°52' to 1°13'
no. 3 gun 1°2' to 1°26'
no. 4. gun 1°13' to 1°41'

(b) +5 to +30 – enfilade barrage
from M.30 a. 4.8 to M.25. c. 5.9

Bearing 55° magnetic

Elevation { no 1. gun 1°41' to 2°57'
no. 2 gun 2°35' to 4°16'
no. 3. gun 3°47' to 6°0'
no. 4 gun 5°22' to 7°27'

Reference Q.N.A. Operation Orders no. 11.
of 27.4.17

Corrections as follows

1. Para 5 for "M.31.c, M.31.d"
read "N.31.c, N.31.d"

2. attached table para 1(a)
for "M.36.c central"
read "M.30.c central"

Copy 1 OXFORDS
2 QNA1
3 QNA3
4 Bde
5 W.D.
6 file

[signature] CAPT
COMDG. 184 COMPANY M. G. CORPS.

Q.M.G. Operation Orders No 11

28. 4. 1917

APPENDIX XVII

1 No "2" Section will relieve No 4 Section in OUTPOST LINE night of 28-29th. Guides to be at No 2 Section H.Q. 7 Pm.

2 No 1 Section will relieve No 3 Section in OUTPOST LINE night of 28-29th. Guides to be at No 1 Sec HQ 7 Pm.

3 Trench boards & Bells will be taken over on relief.

4 Section Sgt + 1 Man per Gun team No 4 Section will be left in the line 12 hours after relief.

5 Rations for 29th will be taken up by Sections relieving.

6 Completion of relief to be reported by wire.

Code:-

"SALLY IN OUR ALLEY."

ACKNOWLEDGE

W Napier

CAPT

COMDG. 184 COMPANY M. G. CORPS.

Vol 12

C O N F I D E N T I A L.

W A R D I A R Y - V O L U M E X11

----- of ------

184TH COMPANY, MACHINE GUN CORPS

------ For -------

PERIOD MAY 1ST to MAY 31ST

1917.

****

Instructions regarding War Diaries and Intelligence Summaries are contained in F. S. Regs., Part II. and the Staff Manual respectively. Title pages will be prepared in manuscript.

184 M.G. Co

WAR DIARY
or
INTELLIGENCE SUMMARY.
(Erase heading not required.)

Army Form C. 2118.

Place	Date	Hour	Summary of Events and Information	Remarks and references to Appendices
RAILWAY EMBANKMENT X.11.D.2.0 (Sheet 62D.SE) near HOLNON.	1		All guns of the company in the line: eight in outpost and eight in BROWN line	APP. A (Map)
		12.0 noon	Orders issued for relief of the company by 183 Company on night of 1st/2nd. Relief complete at 2 am. 2nd inst.	APP. 1.
FORESTE	2	6.0am	Company H.Q. to FORESTE (ST QUENTIN 1/40000 sheet) Company in billets in stables, cellars &c. Casualties nil. 3 O.R. reported arrival	
–	3.		Company employed in cleaning up guns, equipment, overhauling belts &c brought out of the line. 4 O.R. reported arrival	
–	4		Training in elementary gun drill, auxiliary mounting drill, use of ground & cover & range practice (stoppages) carried out	
–	5.		Training: squad & arms drill, points B.D.A, advanced drill. Preparation for inspection by G.O.C. 61st Division. 12 O.R. reported arrival	
–	6	10am	Company and transport equipment &c inspected by Sir Colin McKenzie G.O.C. 61st Division who expressed his satisfaction with the company and transport. Two Military Medals awarded to Sgt Hawkins and Cpl Green presented by G.O.C. 61st Div. {16 men attached to the company from infantry units. (These men were afterwards returned to units by G.O.C. 61. Division).	

A5834 Wt. W4973 M687 750,000 8/16 D. D. & L. Ltd. Forms/C.2118/13.

Instructions regarding War Diaries and Intelligence Summaries are contained in F. S. Regs., Part II. and the Staff Manual respectively. Title pages will be prepared in manuscript.

WAR DIARY
or
INTELLIGENCE SUMMARY.
(Erase heading not required.)

Army Form C. 2118.

Place	Date	Hour	Summary of Events and Information	Remarks and references to Appendices
FORESTE	7		Training in advanced drill, I.A, squad drill. Lecture to N.C.O.s in use of AA. sights. Afternoon devoted to recreation	
	8.		Training: Arms drill, Physical training, gas drill, testing guns & preparation for brigade parade on the 9th Lecture to N.C.O.s on "Map reading" & to officers on "use of A.A. sights"	
	9.		Training: Packing and cleaning of limbers, revolver practice, lecture on "Machine Guns in Open Warfare" by section officers.	
		2.45pm.	Company paraded at a brigade parade under Lt.Col. Balfour Cmdg. the 184 Bde. for inspection by the G.O.C. 61st Division & presentation of parchments.	
	10.		Training: Physical training, use of ground & cover, Company drill, Pts. B.D.A afternoon devoted to company sports.	
	11.		Training: Sections training under section officers, general overhauling of guns &c in view of possible relief.	
			2/Lt URQUHART reported arrival.	

A5834 Wt. W4973/M687 750,000 8/16 D. D. & L. Ltd. Forms/C.2118/13.

Instructions regarding War Diaries and Intelligence Summaries are contained in F. S. Regs., Part II. and the Staff Manual respectively. Title pages will be prepared in manuscript.

WAR DIARY
or
INTELLIGENCE SUMMARY.
(Erase heading not required.)

Army Form C. 2118.

Place	Date	Hour	Summary of Events and Information	Remarks and references to Appendices
FORESTE	12		Training comprised Squad + Company Drill, overhauling guns + equipment preparatory to move	
	13	4 a.m.	Company moved to NESLE area in accordance with Operation Orders. Company in huts N.W. of MANICOURT (~~Sheet~~ AMIENS 1/40000)	APP. 2
MANICOURT	14		Company training comprised revolver practice, physical training, company + arms drill. Transport moved in accordance with Brigade orders by road.	
	15.		Company entrained at NESLE for LONGEAU + marched to CAMON. Company in billets in CAMON.	APP. 3.
	16.		Training in close order + arms drill; cleaning + overhauling guns + limbers.	
	17		Company moved to TALMAS (LENS, 11 1/10,000)	APP 4.

A5834 Wt. W4973 M687 750,000 8/16 D. D. & L. Ltd. Forms/C.2118/13.

Instructions regarding War Diaries and Intelligence Summaries are contained in F. S. Regs., Part II. and the Staff Manual respectively. Title pages will be prepared in manuscript.

WAR DIARY

~~INTELLIGENCE SUMMARY.~~

(Erase heading not required.)

Army Form C. 2118.

Place	Date	Hour	Summary of Events and Information	Remarks and references to Appendices
TALMAS	18th		Training. Ammo drill, gun drill and range work	
	19th		Training - attack in conjunction with Battalions. LT. F.R. Parsons off str. to U.K.	
	20th		Preparation for move	
RANSART	21st		Company moved to RANSART (LENS 11 1/100000)	APPENDIX 5
	23rd		Company moved to FOSSEUX (LENS 11 1/100000) LT F. LISMORE reported arrival as 2 i/c	Appendix 6
DUISANS	24th		Company moved to DUISANS (LENS 11 1/100000)	Appendix 7
	25th		Training - Squad drill - stoppages. Cleaning limbers.	
	26th		Training - No1 section with 2/5 Glosters practising attack. Remainder overhauling equipment and range work	
	27th		Training - No2 Section with 2/4 Bucks in attack. Remainder Gas drill, gun drill, indirect fire by night. 3 O.R. arrived. Lt. R.I. McKAY off str. to Hospital	
	28th		Training - No 3 Section with 2/4 Oxford and Bucks in attack. Remainder as on 27th	
	29th		Training - No 4 Section with 2/4 Berks - remainder as before.	
	30th		Training continued	
N10G77	31st		Moved to forward area - guns in line duplicating positions occupied by 111 M.G. Co. Commenced taking up positions at 9.30 p.m. not completed by midnight.	Appendix 8
			Company strength at end of month Officers 11 O.R. 172	SHEET 51B N.W. 51B S.W.

[signature] CAPT.

84 COMPANY

A5834 Wt. W4973/M687 750,000 8/16 D. D. & L. Ltd. Forms/C.2118/13.

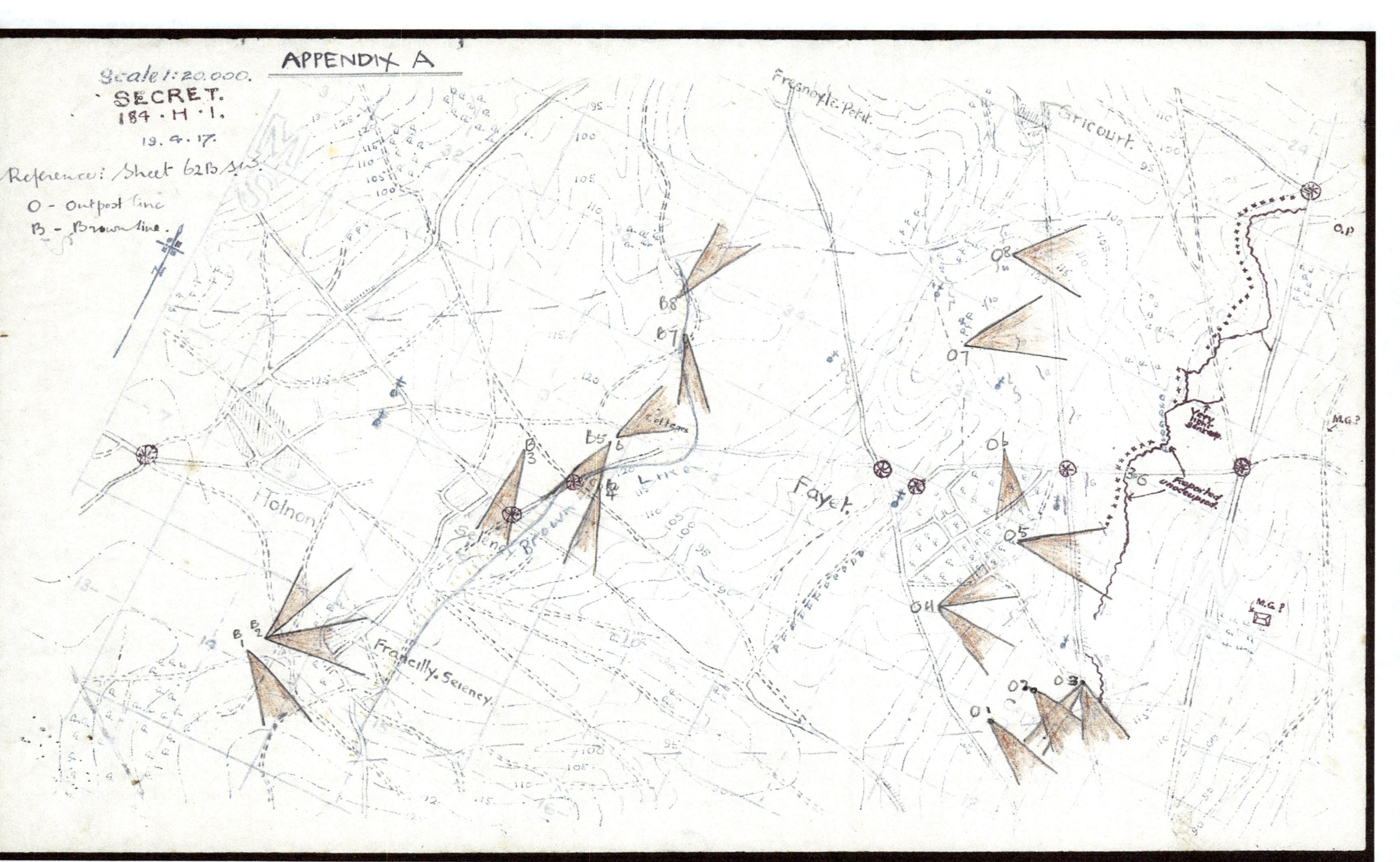
APPENDIX A
Scale 1:20.000.
SECRET.
184 · H · 1.
19. 4. 17.
Reference: Sheet 62B S.W.
O - Outpost line
B - Brown line.
Fresnoy le Petit.
Gricourt.
Fayet.
Holnon
Selency
Brown Line
Francilly. Selency.
Cottages
Reported unoccupied.
Very light sentry
O.P
M.G.?
O1
O2
O3
O4
O5
O6
O7
O8
B1
B2
B3
B5
B7
B8

APPENDIX 1

Handed over & Receipt obtained.

W Napier CAPT.
COMDG. 184 COMPANY M. G. CORPS.

WD.

Operation Orders No 14. APPENDIX 2

184 Coy. M.G. Corps 12.5.17

I The Company will move to the NESLE area tomorrow 13th inst.

2 Parade 4 am in front of Hangars in Transport Lines. Order of march:-

No 1 Section
2 "
3 "
4 "
Headquarters
Transport.

Route:

DOUILLY - MATIGNY - BUNY - VOYENNES

3 Lieut McKay will remain behind and hand over all Maps Sketches & Defence Scheme to incoming Unit.

Copies to O.C. Sections.
1 Copy - 184 Bde
1 " - Transport Officer
1 " War Diary
1 " C.S.M.
1 " C.Q.M.S.

G. Miller Lieut
for Capt
Comdg 184 Coy M.G.C.

Issued at 4.30 pm

~~Company~~ Operation Order No 14
184 Coy M. G. Corps. 12 · 5 · 1917

I The Company will march tomorrow at 13 h to NESLE area.

2 Parade of Coy in front of Limbers in Transport Lines.
Order of March :- No 1 Section
2 -
3 -
4 -
Head Quarters
Transport
Route :- DOUILLY. MATIGNY. BUNY. VOYENNES.

3. Lt McKay will remain behind to hand over all Maps. Sketches & Defence Scheme, to incoming Unit.

Copies to O^s C Section.
1 Copy. 184 Bde
1 " Transport Officer
1 " War Diary
1 " C.S.M.
1 " C.Q.M.S.

G. [illegible]
for Capt
Comdg 184 Coy M.G.C.

Issued at 4 · 30 PM

Operation Orders No. 15 APPEDIX 3

184 Coy M G Corps 14-5-17

1 The Company will march to NESLE Station 15th and will entrain for LONGEAU.

2 <u>Parade 4.30 am</u>

<u>Dress.</u> Full marching order. Steel helmets will be carried on pack.

<u>Order of March.</u> No 1.2.3.4 & HdQrs.

<u>Water Bottles</u> will be filled before marching.

3 <u>Starting Point.</u> X Roads 400 Yds due N of 17 of Maricourt

<u>Route.</u> MARICOURT - NESLE Rd to B of FRES then [illegible] direct to Station.

<u>REF MAP:- AMIENS 17.</u>

Administrative Details in Company Orders.

Copies to Section Officers

1 Copy War Diary

1 " File

1 " 184 Inf Bde

[illegible]

for Lt.

Operation Order No 16 APPEDIX 4
184 Coy M.G.C. [illegible]

1. The Company will march tomorrow 7th to Thieves [illegible]
Route Rivery - Bouchonville - Villers - Bocage.

2. Reveille 2 am
Breakfast 2.45 am
Parade 4.10 am

3. Full marching order. 3.4.2.1 M.G. [illegible] Packs must be carried on limbers.

E J Mills

CAPT.
COMDG. 184 COMPANY M. G. CORPS.

Operation Orders No. 6.   Appendix 5
184 Company M.G. Corps   [illegible] 1917

I   The Company will march to and billet in RAMSART tomorrow 21st inst.
     Route. BEAUVAL. DOULLENS. HAUTE [illegible].

II   Parade. 6.45 am.
     Dress marching order without packs.
          Haversacks slung. Waterproof sheet rolled and strapped under flap of haversack.
          Mess tin in haversack.

III Order of March. 4. 1. 2. 3. HQ. Transport.

IV   There will be a halt from 7.50 am until 8.50 am.

W. Napier CAPT.
COMDG. 184 COMPANY M.G. CORPS.

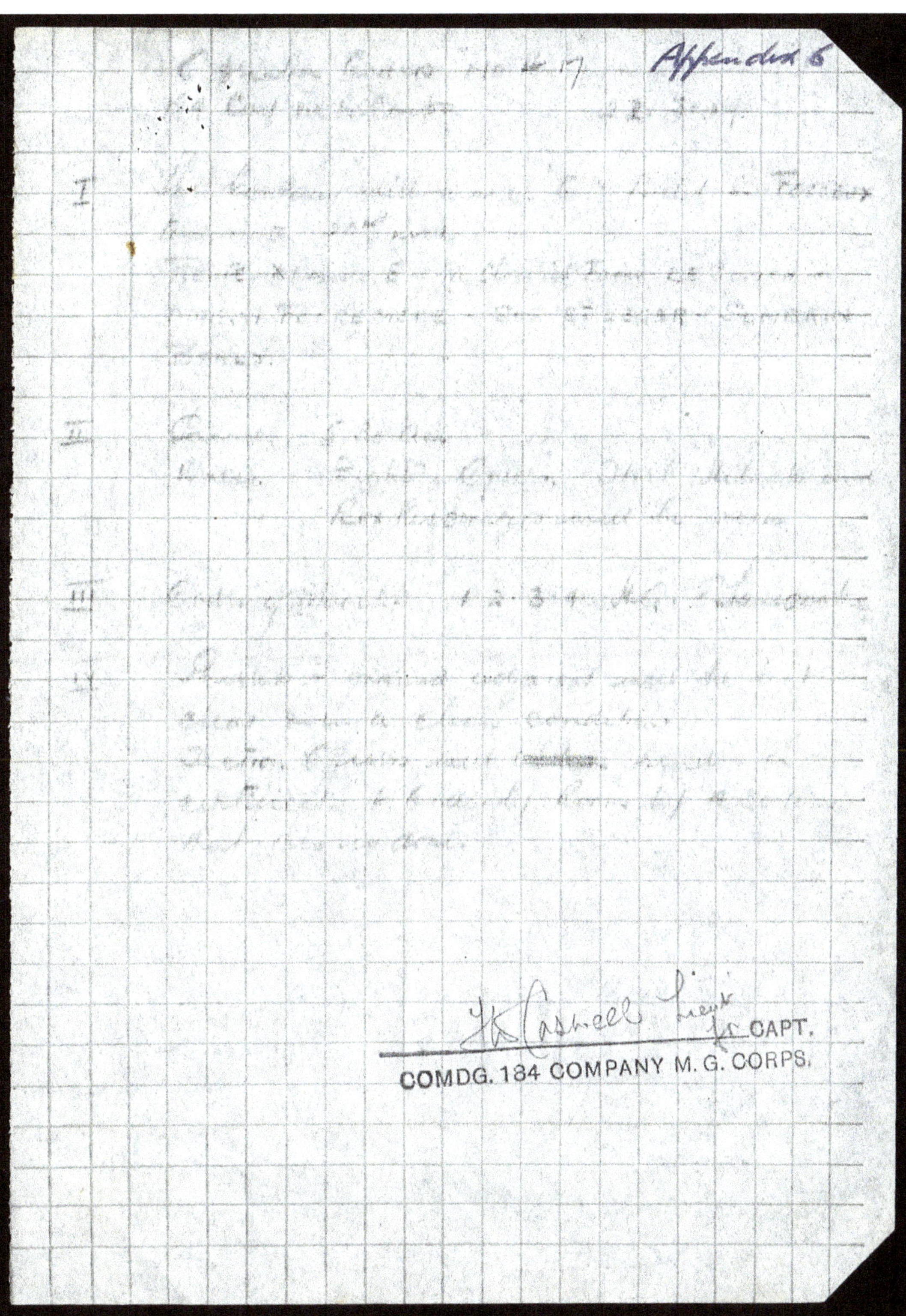

Appendix 6

CAPT.
COMDG. 184 COMPANY M. G. CORPS.

Operation Orders No 18 | Appendix 7

184 M.G. Coy. | 23.5.1917

1 The Company will march to DUISANS area tomorrow 24.5.1917.
Route. WANQUETIN – WARLUS – [illegible]

2 Parade 8.45 am
Dress – Full marching Order with Packs
Steel Helmet & Box Respirators will be worn.

3. Order of march 1.2.3.4, H.Q. Transport.

4 Billets & Ground adjacent will be left clean & in a clean condition.
Section Officers will send a certificate to this effect to Orderly Room by 9 am.

H.L. Caswell Lieut for CAPT.
COMDG. 184 COMPANY M.G. CORPS.

Operation Orders No 18 — Appendix 8
114 Coy. M.G. Corps — 30.5.1917

Ref. France 1/100.000
Sheet 51B N.W. 51B S.W. 1/20.000

1 The 114 M.G. Coy will move on the 31st inst from DAINVILLE to [illegible] area of the 114th Inf Bde.
Starting point [illegible] at DAINVILLE at 8.55 am.

2 The Company will parade at 8.30 am on [illegible] moving off at 8.45 am. [illegible] fighting limbers [illegible] transport fighting formation.
200 yards distance will be maintained between sections from PORTE BOUDEMENT.
Route: [illegible] – [illegible] – [illegible] – BOIS DES BOEUFS – [illegible] ROAD – Track to H10 b 1.4.

3 The regular halts will be made except between DAINVILLE and PORTE BOUDEMENT.
The Company will halt in Bois des Boeufs [illegible] 1.30 pm.

4 Dinners [illegible] will be prepared in Bois des Boeufs and rations for June 1st issued.

5 The following dispositions will be taken over:-

No 3 Section	2 Guns [illegible] Trench
No 4 do less 1 detachment	1 " Section H.Q.
under 2/Lt [illegible] with	2 " [illegible] Trench
2/Lt [illegible]	2 " Rake do

1 detachment No 4
1 do No 2 under
2/Lt Wonderley [?] } 2 Guns GUEMAPPE.

No 2 less 1 detachment — No 1 Gun Posn 40.45.
No 1 Section, under — 23 do S. Cambrai Rd
2/Lt Griffiths — 45 do N do do
64 do TWIN LANE.

6. 1 Guide per detachment of Guns in front of GUEMAPPE will be at WANCOURT CHURCH N23 b 3.2. at 4.30 pm.
1 Guide per detachment for remaining positions will be at HQ 111th M.G. Coy N10 b 4.4. at 9 pm.
7. 1 Man per detachment & 1 Officer per group of detachments of relieving Coy's will remain in the line for 12 hours after completion of relief.
8. Certificates for S.A.A. & other Stores taken over will be signed in duplicate and 1 copy forwarded to Coy H.Q. N10 b 4.4.
9. On completion of Reliefs, Transport will return to Bde Transport lines at G 33 d.
10. Completion of Relief will be reported per runner. Code. SCRAP.

W Napier [?] CAPT.
COMDG. 184 COMPANY M.G. CORPS.

C O N F I D E N T I A L,

Vol 13

W A R   D I A R Y

**** of ***

184th COMPANY, MACHINE GUN CORPS

**** From ****

June 1st, 1917 to J une 30th, 1917.

(VOLUME X111)

****

Instructions regarding War Diaries and Intelligence Summaries are contained in F. S. Regs., Part II. and the Staff Manual respectively. Title pages will be prepared in manuscript.

WAR DIARY

~~or~~

~~INTELLIGENCE SUMMARY.~~

(Erase heading not required.)

184 Machine Gun Company

Army Form C. 2118.

Place	Date	Hour	Summary of Events and Information	Remarks and references to Appendices
ARRAS-GAMBRAI ROAD SECTOR	June 1		Detachments of 111 M.G. Co relieved by 2 a.m. Dispositions taken up :-	Map 51 B S.W. 1/20000
Co Hq N10 G 77			O7 b 23, O7 b 63, O7 b 72, O7 d 54, O7 d 56, O13 b 23, O13 b 26 } Forward group. O19 a 73, O19 a 75 } GUEMAPPE group. N12 b 09, N12 b 08, N12 b 03, N12 b 02, N12 c 36, N12 c 32, N11 d 25 } Rear group	
			ANTI-AIRCRAFT positions prepared near each of rear group guns.	
	2		Detachment at O7 b 63 moved to O7 b 71	
			A·A guns drove back enemy planes on two occasions.	
	3		Our guns active at A·A work - good results - enemy planes turned back repeatedly	
	4		Detachments in Rear group exchanged with those in FORWARD group. Gun at O19a 75 moved to O19a 38	APPENDIX I OO 9 [illegible]
	5		Work commenced on new scheme. Gun positions sited in adjacent shellholes - a dugout shaft, the dug from each meeting in a chamber eighteen to twenty feet below ground. It is necessary to enlarge the shellhole before commencing the dug out. All the work has to be camouflaged each day at dawn.	
	8		Working parties supplied by 183 M.G. Co.	
	9		Shell holes enlarged, occupied and camouflaged at following positions: O7 d 35 22, O7 d 3 2, O13 b 35, O13 b 36 } FORWARD group. N12 c 70 58, N12 b 15 25, N12 b 40 75, N18 a 37 } Rear group	
			A·A guns active each day. Co. congratulated by G.O.C Brigade for good work done in locating enemy M.Gs	

A5834 Wt. W4973 M687 750,000 8/16 D. D. & L. Ltd. Forms/C.2118/13.

Instructions regarding War Diaries and Intelligence Summaries are contained in F. S. Regs., Part II. and the Staff Manual respectively. Title pages will be prepared in manuscript.

WAR DIARY

~~or~~

~~INTELLIGENCE SUMMARY.~~

(Erase heading not required.)

184 Machine Gun Company.

Army Form C. 2118.

Place	Date	Hour	Summary of Events and Information	Remarks and references to Appendices
ARRAS – CAMBRAI ROAD SECTOR	June 10		The following detachments relieved by 8 MG Co. Relief complete by 3 a.m. FORWARD group: O7G53, O7G74, O7G75 45. Rear group: N12G37, N12G04, N12G05, N12G25 75	APP II OO 20 attached
			The following shell hole positions dug camouflaged and occupied – O7G53, O7G74, O7G75 45 – FORWARD GROUP. Rear group: N12C75 55	
	10		The two detachments in front of GUEMAPPE south of the COJEUL RIVER relieved by one detachment of 169 MG Co	APP 3. OO 21
	10		Detachments relieved on 10/11 marched to TRANSPORT LINES G320 GUEMAPPE detachments bivouaced night of 10/11 at BOIS DES BOEUFS TILLOY N2 00	Ref map ARRAS 5E 1/20000
	11		GUEMAPPE detachments marched to TRANSPORT LINES and thence with own detachments relieved on 10/11 to billets in BERNEVILLE	OO 22. APP4.
			Remaining seven detachments in the line relieved by 169 MG Co. Relief complete by 2 a.m.	Map 51GNW 1/20000
	12		Bivouaced at N2 a 04 marching to BERNEVILLE at 2 pm	
BERNEVILLE	13		Resting. Casualties in line: 2 OR KILLED, 3 OR WOUNDED	
	14		Twenty men attached from infantry units – TRAINING COMMENCED – programmes attached	Appendix 7

Instructions regarding War Diaries and Intelligence Summaries are contained in F. S. Regs., Part II. and the Staff Manual respectively. Title pages will be prepared in manuscript.

WAR DIARY

~~or~~

~~INTELLIGENCE~~ SUMMARY.

(*Erase heading not required.*)

Army Form C. 2118.

184 Machine Gun Company

Place	Date	Hour	Summary of Events and Information	Remarks and references to Appendices
BERNEVILLE	14 to 20		Training continued on lines of programme. Twenty infantry from Brigade attached – formed into a class and given elementary instruction on the gun.	Ref Map Sheet 51c/40,000
FROHEN-LE-GRAND	23		Move to FROHEN-LE-GRAND	Appendix 5. O.O. 24
	to 27		Training continued as above	Ref Map LENS 11. 1/100,000.
VAULX	27		Move to VAULX	
	to 30		Training continued on same lines. Barrage schemes practised. Staff rides officers and NCOs under G.O.C.s 184 Bde. and 61st Div.	O.O 25 Appendix 6. Ref Map LENS 11 1/100 000. Training Programme Appendix 4.

A Napier CAPT.
COMDG. 184 COMPANY M. G. CORPS.

A5834 Wt. W4973 M687 750,000 8/16 D. D. & L. Ltd. Forms/C.2118/13.

~~Copy~~ Section Orders No. 19. APP I

No 4 ✓ 4.6.1917

A

I The seven detachments in Reserve Positions will relieve the seven in the forward Positions on the 4.6.1917
The two detachments S.E of GUEMAPPE will remain in Position.

2. 2/Lt CASWELL & 2/Lt HIGHET will relieve 2/Lieut ALLEN and 2/Lt ROWE.
2/Lt CRAIG will relieve 2/Lt GRIFFITHS.
2/Lt URQUHART will relieve 2/Lt HOMERSLEY.

3 The relief of the forward Guns will be at a time fixed by mutual arrangement between 2/Lt ALLEN & 2/Lt GRIFFITHS

4 Only Guns, Spare Parts and 1 tin of water for Rations for the 5th inst will be taken forward by relieving detachments

5 The Officers relieved will remain with the relieving Officers for 12 hours after arrival of the latter.

6 One man per detachment will be left at reserve Position until 9 P.M. 4th inst, they will then report to Reserve Section H.Q. and form a carrying Party for the Rations of their detachments at the forward Positions. They will remain with their detachments on Completion

7 2/Lt Caswell, 2/Lt Highet, 2/Lt Craig & 2/Lt Urquhart will report to Coy H.Q. at 4 P.M. proceeding afterwards to their Positions.

8 Details of work to be done will be handed over in writing to relieving Officers.
Accurate receipts for Articles handed over by each detachment and at Section H.Q. will be exchanged and copies will be forwarded to Coy H.Q. with next Intelligence Summary.

9. Completion of action will be reported by wire
Code Word. "CRUMP"

ACKNOWLEDGE.

Issued at 11.30 am.
By Runner.

Copies:-

No 1 2/Lt Allen
2 do Griffiths.
3. do Womersley.
4 Lt Caswell and Officers in Arras
5 Bde. H.Q.
6 C.Q.M.S.
7. File.
8 War Diary

[illegible] Lt for Capt
Comdg. Q.H.A.

SHEET "ETERPIGNY" APPENDIX 2,

1/20 000.

[illegible] Orders No 20 9.6.1918

1. On the night 9-10th June the detachments [illegible] and the [illegible] of the Brigade Front will be relieved by detachments of the 8. M. G. Company.

2. The following dispositions will be handed over:-

- [illegible] } FORWARD GROUP
- [illegible] } RESERVE GROUP

3. The [illegible] of the Forward Group will each be relieved by a detachment of the 8. M. G. Coy.
The detachments detailed of the Reserve Group will be collectively relieved by one detachment of No 8. M. G. Coy.

4. One Guide per detachment of the three forward guns will be at junction of PICK TRENCH and DRAGOON LANE at [illegible] midnight 9/10th.
No Guide [illegible] required for Reserve Group.

5. Relieved detachments on completion of relief will withdraw to Company H.Q. [illegible] [illegible] DRAGOON LANE [illegible] at 9.15 p.m. on the 10th.

6. Section officer Reserve Group will, from MIDNIGHT 9-10th until relief of detachments of RESERVE GROUP, be in the vicinity of these guns and as soon as the one detachment of No 8 M.G. Company has taken over will order these 4 guns to withdraw.

7. [illegible] [illegible] will be handed over. Receipts [illegible] and forward to Company H.Q. by [illegible]

8. On Completion of the [illegible] the three forward detachments they will come under the orders of the [illegible] Officer [illegible] Group, who will withdraw with them.

9. [illegible] at [illegible] Coy. H.Q. at [illegible] will come under orders of the [illegible] in Command, and will [illegible] to [illegible]

10. [illegible] Right Brigade [illegible] the 10th

10. Rations for relieved detachments will be [illegible] at Coy. H.Q. 9.30 p.m. 9/10

11. Completion of Relief will be reported to Coy. H.Q. [illegible] Code word "[illegible]"

ACKNOWLEDGE.

Issued at 12 noon

Copies to:-

No 1 [illegible]
2 Section Officer Forward Group
3 Sub-Section Officer [illegible]
4 Section Officer Reserve Group
5 Transport Officer
6 O.C. 8 M.G. Coy
7 184 Brigade
8 [illegible]
9 War Diary
10 File.

W Napier CAPT.
COMDG. 184 COMPANY M. G. CORPS.

Copy No 2

App 3.

[illegible] Orders No 21 10/6/1918

184 Company M.G. Corps.

Ref Sheet 51B S.W. 1/20000

I The two detachments of 184 M.G. Coy on South bank of COJEUL RIVER will be relieved on night of 10/11th June by one detachment of the 169 M.G. Coy.

2 The following dispositions will be handed over:-

one detachment O 19 a 9. 4. (old Gun Pit)

do O 19 a 8.4. PANTHER TRENCH.

3 No guides will be required.

4 One Fighting Limber No 2 Section will be at WANCOURT CHURCH at 9.30 PM 10/11th for use of relieved detachments.

5 On relief of Gun Pit position Sub Section Officer 184 Company will withdraw both detachments to BOIS DES BOEUFS TILLOY H 2 a 0.4. where they will bivouac for night moving 10 Am 11th to Transport lines G 32 a.

6. All S.A.A. Trench Stores and Defence maps will be handed over receipt being exchanged by Officers concerned and forwarded to Coy. H.Q. forthwith.

7 Completion of Relief will be reported by runner. Code "OUT"

Issued at 5.30 Pm.

Copies To - 9

1 Sub Section Officer Right Front

2 Section Officer Rear Group

3 " " Forward Group

4 Transport Officer

5 C.Q.M.S.

6 184 Inf Brigade

7 O.C. 169 M.G. Coy

8 File

9 War Diary

[signature] for CAPT.

COMDG. 184 COMPANY M. G. CORPS.

Appendix 4.

Copy No 9 Operation Order No 22

Ref Sheet 51 B S.W. & 51 B N.W. 1/20.000

1. The 184 M.G. Coy less of Detachments and Transport will move to BERNEVILLE on the 12th inst.
2. Starting Point H31.c.6.0.5 at 2 P.M.
3. Parade 1.40 P.M. Dress Fighting Order. Limbers will be drawn up on WANCOURT – TILLOY Road N.W. of N1.b.6.1 in the following order:-
   H.Q. Limbers
   Fighting Limbers No 1
   do do No 2
   do do No 4
4. Route: ARRAS – DAINVILLE – WARLUS – BERNEVILLE
5. A distance of 200 yds between Sections will be maintained E of ARRAS. W of ARRAS this distance will be ~~maintained~~ 100 yds.
6. No regular halts will be made until clear of Railway W of DAINVILLE
7. The 9 Detachments at the Transport Lines and the Transport except as detailed in No 3, will move under 2 Lt Griffiths to BERNEVILLE on afternoon 11th inst. immediately after rations are available. Orders No 4. 5. 6. will apply to this Party
8. Limbers detailed in No 3 will report to a/C.S.M. BOIS DES BOEUFS H2a.0.4 at 5 P.M. 11th inst.
9. They will carry rations for 3 Officers, 9 detachments and for Transport detailed, also all available Water Tins
10. An Officer detailed by 2 Lt Griffiths will report to Staff Captain at TOWN MAJORS Office BERNEVILLE at 12 Noon 11th inst for Billeting

Issued at 10 Am.

Copy No 1 – Section Officer Forward Group
2 – do do Rear Group
3 – 2/Lt Griffiths.
4 Transport Officer
5 a/CSM
6 CQMS.
7 184 Inf Brigade
8 War Diary
9 File.

J. [illegible] C
Comdg 184 Coy.

W.D.

Appendix 5

Copy No. 7 Amendment to Operation Order No. 24 . 20. 6. 1918

Ref Sheet 51c 1/40000

For Paragraphs 7. 8. 10. 11. Substitute

6. The Company less Transport will parade at 7.55 Am outside Billets. Dress: Fighting Order. Steel Helmets. Water Bottles filled. And will be formed up on Right side of Road at 7.50 Am in the following Order from the Right: H.Q. 1. 2. 3. 4. The Company will move off at 8 Am passing Starting Point [illegible] 51 at 8.5 Am.

7. It will proceed via GAUCHETZ – FLORCHET – GOUY-EN-ARTOIS to Station Area Relieving [illegible].

10. All baggage not loaded on Transport will be dumped at Officers Mess at 6.30 Am.

11. Halts will be made from 15 minutes to hour until the Hour.

Issued at 11 Am.

Copy No. 1 Not Issued

2
3
4 Section Officers
5
6 [illegible] & C.Q.M.S.
7 File
8 War Diary

[illegible signature] Lt.

for

CAPT.

COMDG. 184 COMPANY M. G. CORPS

Copy No. 7

184 Company M.G. Corps

Map Sheet 51C 1/40,000
Lens 11 1/100,000

Operation Order No. 24

21. 6. 1917

I The 184 M.G. Company will move on the 22nd & 23rd inst. to FROHEN-LE-GRANDE.

2 The transport will parade under 2/Lt. [illegible] and [illegible] at 4.20 am – Dress Marching Order. Steel Helmets. Rations for the 22nd and 23rd inst. will be carried and will move off at 4.35 am passing starting point G.6.a.5.1. at 4.42 am. It will march via SIMENCOURT – WANQUETIN – AVESNES-LE-COMTE – LE CAUROY to REBREUVE continuing its march to FROHEN LE GRANDE on 23.6.1917.

3 All packs and [illegible] except Officers Baggage [illegible] and [illegible] Cook[s] Gear will be loaded on vehicles by 4 pm 21st inst. [illegible] Officers detailed [illegible] No 2 [illegible] and [illegible] as [illegible]. Balance of Personnel will [illegible] transport – Dress, Fighting Order.

4. The transport will on 22nd inst. under the orders of Major [illegible] ANDERSON 24 Royal [illegible] and on 23rd inst. under those of Major F.J. FOSTER 2/5 WARWICKS.

5. The transport 1st line will meet the Brigade [illegible] at junction of [illegible] and [illegible] Roads at 8.30 am on 22nd [illegible]

6. The Company less transport will parade at 8.20 am on Road outside billets on 23rd – Dress Fighting Order & Steel Helmets with bottles filled in the following order – HQ 1 2 3 4 and will move off at 8.30 am passing starting point G.6.a.5.1 at 8.35 am.

7 It will proceed via SIMENCOURT – WANQUETIN to FOSSEUX LOOP [illegible]

8. It will detrain at AUXI LE CHATEAU marching to FROHEN LE GRANDE [illegible]

9 [illegible] will proceed for billeting on 22nd inst. at 8.30 am by lorry which will be at end of column of lorries for carrying 2/5 [illegible]. This column will be on WARLUS – WANQUETIN Road just outside WARLUS. He will carry rations for 22nd & 23rd, and will meet Company on detrainment at AUXI LE CHATEAU guiding it to billets.

10 Lorry for carrying baggage not loaded in transport will report at Officers Mess before Company parade on 23rd inst. All such baggage will be dumped at [illegible] point before [illegible].

11 Halts will be made from 10 minutes to the hour until the hour as usual.

Issued at 7.30 pm

Copies to

No 1 Commanding Officer
2 Section Officer No 1
3 " No 2
4 " No 3
5 " No 4
6 O/C Sect & C.Q.M.S.
7 File
8 War Diary

[signature] Lt.
for CAPT.
COMDG. 184 COMPANY M.G. CORPS.

Copy No 7

Operation Order 25

26-6-1914
appendix. 6.

[illegible]

1. The 184 M.G. Company will move to Billets at Vaux on 27th June [illegible]

2. Company will parade on Road outside Billets at [illegible] am in the following order from the right. [illegible]

[illegible] Transport will form up on right of Company [illegible] Chateau in the following order from the front. [illegible]

3. The Company will move off at [illegible] am. [illegible] Chateau – Le [illegible] – Vaux.

4. All [illegible] will be [illegible] Billeting Officer will [illegible]

5. [illegible]

6. [illegible]

6 [illegible]

7. [illegible]

[illegible]

[illegible]

Issued at [illegible]

Copies to –

No 1 Officer i/c No 1 Section

2 — 2 .

3 — 3 .

4 — 4 .

5 Transport Officer

6 Comdg [illegible]

7 File

8 War Diary.

[signature] Lt for

CAPT.

COMDG. 184 COMPANY M.G. CORPS,

appendix 4

184 COMPANY
M. G. CORPS.

TRAINING PROGRAMME

TRAINING

	Overhauling Equipment	Belt Filling and Cleaning	Mechanism	Points Before During and After Firing	Range	Range Immediate Action	Gun Drill and Tests of Elementary Training	Tactical Section Drill	Care and Cleaning	Indirect Firing Practice in Preparing for	Night Firing Practice in Preparing for	Advance and Occupation of Position	Packing Limbers	Stripping	Tactical Schemes under R. C. O.	Preparation for Barrage Fire	Repairs and Adjustments	Duties in Trenches and in Action
1st Day 14	3	1					1											
2nd Day 15			1	1	1	1	1											
3rd do 16		1	1		1	1	1											
4th do 17			1	1	1		1											
5th do 18							1						1					
6th do 28						1	1 X	1						1			1	
7th do 25					1			2	1		1							
8th do 4																5		
9th do 5					1	1	1					2	1					
10th do 6					1	1			1	2						5		
11th do 7					1	1												
12th do 8					1	1					1	1			5			
13th do 9															5			1
Total Hours for Each Subject	3	2	3	2	6	6	6	3	2	2	2	3	2	1	10	10	1	1

Remarks

[illegible] will enable [illegible] [illegible] greatest value. Also [illegible] physical training [illegible] [illegible] will be practised. [illegible] special [illegible] NCOs in Discipline will be given [illegible] not shown on the programme.

[signature] for CAPT.
COMDG. 184 COMPANY M. G. CORPS.

Rev. 5.30
Parade 5.45
Brekt 6.30
Parade 8.0
Dinner 12.15
Parm 1.30 & 2.30 p.m.

Vol 14

C O N F I D E N T I A L

W A R   D I A R Y

**** of ****

184 COMPANY, MACHINE GUN CORPS.

From 1st July 1917 to 31st July,1917.

(VOLUME XlV)

****

184 Company M.G. Corps

WAR DIARY
or
~~INTELLIGENCE SUMMARY.~~

(Erase heading not required.)

Army Form C. 2118.

Instructions regarding War Diaries and Intelligence Summaries are contained in F. S. Regs., Part II. and the Staff Manual respectively. Title pages will be prepared in manuscript.

Place	Date	Hour	Summary of Events and Information	Remarks and references to Appendices
	July			
VAULX	1 to 6	-	Training continued. Attached infantry examined by GO and sent to sections. Company exercised in:- field firing, tactical schemes and barrage work	Ref Map LENS 11 1/100000
	7	-	Barrage scheme and demonstration. GOC Bde and GO. infantry battalions present. Detailed orders attached	Appendix I
	8 to 20	-	Training continued. One subsection daily with battalion in attack. Company exercised in:- Consolidation of shell holes, field firing, range practice, use of pack transport, action from limbers, revolver shooting. Night firing carried out once each week by every section. Company concerts and sports held.	Ref map TRAINING MAP HOXI-LE-CHATEAU 1/20000
	21	-	Company cooperates with Bde. in attack scheme. Operation order attached	Appendix II
	22 23 24		Preparing for move	
	25		Move to BUYSSCHEURE. Operation order attached.	Ref map HAZEBROUCK 5A 1/100000
	26		Arrived at new billets	Appendix III O.O.
	27 to 31		Training continued. Special attention given to - Attack and defence of strong points, intensive digging and consolidation of shell holes also anti-gas defence.	

	Officers	OR including attached
Strength at commencement of month	11	187
Strength at end of month	11	201
Drafts from base	-	12

A5834 Wt. W4973 M687 750,000 8/16 D. D. & L. Ltd. Forms/C.2118/13.

[signature] CAPT.
COMDG. 184 COMPANY M. G. CORPS.

APPENDIX I

Special Order.

7. 7. 1917.

1. The 184 M.G. Coy will carry out a barrage demonstration on 7th July 1917.
2. The Company will form up with limbers on road to training area at 7.30 am in following order H.Q. 1. 2. 3. 4.
   Dress: Fighting Order.
3. Sections will move off independently and will take up dispositions indicated to them today. Limbers will [illegible] up under cover close to the gun positions.
   Guns will be ready for firing at 9 am.
4. Arrangements will be made by Section Officers for the supply of ammunition to the guns and the immediate refilling of belts.
5. Lieut Caswell will be in charge of the four sections throughout the operations and will keep in close touch with the forward observing station.
6. No 1 and No 4 sections will move forward at Zero + 5 to the positions shown to the Section Officers concerned today and will reopen fire as soon as possible afterwards.
7. Fire orders are attached.
8. C.S.M. will detail 1 N.C.O. and 7 men as party for picketing roads. This party with the 4 Signallers attached from Brigade will parade with H.Qrs party under C.S.M. Bicycles and all available flags will be taken.
   Pte Semple will open communication with Forward Observing Station immediately on arrival. The remainder of the party will proceed to Forward Observing Station reporting there to Lieut. F. Lismore.
9. At 9 am guns will be registered on targets
10. Probable time of Zero is 10 am.

Issued at 12 Midnight

(1) Section Officer No 1
2 " " 2
3 " " 3
4 " " 4
5 File
6 War Diary
7 C.S.M.

F. Lismore for

CAPT.

COMDG. 184 COMPANY M.G. CORPS.

Barrage Demonstration

184 M. G. Coy. 4. 4. 1918.

1 The enemy is holding an outpost position from M2c 8 7. to M3c4.6. and a line of resistance from M3c5 9 to M3c4.9.
The 184 Infantry Brigade is detailed to dislodge and occupy the latter position.

2 1 Infantry Battalion is detailed for the assault which is to be covered by 16 guns of the 184 M. G. Coy.

3 A copy of fire orders issued to Section Officers is attached also rough sketch map.
These fire orders are liable to alteration at any time during the operation as direct observation will be obtainable throughout

4 It is to be noted that only a limited area of ground can be fired on and no oblique fire can be brought to bear on the objectives owing to considerations of safety for the civilian population.

W Napier CAPT.
COMDG. 184 COMPANY M. G. CORPS.

Fire Orders.

184 M. G. Coy
Barrage Demonstration 4/7/1917

No. of Section	No. of Guns	Commander	Timing From	Timing To	Target	Rate of Fire	Distance gun to target	Bearing Chart	Angle of Elevation	Bearing of Ref. Object
FIRST PHASE										
1	4	2/Lt. Griffiths	Zero	Zero + 5	Blue Flags.	1 belt per gun per two mins	1800x	355° to 358°	2° 5' to 2° 15'	3° [illegible]
2	4	Lt. Caswell	do	do	do	do	do	353° to 355°	do	do
3	4	2/Lt. Allen	do	do	do	do	do	350° to 353°	do	do
4	4	2/Lt. Craig	do	do	do	do	do	347° to 350°	do	do
SECOND PHASE										
2	4	Lt. Caswell	Zero + 5	Zero + 10	White Flags	1 belt per Gun per minute	1900x	do	2° 15' to 2° 20'	do
3	4	2/Lt. Allen	do	do	do	do	do	do	do	do
2	4	Lt. Caswell	Zero + 10	Zero + 20	do	1 belt per Gun per 2 minutes	do	do	do	do
3.	4	2/Lt. Allen	do	do	do	do	do	do	do	do
1	4	2/Lt. Griffiths	Time of taking up the position	Zero + 20	do	do	1800	Traversing	movements on target	—
4	4	2/Lt. Craig		do	do	do	[illegible]			

[illegible signature] CAPT.
COMDG. 184 COMPANY M. G. CORPS.

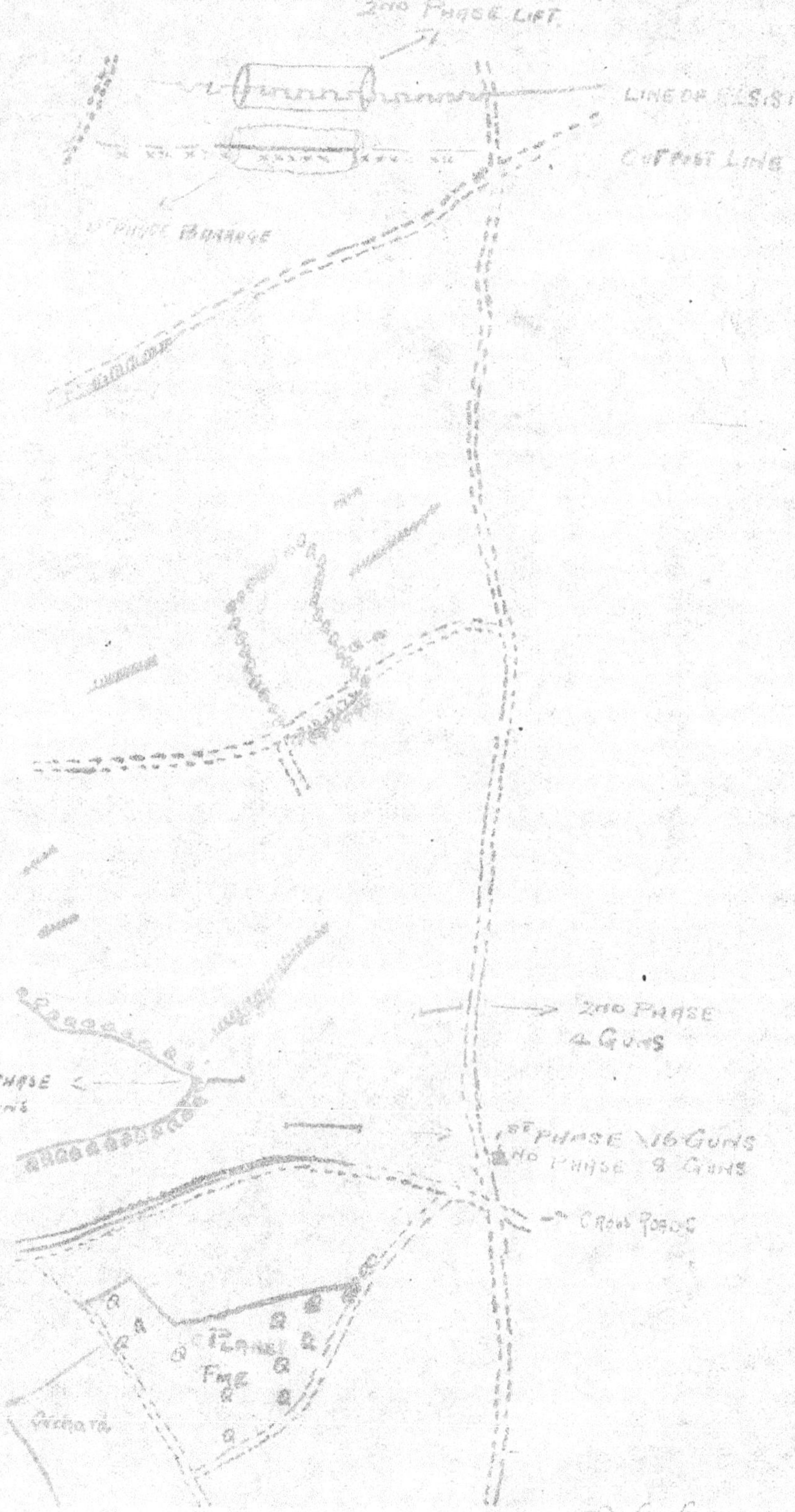

2ND PHASE LIFT
LINE OF RESISTANCE
OUTPOST LINE
1ST PHASE BARRAGE
2ND PHASE
4 GUNS
2ND PHASE
4 GUNS
1ST PHASE 16 GUNS
2ND PHASE 8 GUNS
CROSS ROADS
PLANE FME
ORCHARD

18th M. G. Co.
BARRAGE
DEMONSTRATION
7-7-17

ROUGH SKETCH MAP
APPROX SCALE 1/20000

APPENDIX II

Operation Order No 24 Copy No 8

Ref/Map Sketch map attached

1 The 184 M.G. Coy will cooperate in an attack being made by 184 Brigade on trenches protecting VAULX from M14b 25 55 to M4d 89. 1st Brigade will attack on left of 184 Brigade. 182nd Brigade will attack on right of 184 Brigade.

2 The 184 Brigade will attack with a two battalion frontage, Glosters on right Royal Berks on left. dividing line between battalions being line joining M18b 21 M8C42 M8C74

3 Zero will be at 10.30 Am infantry advancing at that hour.

4 Objectives.

1st Wave to 2nd objective			HANS TRENCH
2nd do to 1st		do	FRITZ TRENCH
3rd do to 3rd		do	KAISER TRENCH
4th do to 3rd		do	KAISER TRENCH

5 1 Sub Section of No 1 Section under 2/Lt Griffiths will report to O.C. Glosters at 9 Am.
1 Sub Section of No 2 Section under Lt Boswell will report to O.C. Royal Berks at 9 Am.
These sub sections will advance from FACE TRENCH as the 3rd wave of their respective battalions passes over, and on their objective being reached will take up position approximately as follows:—

1 M4d 49

2 M8C 5.5

3 }
4 } about M14b 44

6 The Glosters and Royal Berks will each provide 12 men as ammunition carriers and escorts for the sub-section advancing with them.

7 2 detachments of No 1 Section under 2/Lt Urquhart will be in position about M 8 b 1.5. and M 8 b 4.3.
2 detachments of No 2 Section under Lt McKay will be in position about M 8 d 8.7 They will be prepared to break up an attack on our line should the operation prove a failure.

8 On the 3rd objective being taken these 4 guns mentioned in para 7 will be relieved by 4 guns from the barrage group they will then move forward and report to their respective Section Commanders who will organize defence in depth based on strong points to be dug at:-

No 1 M 7 d. 6.8.
2 M 7 d 9.0.
3 M 14 a 3.8.
4 M 14 a 9.4.

9 8 guns of No 3 & 4 Sections under 2/Lt Allen will be in position at M 9 a 4.4. at 9 am. They will place a barrage on line from M 13 b 9.9 – M 14 a 7.0 from Zero to Zero + 9 in accordance with attached table.
At Zero + 9 No 4 section will return 4 guns as detailed in 8.
No 3 Section will remain in their position and become Brigade Reserve.

10 Company H.Q will be at M 8 b 8.4 to which point all reports will be sent.
At Zero + 60 Company H.Q. will move to M 8 c 4.8

11 Company dump under C.S.M. will be at M 8 b. 8.5.
No 1 Section H.Q. M 8 d 5.7.
2 do H.Q M 8 a 9.5.
Advanced dumps at No 1 & 2 section H.Q. arrangements to be made by section officers concerned.

12 Details of load to be carried by each advancing detachment and of material at section and company dumps are attached.

13 Acknowledge.

W Napier Capt
OC 184 MG Coy

Copies to:-

No 1 O.C. No 1 Section
2 O.C. No 2 do
3 O.C. No 3 do
4 O.C. No 4 do
5 184 Inf Bde
6 C.S.M.
7 File
8 War Diary.
9 O.C. Glosters
10 O.C. Berks.

20.7.17

Issued at 6pm

No of Guns	Arrangements	Time From	Time To	Rate of Fire	Distance from to Target	Quantity [illegible]	Quadrant Angle of Elevation
4	[illegible]	[illegible]	[illegible]	[illegible]	1500	[illegible]	1° 25'
4	[illegible]	do	do	do	do	do	do
4	[illegible]	[illegible]	[illegible]	do	1700	do	2° 12'
4	[illegible]	do	do	do	do	do	do
4	[illegible]	[illegible]	[illegible]	do	do	do	do

184 M.G Company.

Copy No - 8 -

Operation Order No 28

Appendix III

Map. LENS 11 1/100.000
HAZEBROUCK 5A 1/100.000

1. The 184 M.G. Company will march to AUXI-LE-CHATEAU on night of 25th/26th July 1917, will entrain there by train leaving at 10.20 pm and detrain at ST OMER.

2. On arrival at St OMER the unit will march to BROXEELE area.

3. The transport will parade under orders of the Transport Officer and will arrive at the station AUXI-LE-CHATEAU at 7.15 pm. One horseholder will be allotted to each animal. To provide for this. CSM will detail 25 men to report to Transport Officer at 2 pm. These will be attached to transport until the completion of the detrainment. Dragropes will be carried for use as breast ropes in covered trucks.
The supply wagon will entrain with the transport.

4. Company less transport will parade at 7 pm and will arrive at the station AUXI-LE-CHATEAU not later than 8.45 pm. Order of March. 1.2.3.4. HQ.

5. Lieut Lismore will report to R.T.O AUXI-LE-CHATEAU at 7 pm and will act as entraining officer for the company.

6. Refilling will take place twice on 25th. Rations for 26th will be drawn at refilling point S of AUXI STATION at 6 pm and will be issued at the station. Rations for the 27th will then be drawn and carried on supply wagon.

7. The water cart and water bottles will be full on entrainment.
No lights will be lit on the train.

Copies Nos 1-4 Section Officers
5 Transport Officer
6 C.S.M
7 C.Q.M.S
8 War Diary
9 File

W [illegible] Capt
Comdg 184 Coy M.G.C.

24.7.17

1 3rd Wave guns under
2/Lt Griffiths. Lt Caswell.
1 Gun with case (1 spare barrel
and 1 cleaning rod Sn. St Section.
1 Tripod
1 Spare Parts case
1 condenser complete.
1 water tin
12 Belt Boxes
2 Picks
2 Shovels.
Sandbags.

2. Front Section Dump. (each i/c of N.C.O)
2 spare Barrels
2 spare cleaning rods
4 spare parts-cases.
4 Water Tins
4 S.A.A.
1 Rangefinder in box
Spare oil

3. Front line guns under 2/Lt Urquhart
and Lieut McKay.
1 gun with case containing:-
spare barrel & cleaning rod.
1 Tripod
1 spare parts case
1 condenser complete
1 water tin
6 belt boxes
2 Picks
2 Shovels.

4 Barrage guns to move to front line under 2/Lt Craig.
1 gun with case containing:-
spare barrel & cleaning rod
1 Tripod
1 spare parts case
1 condenser complete
10 belt boxes

5. Company Dump
16 Boxes S.A.A
5 Water Tins
1 Tin. Oil
4" x 2"
Sandbags.

Vol 15

CONFIDENTIAL

W A R D I A R Y

*** of ***

1 8 4 C O M P A N Y , M A C H I N E G U N C O R P S

From 1st August, 1917 to 31st August, 1917.

VOLUME XV.

Instructions regarding War Diaries and Intelligence Summaries are contained in F. S. Regs., Part II. and the Staff Manual respectively. Title pages will be prepared in manuscript.

WAR DIARY
or
~~INTELLIGENCE SUMMARY.~~
(Erase heading not required.)

184 M. G. Coy

Army Form C. 2118.

Place	Date	Hour	Summary of Events and Information	Remarks and references to Appendices
BUYSSCHEURE	August 1		Training continued on same lines - special attention being given to Barrage Drill	Ref. map 5A HAZEBROUCK 1/100000
	7		Cooperated in Brigade attack scheme - operation order attached	APPENDIX I
	10		Inspection by G.O.C. 184 Inf. Bde	
	14		Training continued. Lt Griffiths to CCS sick	
	15		Move to WATOU No 1 area. Operation order attached	APPENDIX II
	16		Preparing for line	
	17		Move to GOLDFISH CHATEAU — area YPRES NORTH - operation order attached	APPENDIX III
	18		No 1 and 3 sections moved to line and relieved two sections 107 MG Co. Guns in barrage positions in vicinity of JASPER Fm - advanced company headquarters - JASPER Fm - operation order attached	Ref. maps 28 NW 1/20000 27 1/40000
	20	10 pm	No 2 and 4 sections moved into line and took up positions of assembly for Brigade attack. No 1 and No 3 took up positions for barrage with guns of 182 MG Co and 183 MG Co respectively.	APPENDIX IV.
	21		Preparing for attack	
	22		Brigade attacked enemy positions. 48th Division on left 15th on right - operation orders attached No 4 section advanced behind 2/Bucks on right to vicinity of SOMME and consolidated there Subsection No 2 pushed forward before ZERO to position on flank SEW HILL Remaining subsection No 2 ready to consolidate at POND FARM but that place not captured until 4 pm No 3 section moved from barrage positions to positions covering jumping off line. No 4 and No 2 sustained heavy casualties By the close of the day the following dispositions had been taken up 2 guns SOMME (2 out of action) 6 guns DONT TRENCH 2 guns near POND Fm 2 guns SEW HILL 4 guns in reserve GALL RESERVE TRENCH Several satisfactory targets were obtained on enemy counter attacks and retiring troops	APPENDIX V Ref map FREZENBERG 1/10000 APPENDIX VI Report on operation
	23		again targets were obtained.	
	24		A counter attack developing towards SEW HILL dealt with effectively. Two guns moved from DONT TRENCH to SEW HILL	
			Relief of ten detachments by eight detachments of 182 MG Co leaving 2 guns SEW HILL & GALL RESERVE. The ten 6 detachments withdrawn to BRANDHOEK - operation order attached	APPENDIX VII

A5834 Wt. W4973 M687 750,000 8/16 D. D. & L. Ltd. Forms/C.2118/13.

Army Form C. 2118.

WAR DIARY

~~or~~

~~INTELLIGENCE SUMMARY.~~

(Erase heading not required.)

Instructions regarding War Diaries and Intelligence Summaries are contained in F. S. Regs., Part II. and the Staff Manual respectively. Title pages will be prepared in manuscript.

Place	Date	Hour	Summary of Events and Information	Remarks and references to Appendices
~~[illegible]~~ BRANDHOEK	August 25	-	Overhauling and repairing guns. Casualties in action Officers 3 wounded O.R 4 killed 19 wounded	
			Officers wounded 2Lt Craig 2 Lt Rowe 2Lt Martin	
	26		Refitting and resting	
			Six detachments in line withdrawn	
	27		Refitting and resting	
	28		Refitting and resting	
	29		Return to line to relieve 182 M.G. Co. Strength on 29th Aug. Off 7 OR 159 OR 33 attd.	

[illegible] Capt
Comdg 184 M G Coy

A5834 Wt. W4973 M687 750,000 8/16 D. D. & L. Ltd. Forms/C.2118/13.

Operation Order No 30 Copy No......

Ref Sheet Sketch Map attached 1/10.000

APPENDIX I

1 The Brigade will attack Enemy defences from G28c.2.4 to G33 b 9.2. on a two Battalion front.

BUCKS - RIGHT

OXFORDS - LEFT

Zero hour 10. Am.

2. M.G. Company will co-operate as follows:-

3 Two guns No 4 Section.

Two guns No 3 "

will advance by bounds with BUCKS & OXFORDS respectively starting off from ROAD TRENCH with 3rd wave. Officers i/c S. Sections will report to O.C. BUCKS & OXFORDS at 8.45 Am.

Advancing battalions will furnish 6 men per detachment as carriers. These men will report as follows:-

12 Men BUCKS TO Section Officer No 4 Section G36 a 3.6. ROAD TRENCH.

12 Men OXFORDS to SECTION Officer No 3 " G36 c 5.9. " "

4 OBJECTIVES. These 4 guns will consolidate in the vicinity of:- (1) GREEN DOTTED LINE. G28 d 3.8. - G34 b 2.0.

(2) RED. LINE G24 d 9.4 - G34 a 0.3.

as soon as possible after these objectives have been taken.

5 The remaining 4 guns of Nos 3 & 4 Sections will be in following positions near front line.

No 4. (1) G29 d 4.3 & G35 d 8.8.

No 3 (2) G35 b 8.4. & G35. b. 9.4.

Section HQ. at G 35 b. 8.5.

6 2/Lieut CRAIG will report to Advanced Bde H.Q. at 8.45 Am. He will accompany an R.E. Officer [illegible] to Site 2 strong points. As soon as these strong points have been sited 2/Lt CRAIG will move up the 4 guns mentioned in para 5 above and will arrange a line of defence based on the 2 strong points.

Glosters will supply carrying party of 24 men to assist in this move, these will report at 8.45 Am, at G35 a 9.5.

7 COMMUNICATIONS. Runners should be used sparingly and advantage taken of Battalion communication arrangements. TELEPHONIC. VISUAL SIGNALLING. RUNNERS.

8. Nos 1 & 2 Sections will represent two Batteries of 8 guns each.

No 1 Section A Battery 4 guns. Position H31.a 1.1.

No 2 " B. Battery 4 " " G35 b.9.4.

Orders & time tables attached. (APPENDICES 1 & 2)

These positions will be in communication by telephone with Coy. H.Q.

9 Company HQ will be at FARM G36 a 9 5.

No4 Section H.Q. ROAD TRENCH G36 a 3.6.

No3 " " " " G36 c 5.9.

All positions will be taken up by 8.40. am.

10 Dumps will be established as follows:–

Company Dump under CSM. at G 35 b. 4.4.

Section dumps at No3 & 4 Sections HQ. arrangements to be made by S.O.s concerned.

11 Watches will be synchronised at 9 am.

12 Location reports to Company HQ when in position, and as soon as established in objectives.

Situation reports half hourly from Zero.

13 Details of load to be carried by each advancing detachment and of material at Company & Section Dumps, are attached (appendix 3)

14. ACKNOWLEDGE

Issued at 9.45 pm.

Copies to:-

No 1 - 4 Section Officers

5 184 Inf Bde

6 Glosters

7 Oxfords

8 Royal Berks

9 Bucks

10 D.M.G.O

11 War Diary

Dated: 12 File

7. 8. 1917. 13 Transport Officer

14 C.S.M.

W Napier Capt
Comdg 184 Coy M.G.C.

Note. Appendices attached to copies 1-5. 10-12. & 14

M.G BARRAGE. TIME TABLE. Officer i/c Firing Lt Caswell.

B. BATTERY. APPENDIX. 2.

Gun No	Target	Elevation: Range to Target in Yards	Q.E. in Minutes	Range for Q.E. in Yards	Clearance over own troops: Range to own Troops in Yards	Traj Height in Yards	Clearance Obtained	Clearance Required in Yards	Direction: Compass Bearing or D.D Reading	Time of Firing	No of Rounds Fired	Remarks
1st PHASE												
1	G33D4.8 to	2100	288	2100	1400	46.4	46.4	43	240-244	030.24	45 Rds per min.	
2	G33B4.2.	"	"	"	"	"	"	"	268-241	"	"	
3	"	"	"	"	"	"	"	"	266-269	"	"	
4	"	"	"	"	"	"	"	"	264-264	"	"	
2ND PHASE												
1	G34c.4.0 to	2500	444	2500	2000	101	101	52	241-244	024-30	100 Rds per min	
2	G33a4.2.	"	"	"	"	"	"	"	268-241	"	"	
3	"	"	"	"	"	"	"	"	266-269	"	"	
4	"	"	"	"	"	"	"		264-264	"	"	

M. G. BARRAGE

APPENDIX 2.

A BATTERY.

Officer i/c Guns. Lieut Griffiths.

GUN No	ELEVATION.				CLEARANCE OVER OWN TROOPS				DIRECTION			REMARKS
	TARGET.	RANGE TO TARGET IN YARDS	Q.E. in MINUTES	RANGE FOR Q.E. IN YARDS	RANGE TO OWN TROOPS IN YARDS	TRAJ HEIGHT IN YARDS	CLEARANCE OBTAINED	CLEARANCE REQUIRED IN YARDS	COMPASS BEARING OR D.D. READING	TIME OF FIRING	No OF ROUNDS FIRED	
1ST PHASE												
1	G35a 1.8.	2000	256	2000	1600	40.3	40.3	40	246–249	Z–Z0.10	100 Rds per MIN.	
2	to G34b 6.2.	2100	288	2100	1400	46.4	46.4	43	243–244	"	"	
3	"	2200	322	2200	1800	55.4	55.4	46	240–244	"	"	
4	"	2300	360	2300	1900	63.4	63.4	49.	264–241	"	"	
2ND PHASE.												
1	G28c 4.1.	2400	551	2400	2200	131	131	80	244–248	Z10–0Z0	"	
2	to G34a 9.1.	"	"	"	"	"	"	"	242–245	"	"	
3	"	2600	496	2600	2100	114	114	"	240–243	"	"	
4	"	2500	444	2500	2000	101	101	80	268–241	"	"	

Stores at Dumps

APPENDIX 3

1. 3rd Wave guns under 2/Lt Allen + Lt Womersley.

1 Gun with case (1 spare barrel and cleaning rod Er. S. Section.

1 Tripod
1 Spare parts Case.
1 Condenser. complete.
1 Water Tin.
12 Belt Boxes
2 Picks
2 Shovels
Sandbags.

2. Front Line guns under 2/Lt Craig.

1 Gun with case containing:– " spare barrel + cleaning rod.

1 Tripod
1 Spare parts case
1 Condenser complete
1 Water Tin.
6 Belt Boxes.
2 Picks
2 Shovels.

3. Front Section dumps (each i/c N.C.O.)

2 Spare barrels.
2 " Cleaning rods.
4 Spare Parts Cases
4 Water Tins.
4 Boxes S.A.A.
1 Rangefinder in box.
Spare Oil.

4 Company Dump under C.S.M.

16 Boxes. S.A.A.
5 Tins Water.
1 Tin Oil.
4" × 2"
Sandbags.

COPY No. __________

SECRET. 184th BRIGADE ORDER NO.1000

Ref. Map. Sketch attached. July 31st, 1917.

1. The BRIGADE will attack enemy Defences from G. 28.c.2.7. to G.33.b.9.2.
The 1st BDE. - Left attacking Battalion 1st BLACK WATCH will attack simultaneously on the immediate right.
The 182nd BRIGADE- Right Attacking Battalion 2/6th WARWICKS will attack simultaneously on the immediate left,

2. The BRIGADE ATTACK will be divided into :-

Right Attack.
Left Attack.

Dividing Line between the two will be as shown by a BLACK & RED DOTTED LINE on sketch.

3. The BUCKS will attack on the right.
The OXFORDS " " " left.
Each in normal formation with 2 Coys. in 1st and 2nd waves; 2 Coys. in 3rd and 4th waves.
1 Coy. less Coy.H.Q., GLOSTERS will be allotted to each Attacking Battalion as Carrying Coy.
2 M.Guns of the 184 Machine Gun Coy will be detailed for immediate cooperation with each Attacking Battalion, under the orders of O.C. 184 Machine Gun Coy. (vide para.)
2 Sections (4 Guns) Stokes Mortars will be allotted to BUCKS
1 Section (2 Guns) " " " " " OXFORDS
A party of 2 N.C.O's, 10 O.R. GLOSTERS will accompany each Stokes Mortar.
The Carrying Coys, and Stokes Mortars, will come under the orders of Attacking Battalions to which they are attached at 10 p.m. 2nd inst.
Each Attacking Battalion will find its own MOPPERS UP

4. ZERO will be at 1 0 a.m.
The 1st wave of each Attacking Battalion will advance at ZERO.
The 2nd Wave will follow the 1st Wave.
The 3rd Wave will advance at ZERO- MINUS 2 Min. in the case of the BUCKS, and at ZERO. MINUS 2 Min. 30 secs. in the case of the OXFORDS.
The 4th Wave will follow the 3rd Wave.
In both cases the Left Coys. in the 3rd Wave of each Attacking Battalion will advance slightly more rapidly than Right Coys. in the same Wave, so as to bring the line parallel to that of the 1st and 2nd Waves.

DISTANCES - Between WAVES 70 yards) till 1 st objective
" LINES 15 yards) is gained.

5. OBJECTIVES.

There will be two objectives for Attacking Battalions -

1. GREEN LINE and GREEN DOTTED LINE.

2. RED LINE.

Barrage will stand for 30 Min. approx 200 x W. of GREEN DOTTED LINE.
" " " " " " 200x W. of RED LINE.

~~These~~ This first halt marks two distinct periods for Attacking Battalions.
The approx. barrage halts are shown- yellow and green , and

brown and green on sketch.

1st PERIOD.

1st Wave to HUN TRENCH.

2nd " " SHELL HOLE LINE.

3rd " " GREEN DOTTED LINE.

4th " " GREEN LINE.

After reaching the above objectives, during the barrage halt, the 1st wave will occupy a general line 200x in rear of the 4th Wave.

the 2nd Wave " " " " 250x in rear of 1st Wave.

These distances will be maintained during the advance to the 2nd objective, so as to enable the rear waves to manoeuvre against the strong points, if required.

2nd PERIOD.

3rd Wave to RED LINE.

4th " " RED LINE

1st " " approx. 100 yards E. of RED LINE.

2nd " " " " " " "

The STRONG POINTS W. X. and Y. must be taken before these objectives can be gained.
As soon as the RED LINE is gained it will be consolidated on the above approx. objectives.
The two lines selected will be the most suitable for DEFENCE (vide para.9).

6. BATTALION IN SUPPORT - R.BERKS. ~~will advance in artillery~~ formation at ZERO plus 1 hour 12 min.
One Coy. will support the attack of the BUCKS on Strong Points W. and X. if required.
One Coy. will support the attack of the OXFORDS on Strong Point Y. if required and will capture Strong Point Z.
These two Companies will then move forward to their FINAL OBJECTIVE- RED DOTTED LINE, as soon as the barrage moves forward from the second halt marked brown and green on sketch and will take up an outpost position there.
The remaining two Coys will -

(a) be prepared to drive home the attack on the strong points if necessary.

(b) be prepared to support the two leading Coys. in gaining the RED DOTTED LINE, if necessary.

(c) If not required for either (a) or (b), will occupy a line of shell holes approx.200 yards E. of the Track through G.28.c. and G.34.a. and will be held in readiness to drive back any counter-attack during the period of consolidation (vide para.9(2))
These two Coys. will be kept intact as long as circumstances permit.

R.BERKS will send out patrols to get information and keep in touch with enemy beyond RED DOTTED LINE.
One Section (2 Guns) Stokes Mortars will be allotted to R.BERKS, and will come under its orders at 10 p.m. 2nd inst.
A party of 2 N.C.O's. 10 O.R. GLOSTERS will accompany each Stokes Mortar.

7. M/G.COY.

(a) Will detail 2 guns for immediate cooperation with each Attacking Battalion.
Officers i/c those Subsections will report to O.C. Attacking Battalions as arranged between O.C. Battalions and O.C. Machine Gun Coy. who will also arrange with Attacking Battalions for small Carrying Parties.

(b) 4 Guns will remain in their present position about O.B.1 until moved forward to S.P's constructed by GLOSTERS (vide para.9 (3)).

(c) 8 Guns will be under orders of Div. for barrage purposes.

1 Officer will be detailed to accompany the R.E. Officer i/c strong point working parties to assist him in selecting sites.
This Officer will report at ADV. BDE. H.Q. at 9-45 a.m.

8. L.T.M.B.

Two Sections will be under orders of BUCKS.

One Section " " " " OXFORDS.

One " " " " " R.BERKS.

A party of 2 N.C.O's. and 10 men of GLOSTERS will accompany each Stokes Mortar and will be under the immediate orders of O.C. Sections concerned.

FORWARD DUMPS will be made by the Carrying Parties attached to Sections.
As soon as these Dumps are formed the Carrying Parties will return for fresh supplies.
All Sections will come under orders of Battalions to which they are attached from 10 p.m. 2nd inst.

9. CONSOLIDATION.

(1). BUCKS and OXFORDS on approx. RED LINE.
Two general lines selected for defence on a reverse slope if possible (vide para. 5).

(2). R.BERKS (1) on approx. RED DOTTED LINE with two Coys. as an Outpost line- selected for observation.
(2). on approx line 200 yards E. of the track through G.28.c., G.24.a. (vide para.6.c.)

(3). Two strong points will be constructed by GLOSTERS who will detail 2 Officers, 100 O.R. for each S.P.
As soon as the RED LINE is definitely reported taken the R.E. Officer detailed for the purpose will arrange for the above mentioned working parties of the

GLOSTERS assembled off NORTH & SOUTH ALLEYS to move forward to their allotted S.P's at about G.28.c.7.5.and G.34.a.7.6.

(4). As soon as the strong points are nearly completed, they will each be garrisoned by 2 M.G's from O.B.1. and by 1 Platoon (not less than 30 O.R.) of BUCKS and OXFORDS respectively,

10. All captured documents etc, will be forwarded to ADV.BDE. H.Q. or BDE.FORWARD STATION.

11. Attacking Battalions will render short Situation Reports as soon as possible after they have ~~established~~ themselves on the GREEN and ~~RED LINES to ADV.BDE.H.Q. and subsequently~~ at half hour intervals to BDE.FORWARD STATION, until ZERO plus 3.30, after that every hour.

12. ACKNOWLEDGE.

Issued at-:- 8 p.m.

G Moore

Captain
Brigade Major
184 Infantry Brigade.

GENERAL NOTES.

1. SITUATION.

German front line system has been carried.
The BRIGADE, with the 182 BDE. on its left, and the 1st BRIGADE on its right, is ordered to attack a semi-organized Trench system in rear of the above system.
The Battalions on our immediate flanks are :-

Right - 1st BLACK WATCH.

Left - 2/6 WARWICKS.

2. GERMAN DEFENCES are :-

		Shown by
A.	Front line shell holes.	Short lengths of tape on sticks.
BP.	Second Line-(HUN TRENCH) Continuous Trench- Wire well cut.	Continuous taped line.
C.	Line of Strong Points. Wire partly cut. (Surprise wire may be expected here)	"Surprise" Wire. String with knots of paper.
D.	M.G.'s.	M.G.'s. of another Bde. Coy.

3. German Trenches will be marked out on the evening before the attack.
No reconnaissance of the enemy's position will take place beyond the British Front Line.

4. Troops will not go outside the Training Area during the Attack.

5. Men will not lie down in standing crops.

6. It will be noted that direction will be difficult to keep during the attack. Attention will be given to Compass bearings and direction marks on the ground in Battalion Orders or Instruction s.

7. The BUCKS will be Right Attacking Battalion.

The OXFORDS will be Left Attacking Battalion.

The ROYAL BERKS will be in BDE. RESERVE.

The GLOSTERS will supply Carrying Parties etc.

184TH INFANTRY BRIGADE INSTRUCTIONS.

1. ARTILLERY.

(a). The Brigade Attack will be supported by the --- Artillery Group.

(b). The preliminary bombardment will spread over two days before the attack and will include destructive fire on specially chosen points- both by heavy and field artillery.

(c). One Artillery Officer (imaginary) will be attached to each Battalion H.Q. for liaison purposes.

2. BARRAGE TIMES, as follows:-

A. FIRST PERIOD.

0.- 06	On SHELL HOLES.
06 -24	Advance by lifts of 50 yards per minute to HUN TRENCH.
24 -26	On HUN TRENCH.
26 -42	Advance by lifts of 50 yards per 2 minutes to a line 200 yards W. of DOTTED GREEN LINE.
42 - 1.12	Barrage will stand on this line.

B. SECOND PERIOD.

1.12 -1.36	Advance by lifts of 50 yards per 2 minutes to a line 200 yards W. of RED LINE.
1.36 -2.10	Barrage will stand on this line.

C. THIRD PERIOD.

2.10 -2.34	Advance by lifts of 50 yards per 2 minutes to a line 300 yards W. of RED DOTTED LINE.
2.34 -3.00	Barrage will stand on this line, and will then cease except for S.O.S. signals, which will bring it back on to this line.

The pace of the barrage will regulate that of the Infantry.

As the enemy trenches are not straight the barrage may lift from them in some places, while still on them in others The Infantry must follow closely on the barrage on their immediate front, and not wait for the barrage to lift which may still be down on their flanks.

M.G.BARRAGE.

32 Guns will barrage 400 hundred yards in front of the leading wave, commencing on HUN TRENCH, and finishing 400 yards W. of the RED DOTTED LINE.

3. C.P.A's.

C.P.A's. of the 1st Flying Squadron, R.F.C. will call for flares by succession of AAA on KLAXON or by firing VERY LIGHTS.

A. C.P.A' s are distinguished by

3. C.P.A's. (Contd).

A.(Contd). On no account will flares be lit on call by any other Aeroplane and only on above signal. E. A's often try to deceive our Infantry. All ranks to be warned accordingly.

B. Only Infantry in the FRONT LINE to light flares.

C. All flares must be lit within half a minute of call or they are useless as our Aeroplanes cannot see them.

D. Each Platoon will have a special Sentry to look out for our Aeroplanes.

E. Messages will be sent by shutter from BRIGADE and BATTALION H.Q. and acknowledged by C.P.A's. in the usual manner.

4. TANKS: (imaginary).

4 Tanks will assist the Brigade attack.
2 will start with the fourth wave and assist Infantry as far as the GREEN DOTTED LINE. They will then return.
2 will start with the R.BERKS and will assist in the capture of the strong points, if required, and in the subsequent occupation of the final outpost position on the RED DOTTED LINE.

N.B. All ranks will be made acquainted with TANK SIGNALS in case they may be doubtful about them, vide Card 2nd Edition " TANK coloured disc and light code" which supersedes S.S.148.

5. CAVALRY SQUADRON. (imaginary).

Will co-operate with the Division.
It will dismount and help Infantry to drive back counter-attack, if necessary, and will not fall back under protection of the Infantry.

6. COMMUNICATIONS.

A. BDE. H.Q. will be at BRIGADE OFFICE, BUYSSCHEURE.
ADVANCED BDE H.Q. will be at WINDMILL, G.36.Central.
BDE. FORWARD STATION will be established about G.34.b.9.8. at the WUNDER WERK DUGOUT and will be marked by 2 BLUE & WHITE FLAGS.
The BDE.FORWARD PARTY will not move up until the RED LINE is reported definitely to have been taken.
BATTALION FORWARD C.P. of OXFORDS will be established within 150 yards of B.F.S. and will be marked by one WHITE FLAG with RED CIRCLE with sticks at both ends.
BATTALION FORWARD C.P. of BUCKS will be established as near as convenient to B.F.S., and will be marked by One WHIT E FLAG with BLACK CIRCLE with sticks at both ends.

B. WIRELESS

One set will be at ADVANCED BDE.H.Q. and will move to B.F.S. under arrangements with BDE. SIGNALLING OFFICER. This set will work back to a directing station at H.32.a.2.9.

C. VISUAL.

A DIV.VISUAL STATION will be situated at

It will not work forward except to send R- D.

BDE. SIGNALLING OFFICER will arrange visual communication therewith from B.F.S.
Battalions can communicate by visual with DIV[l] VISUAL STAT ION .

D. AMPLIFIERS & POWER BUZZERS.

2 AMPLIFIERS and 2 POWER BUZZERS will be placed at BDE. SIGNALLING OFFICERS disposal, one of each will move to B.F.S. with which Battalions can communicate.

1 Power Buzzer will be allotted to BUCKS.
1 " " " " " OXFORDS.
2 " " " " " R.BERKS.

E. PIGEONS. (imaginary).

4 Birds will be allotted to BUCKS.
4 " " " " OXFORDS.
4 " " " " R.BERKS.
4 " " " " BDE.H.Q.

BUCKS will send a report of the situation during the time when the barrage is standing 200 yards beyond the GREEN DOTTED LINE by 1 pair of Birds.
OXFORDS and R.BERKS will send a Situation Report during the time when the Barrage is standing 300 yards beyond the RED DOTTED LINE.

F. CODE CALLS.

After ZERO the ordinary Station Calls as laid down in Training Manual of Signalling will be used.

G. RELAY POSTS.

Battalions will establish relay posts under Battalion arrangements, but care will be taken to ensure that :-

1. Men in these posts are kept under cover as much as possible when not on duty.

2. All men so employed are made acquainted with position of other relay posts, Battalion forward Command Posts, Battalion H.Q., Bde. F.S., and Adv. Bde.H.Q.

3. Relay Posts will be marked by b oards or small flag.

H. REPORTS.

Every effort will be made to send back reports as frequently as possible in addition to those specified in sub-para (E) above.
Attacking Battalions will render short reports every half hour after they have established themselves on the RED LINE until ZERO plus 3.30 , after that every h our.
Negative information will be of v alue.

I. SPECIAL PARTIES.

GLOSTERS will detail :-

1. 1 officer and 4 O.R. to report to BDE. SIGNALLING OFFICER at ADV.BDE.H.Q. at 3-45 a.m. for cipher and code work- He will

be acquainted with B.A.B. and PLAYFAIR CODES.
This party will be responsible for the forward movement of the WIRELESS SET vide sub-para (B) above.

ii. 2 Officers - each with 2 Orderlies, to report to the BRIGADE MAJOR at ADV.BDE.H.Q. at 8-45 a.m. These Officers will have important liaison work to carry out, and should be carefully selected. They will carry A.F.C. 2121, Sketch Maps, Field glasses, Revolvers, Box Respirators, and be otherwise lightly equipped.
They will bring their own rations, and water or other drink with them.

iii. 1 N.C.O. 3 O.R. to be in charge of AMPLIFIER SETS vide sub-para.(D) above.
to report to BDE. SIGNALLING OFFICER at ADV . BDE.H.Q. at 8-45 a.m.

7. SPECIAL LIAISON.

BUCKS will detail Special Liaison Parties of not less than 1 Officer and 6 O.R. to meet parties of 1st BLACK WATCH -1st BDE.- 1st DIVISION at following points:-

i. ORCHARD CORNER . G.2 9. c.2.6.

ii. G.28.Central.

iii. On Track at G.27.d.8.7.

OXFORDS will detail similar parties to meet parties of 2/6 WARWICKS- 182 INF.BDE.- at following points:-

i. Road junction G.35.c.9.7.

ii. On Road at G.34.Central.

iii. On Road at G.33.b.7.0.

The Officers in charge of above parties will meet Officers of the Battalions, with whom they have respectively to establish liaison at - a.m., the - inst at____ in the case of the BUCKS, and at --- a.m. the ____ inst at_____ in the case of the OXFORDS.
Careful arrangements will be made to ensure that reports of liaison having been established are sent to BDE. (REAL messages will be sent).

8. LIAISON WITH ATTACKING BATTALIONS.

R.BERKS will attach One Officer and 2 O.R. to OXFORDS and to BUCKS H.Q. who will report on Situation to their own Battalion when it moves forward, under Battalion arrangements.

9. TRAFFIC.

NORTH ALLEY is allotted to BUCKS and) For all IN Traffic.
SOUTH ALLEY " " " OXFORDS.)

As soon as the last wave of the two above Battalions has crossed BRITISH FRONT LINE, NORTH ALLEY will be open for all OUT TRAFFIC.
SOUTH ALLEY will remain for IN TRAFFIC only.
All Traffic will give way to Runners on duty.
GLOSTERS will establish CONTROL POSTS of 1 N.C.O. and 4 men as follows by 9 a.m.

i. Near junction of NORTH ALLEY & BRITISH FRONT LINE.

ii. Near junction " SOUTH ALLEY " "

iii. Near junction of NORTH ALLEY & ROAD TRENCH.

iv. Near junction " SOUTH ALLEY & " "

These Posts will be furnished with written orders as follows:-

i. On no account to allow any OUT TRAFFIC down NORTH or SOUTH ALLEY until the fourth wave of Attacking Battalions has passed over the British Front Line.

ii. To open NORTH ALLEY for OUT TRAFFIC only, after the fourth wave has passed over our front line.

iii. To send back to their Units all stragglers.

iv. To prevent more than One British to 10 Germans in small and One British to 15 Germans in large parties of Prisoners.

v. To control traffic generally and prevent blocks in C.T.'s.

vi. To give facilities as above to all Runners on duty.

CONTROL POSTS will not remain bunched together near junctions of Trenches.

10. ASSEMBLY.

All Units will be responsible for the preparation of their own assembly trenches.
All Units will be in positi on by 9 a.m.
All movement will be by allotted C.T.'s (vide para 9).

(a). ATTACKING BATTALIONS

1 st WAVE	BRITISH FRONT LINE	3rd WAV E	ROAD TRENCH.
2nd WAVE.		4th WAVE	

Assembly of subsection M.G's attached to and section of L.T.M.B. under orders of Attacking Battalions, will be under arrangements of those Battalions.

Carrying parties of 2 N.C.O.'s 10 O.R. GLOSTERS for each Stokes Mortar will assemble un der arrangements of Attacking Battalions.

(b). Carrying Coys. less Coy.H.Q. of GLOSTERS allotted to Attacking Battalions will assemble in slit trenches and shell holes off NORTH & SOUTH ALLEYS respectively between BRITISH FRONT LINE & ROAD T RENCH.

(c). One Section of R.E. and Strong Point Working Parties of GLOSTERS- 2 Officers and 100 O.R. in each party , will assemble off NORTH & SOUTH ALLEYS in shell holes imm diatel in rear of the Carrying Coys.

Support Battalion - ROYAL BERKS - will assemble about G.24. central near ADV.BDE.H.Q.

11. PRISONERS.

Will be evacuated over the top as much as possible to ADV. BDE. H.Q.
Not more than 1 British to 10 Germans in small and 1 British to 15 Germans in large parties.
Slightly wounded British to be used if possible.
Special measures may be necessary in the case of enemy officers.

12. MAPS, DOCUMENTS, ETC.

(1). Officers will take with them into action the following MAPS :-

(a). 1/10,000 Trench Maps shewing ground over which he himself has to pass and the ground for at least 1,000 yards on each side of that area.

(b). 1/10,000 or 1/20,000 Map shewing ground for at least 1 mile beyond the final objective, and the ground on the flanks.

(c). 1/100,000 Map shewing Back Areas, etc.

(2). Officers will carry 6 Message Form Pads A.F.C. 3481. Notebook, Envelopes, Field Service Pocket Book, and B.A.B. French Code (Coy.Commander only).

(3). No Letters or Documents likely to give information to the enemy will be taken into action.

13. DRESS & EQUIPMENT.

As in S.S.135 for Fighting Order.
MOPPERS UP will carry 1 P.Bomb, and 4 Mills Bombs each.
RUNNERS will carry Rifle, Bayonet, Water Bottle, 50 rounds S.A.A. and Box Respirator only.
All distinguishing marks will be worn.
A plentiful supply of Rifle Grenades and Smoke Bombs will probably be required to assist in carrying the Strong Points.

14. SYNCHRONIZATION OF WATCHES.

(a). Watches will be synchronised under arrangements made by BDE. SIGNALLING OFFICER at 9 a.m. and 9-30 p.m.

(b). The utmost care will be taken to ensure that the synchronization is absolutely correct.
As the 3rd and 4th Waves of Attacking Battalions will have to leave ROAD TRENCH before ZERO, any mistake in timing may have serious consequences.

184 M.G. Coy's
Operation Order No 31.

No ---- 12 14.8.1917

APPENDIX II

Sect. HAZEBROUCK 1/40.000.

1. The 184 M.G. Coy will move to WATOU. No 1 AREA on 15th inst. The company less transport will proceed by ~~road and~~ train, the Transport by road.

2. Starting point - Company less transport, Cross Roads at PONT DU JOUR at 4.15 am.

Transport - Cross roads 300x N.W of church BUYSSCHEURE at ~~9.15am.~~ 9.20am

3. Company less transport will parade in column of sect's 2.3.4.1. HQ at 3.45 am on road to PONT DU JOUR. Head of column facing N and 300x from Cross Roads near C.Q.M. Stores. - Dress marching order, caps, helmets on packs, one days rations in haversack, full water bottles.

Transport will parade at 8.45 am, on road to PONT DU JOUR. head of column on Cross Roads near C.Q.M. Stores and facing S. in following order. Fighting limbers 1.2-3-4. Nos 3's 1.2.3.4 HQ. Cooks Cart, Water Cart G.S. wagon. - Dress fighting order, caps helmets on packs on limbers.

4 Route - Company less transport - PONT DU JOUR - LE MENEGAT entraining at ARNEKE, detraining at ABEELE - hence to WATOU. No 1 Area.

Transport - X Roads 300x N.W of Church BUYSSCHEURE - BALEMBERG. - LE-MENEGAT - HEMAERE - CAPPEL - HARDIFORT - OUDEZEELE - STEENVOORDE - ABEELE - HILLEHOEK.

5 Transport will for the move come under the orders of Major H.S. BENNETT 2/4 Oxf Bucks L.I.

6 There will be a halt of 15 mins before each clock hour. Transport will also halt, as soon as the head of the column reaches LE TEMPLE (S.E. of OUDEZEELE) for two hours to water and feed.

7 All transport will maintain a distance of 200x between Battalions, or equivalent number of vehicles throughout the march. After detrainment at ABEELE 500x will be maintained between battalions.

8 Billets will be cleaned by 9 pm on 14th inst and again cleaned before 2.45 am 15th inst. Certificates will be rendered by S.O's at this time.

8. (Contd) C.Q.M.S will arrange to collect and load all Officers Valises, these will be dumped at C.Q.M Stores or left outside Officers billets.
Section Officers will detail 1 brakes man for the 3 section limbers.
C.S.M. will detail 1 brakes man for each G.S. Wagon & H.Q. Limber.

9. ACKNOWLEDGE.

Issued at 7.45 Pm.

Copies to:-
No 1-4 Section Officers
5. Transport Officer
6 C.S.M.
7 C.Q.M.S.
8 War Diary
9 File.

[illegible] Capt.
Comdg 184 Coy. M.G.C.

APPENDIX III

184 Machine Gun Company
Operation Order No

17th August 1917
Ref. map 28 N W
27

1 The 184 M G Co will move to a camp near GOLDFISH CHATEAU H 11 central on 17th August

2 Starting point Road junction on ABEELE POPERINGHE RD at L 22 a 88 at a time to be notified later. Route POPERINGHE – VLAMERTINGHE

3 Co will parade at a time to be notified later and will move off in following order 3 4 1 2 Hqs. Fighting Limbers ~~1 2 3 4~~ No 1 ~~2 3 4~~ Hq. ~~G S wagon~~ water cart G S wagon.
Dress Fighting order.

4 Mess cart and ~~[illegible]~~ No 1 and 2 will move to new area at 11 a.m under 2 Lt Graig. He will ~~f~~ commence preparations for dinners on arrival at the new camp.

5 Advance party will report to OC 184 MG Co at GOLDFISH CHATEAU and will guide the unit on from there.

Issued at 10.50 a.m
Copies to
1 S Os com
2 File
3 War Diary

J Lismore Lt
for
OC 184 MG Co

Appendix IV

Pty No 7

184 M.G. Coy's

Operation order No 33.

14.8.1917

Ref Sheet 28 NW 1/20.000.

1. Nos 1 & 3 Sections. 184 M.G. Coy will relieve 8 guns of No 107 M.G. Coy in Barrage positions JASPER FARM. C 29 b 5.7 on morning of 18th inst.
2. Guides will be at Dressing Station 300x yds W. of WIELTJE 5.30 am.
3. Parade 4 am. Dress fighting order. two days rations will be carried. March off 4.15 am.
Route:- H 11 (Central) I 7 c (central) I 7 c 8.9. I 7 a 4.5. thence direct via ST JEAN.
4. Intervals of 200x yds between sections up to ST JEAN and thereafter 200x between subsections.
Limbers will be unloaded at BILGE TR 300x W of WIELTJE and sent back to transport lines immediately
5. All MAPS, DEFENCE SCHEMES & BARRAGE LINES will be taken over, also all tripod platforms & S.A.A. and a list forwarded to Coy. H.Q.
6. Completion of relief to be reported advanced Coy H.Q. JASPER FARM.
7. Acknowledge.

Issued at

Copies to:-

No 1 O.C No 1 Section
2 " 3 "
3 184 Bde
4 107 M.G. Coy
5 DMGO
6 War Diary
7 TOC
8 C.S.M.
9 C.Q.M.S.
10 183 Bde

W. Napier Capt
Comdg 184 Coy M.G. Corps

Ref Map FREZENBERG 1/10.000 20. 8. 1917

APPENDIX V

The Brigade will attack enemy's defences from D14C.6.4. Point in DEEP DRIVE 60 yds due N of H in MARTHA HOUSE to D4C3.5. road junction 100 yds S of W in WINNIPEG. both inclusive
The 44th Inf BdE, 15 DIV, will attack on the right - left attacking Battalion 7th Cameron Highlanders. Zero hour will be at about 4.45 am. Exact hour will be notified later.
The 143rd Inf BdE 48th DIV. will attack on the left.
Division between 44th Inf Bde and 184 BdE will be a line drawn through D19a 3.4 - D13d 42 (GALLIPOLI exclusive to 184 BdE) D14 Central (MARTHA HOUSE) inclusive to 184 BdE)
Division between 143 Inf Bde + 184 Inf BdE. will be a line drawn through C18a 2.1. - C18 b 6.8 (BORDER HOUSE exclusive to 184 BdE) - road junction D4C 3.5 (inclusive to 184 BdE)
The Bucks will attack on the right.
The Oxfords will attack on the left.
The Bucks will attack with 2 companies, forming 1st + 2nd waves, and 2 Coys forming 3rd + 4th waves.
The Oxfords will attack with 3 Coys forming the first + second waves. and one Coy. forming the third wave.
2/Lt WOMERSLEY with 2 guns No 2 Section will take up a position about JEW HILL before ZERO hour. These guns will cover the front from WURST FARM to NILE.
After objectives have been taken, guns will move as follows:-
Lt CASWELL with 2 guns No2 Section to vicinity of POND FARM, covering from WINNIPEG TO WURST FARM.
No4 Section under command of 2/Lt CRAIG will advance to SOMME FARM where 2 guns will take up a position covering front from D4 Central to AVIATIK FARM.
2 guns under 2/Lt MARTIN will act under orders of O.C. BUCKS
2/Lt MARTIN will keep in close touch with battalion Commander throughout the operation.
Guns for advance will move to front line system on night of 20th/21st under Section arrangements.
No1 Section will be under orders of O.C. No 182 M.G. Coy for Barrage purposes
No3 Section will be under orders of O.C. " 183 " " " for " "

5 Position of Section HQ & Section dumps will be notified later.
Company HQ will be in CALL Reserve C23C 7.8 from 9 pm
21st/22nd, up to that time it will be at JASPER FARM.
Instructions and special information are attached to Copies 10 & 11.

6 ACKNOWLEDGE.

Issued at

Copies to:-

Nos 1/4 Section Officers
5/7 Sub. Section Officers
8 Transport Officers
9 184 Bde
10 D.M.G.O
11 183 M.G. Coy
12 182 " "
13 O.C. 2/5 Glosters
14 OC Oxfords
15 O.C. Royal Berks
16 OC Bucks.
17 C S M
18 C.Q.M.S.
19 War Diary
20 File.

A S Napier CAPT.
COMDG. 184 COMPANY M.G. CORPS.

Instructions & Information
regarding operations of the 184 Bde 20.8.17
Issued with Operation Order No 34.

1. Detachments advancing will carry the following:-
1 Gun
1 tripod
1 Spare parts case & barrel
10 belt boxes 2 picks
1 Condenser complete 4 Shovels
Sandbags.
Each section will take a range finder.

2 All ranks will wear fighting order.
Men of detachments advancing will carry besides the contents of the pack as laid down:-
2 lemons
1 tin solidified alcohol each gun team.
1 days rations.

3 No 2 & 4 Sections will form section dumps consisting of:-
8 Tins of water
1 days rations of section.
2 spare parts boxes
10 boxes of S.A.A.
under section arrangements during 21st.

4 A dump of water tins will be formed near dressing Station at WIELTJE.
Sections attached to 182 & 183 will draw rations for 3 days and lemons and solidified alcohol from 184 at 4 30 am on 21st.
Water Tins will be supplied during 21st and 22nd in limited numbers on the requisition signed by an Officer of 184 M/G Coy.

5 Section Officers 2 & 4 will immediately prepare range cards, showing range and compass bearings from points to which they will move their guns for the operation.

6 A Bde relay post No 3 will be established at BRIDGE HOUSE. It will be able to transmit to adv Bde HQ any message handed in by runner, visual or phone.
Battalion HQ are in communication with this post by telephone, visual & runners.

No 6 (Contd) Company H.Q. will be in communication with adv. Bde HQ by telephone & runner.
During the operation, battalion advanced stations will be formed at C 18 b 4/2.2. OXFORD.
SOMME. BUCKS.
adv Bde HQ will move to about C 18 d 5.6.

7. Reports will be sent:-
(1) on night of 20/21 as soon as sections take up positions in front system.
Location of dumps will be given.
(2) Frequent reports during operation, particularly
(1) on moving forward.
2 on arrival at objective.

8. Information about TANKS is attached. this will be destroyed as soon as noted.

9 Section officers will satisfy themselves that their gunners know the arrangements for communication.

10. Coy H.Q will be at JASPER FARM until 9. PM. 21-22ND

11. Silence will be observed during moving in on 20/21 and until the operation

12 S.O.S. Green 1" Very Light fired until guns open.

13 Envelopes addressed to recipients will not be taken into action.

14 TANK SIGNALS.

HAVE reached my objective	RED GREEN
AM. Broken down.	R. R. R
No Enemy in sight	RED. W. W.

15. Contact aeroplanes will be marked with two black projections on each lower wing.

16. A repair shop will be established in CALL RESERVE TR C23C 7.8. This is primarily for the Barrage Guns.

W. Napier Capt

APPENDIX VI

Report on action by 184 M.G. Coy during operations from 22-8-17 - 29-8-17.

In accordance with Company Operation Order No 34. 20-8-17, 2 Guns No 2 Section under 2/Lt Hanners(?) occupied JEW HILL C.12.d.2.3 before dawn 22-8-17.

These guns did not come into action during 1st phase of the operation, but when the infantry fell back they opened fire on the enemy in the vicinity of WINNIPEG X Rds. SCHULER FARM, and ground between these two places, and prevented the left flank of the Oxfords from being turned.

On 23rd Enemy were caught retiring from POND FARM, carrying machine guns. About 20 of them were shot down.

On night of 23rd inst 2 guns No 1 Section were sent out to JEW HILL, and the 4 guns laid on S.O.S. barrage line HANNEBECK RIVER.

On morning of 24th inst Enemy counter-attacked our line of out posts to the N.E. of JEW HILL with Flamenwerfer. All 4 guns opened fire and prevented the enemy from advancing inflicting heavy casualties.

2 guns under 2/Lt Craig advanced to SOMME FARM after it had been taken. They took up positions at D13c34 & D13c54. As GALLIPOLI and Hill 35 were not taken on the right and POND FARM on the left, the flanks of this position were very exposed. The officer and Sergeant became casualties and 1 gun was put out of action.

On this information reaching O.C. Bucks he ordered his reserve two guns under 2/Lt Martin to move up to SOMME FARM to protect his right flank.

During the advance 2/Lt Martin and his Sergeant became casualties and the command of the 4 guns devolved on the remaining N.C.O. Cpl Rutherford who reorganised the section and 2 guns which had been put out of action.

This N.C.O showed great coolness & presence of mind and by his good example and energy undoubtedly prevented the survivors of his section from retiring. He remained in command for 3 days during which time the reports he sent back were very useful. He was also in close touch with the battalion Commander throughout.

No 3 Section were attached to No 183 Coy and formed part of barrage battery in CAPRICORN TRENCH.

No 1 Section were attached to No 182 Coy and formed part of Barrage battery. CALL RESERVE.

2/Lt Allen with 2 guns was ordered to move from Barrage position in CAPRICORN TRENCH to DONT TRENCH and took up position there night of 22nd - 23rd inst.

. The Company less 6 detachments were relieved by 182 M.G. Coy on night 24th inst.

Casualties Officers 3. Other Ranks 23.

28-8-17.

Cop: No

184 M G Coy
Operation Order No 35

24. 8. 1917

Ref map Sheet FREZENBERG ypres
28 N.W. 1/20.000

APPENDIX
VII

1. Eight detachments of the 182 M.G. Coy will relieve 14 detachments of 184 M.G. Coy in the line night of 24/25th inst.

2. The following dispositions will be handed over:

2 Guns SOMME { D.13.C.50.35 / D.13.C.40.20 }

2 do DONT TRENCH { D.13.C.30.15 / D.13.C.10.15 }

4 Guns JEW HILL { C.12.d.20.15 / C.12.d.20.25 / C.12.d.15.30 / C.12.d.15.40 }

3. 1 Guide for section relieving the 2 guns near SOMME and the 2 guns near DONT TRENCH, will be at the dressing station WIELTJE at 7.30 pm. This guide will take the section to JASPER FARM where 1 guide per detachment will meet them and take them to their positions. 2 guides will be at dressing station WIELTJE at 8 pm for the 4 guns at JEW HILL.

4. 10 Belt boxes per gun will be handed over at each position. All S.A.A. range cards and S.O.S. lines, also a diagram for each position showing situation of front line and infantry, will be handed over. Transport Officer 184 M.G. Coy will take over 80 full belt boxes from T.O. 182 M.G. Coy at transport lines of the latter.

5. Transport Officer 184 M.G. Coy will meet T.O. 182 M.G. Coy on morning of 24th inst. and will arrange to take over transport lines and billets.

6. Guns except those detailed in para 2 will withdraw at dusk to dump.

7. Company on relief will proceed, probably by train from WIELTJE, to billets at G.6.d.5.0 vacated by 182 M.G. Coy.

8. Detailed orders to section officers attached.

9. Coy H.Q. will move from JASPER FARM to WIELTJE dump at 8 pm 24/25th and to new area on completion of relief.

10. Completion of relief will be reported by outgoing Section Officers as they pass WIELTJE and to D.M.G.O. by word "CORSE LEEKED".

11. Acknowledge.

12. Issued at 9.30 am.

Copies to:

1. 2/Lt Urquhart
2. Lt Creswell
3. 2/Lt Womersley
4. " Allen
5. Transport Officer
6. 184 Bde H.Q.
7. 182 "
8. [illegible] M.G.O.
9. C.S.M.

10/11 War Diary + File.

Instructions to
Section Officers & Transport Officers.

Issued with Operation Order 35.

24.8.1917.

1. Every article of equipment except 80 belt boxes handed over, will be brought out of the line.
2. Section Officers concerned will make certain guides are at places appointed in time, and will provide each guide with a piece of paper on which the name of the guns position is shown.
   H.Q. will provide the guide from the dressing station to JASPER FARM.
3. Limbers will report at dump as follows and will return to BRANDHOEK area at orders of Section Officers as soon as loaded:-

SECTION OFFICER	SUB SECTION	LIMBER	TIME AT DUMP
2/Lt Urquhart	S.S. 1 S.S. 3	1/1	10 PM.
Lt Caswell } 2 Lt Allen }	{ S.S. 2 { S.S 3 S. 4.	3/1 4/1	9.30 PM.
2/Lt Womersley	S.S. 2 S.S. 1	2/1	10.30 PM.
Hd. Qrs	H.Q.	H.Q.	9. Pm.

All fighting limbers will be empty except for 4 gun boxes.
Each lead mule will be accompanied by one loader and will carry a pack saddle.

4. Personnel will take such cover as available pending ~~arrival~~ of orders as to transport by train.
5. Transport will see that cooks prepare hot food on arrival at new area.

for Capt
Comdg 184 M. G. Coy

Vol 16

C O N F I D E N T I A L

W A R   D I A R Y

**** of ****

184TH COMPANY, MACHINE GUN CORPS

From 1st Sept, 1917 to 30th Sept,1917.

VOLUME XV1.

****

Instructions regarding War Diaries and Intelligence Summaries are contained in F. S. Regs., Part II. and the Staff Manual respectively. Title pages will be prepared in manuscript.

WAR DIARY
~~or~~
~~INTELLIGENCE SUMMARY.~~
(Erase heading not required.)

Army Form C. 2118.

184 M. G. Co.

Place	Date	Hour	Summary of Events and Information	Remarks and references to Appendices
WIELTJE SECTOR	August 30	-	The following dispositions taken over from 182 M. G. Co. 183 Bde Holding Line. 4 guns JEW HILL 2 guns POND FARM 2 guns SOMME 4 guns HILL 35 Headquarters of Co. at WIELTJE 4 guns JASPER FARM	Ref MAPS 5A HAZEBROUCK 1/100000 28 NW 1/20000
	31	-	Dispositions altered to the following 183 Bde relieved by 182 Bde 4 guns JEW HILL 2 guns POND FARM 2 guns SOMME 1 guns POMMERN REDOUBT 4 guns JASPER FARM 3 guns CAMEL AVENUE The gun in POMMERN (No 3 Section) cooperated in an enterprise of the right Battalion against HILL 35 gun pits. The enterprise failed and gun returned to its previous position in POMMERN. Moved forward the guns in vicinity of POND and DONT Trench to more suitable positions in the neighbourhood	FREZENBORG 1/10000 27 1/40000 FRANCE 51B 51C 1/40000 LENS 11 1/100000
	Sept. 1	-	The right Battalion again attacked gun pits on HILL 35. The gun in POMMERN moved to a flank to guard against a counter attack from IBERIAN — the attack was without result and the gun resumed its former position.	
	2	-	Established a visual signal station at the guns on JEW HILL in communication with CALL RESERVE. Hence by wire to WIELTJE.	

A5834 Wt. W4973 M687 750,000 8/16 D. D. & L. Ltd. Forms/C.2118/13.

Instructions regarding War Diaries and Intelligence Summaries are contained in F. S. Regs., Part II. and the Staff Manual respectively. Title pages will be prepared in manuscript.

WAR DIARY

~~or~~

~~INTELLIGENCE SUMMARY.~~

(*Erase heading not required.*)

Army Form C. 2118.

Place	Date	Hour	Summary of Events and Information	Remarks and references to Appendices
WIELTJE SECTOR	Sept. 3	-	The right battalion again attempted to take gun pits on HILL 35 at 10 p.m. Cooperated with two guns – one in vicinity of SOMME keeping up fire towards GALLIPOLI the other on the right flank moving to where it could protect against a counter attack from IBERIAN. The attack was without result and guns took up usual dispositions by dawn. Bombs dropped on transport lines by enemy planes. Casualties 2 OR wounded. Horses 3 killed 10 wounded. During tour from Aug. 30th to Sept 4th an average of 10000 rounds fired nightly on tracks and roads behind enemy lines: hot food carried each night to all sections except that in POND FARM.	[initials]
	4		Relieved in line by 182 M.G Co. and 183 M.G. Co. O.O. attached	Appendix No. 1
BRANDHOEK G.5.c 4.4			returned to camp at BRANDHOEK by light railway. Casualties during tour 7 OR wounded.	[initials]
			Refitting and training.	
	8		Two sections 183 M.G. Co in right subsector relieved by two ~~detachments~~ sections. Dispositions taken up: 4 guns JASPER FARM; 3 guns CAMEL AVENUE; 1 gun POMMERN. O.O. attached	Appendix No. 2
			O.C. 184 M.G. Co took command of M.Gs in line – two sections of 183 M.G Co being in left subsector.	
	9		Two detachments from CAMEL AVE moved to forward position near POMMERN by 12 midnight in preparation for an advance to gun pits on HILL 35 when they had been captured on 10th. O.O. attached. Military medal awarded Cpl Rutherford for gallantry Pte. ALLEN in action 26th Aug	Appendix No. 3 [initials]
	10		Gun pits on HILL 35 attacked by Oxfords at 4 p.m. Attack unsuccessful – 2LT SIMKIN wounded going forward to ~~occupy~~ situation at 4.20 p.m. Guns returned to usual dispositions by 2 am.	[initials]

A5834 Wt. W4973 M687 750,000 8/16 D. D. & L. Ltd. Forms/C.2118/13.

Instructions regarding War Diaries and Intelligence Summaries are contained in F. S. Regs., Part II. and the Staff Manual respectively. Title pages will be prepared in manuscript.

WAR DIARY

~~or~~

~~INTELLIGENCE SUMMARY.~~

(Erase heading not required.)

Army Form C. 2118.

Place	Date	Hour	Summary of Events and Information	Remarks and references to Appendices
WIELTJE sector	11			[initials]
	12		Two sections (JEW HILL POND FARM SOMME) of 183 M.G. Co relieved by two sections 184 M.G. Co. Complete company now in line. OO attached	[initials] Appendix No. 4
	13		Military Cross awarded 2nd Lt. R.W. GRAIG for gallantry in action 21st August.	[initials]
	14		Co relieved by 166 M.G. Co. Relief complete by 11 p.m. Returned to camp at BRANDHOEK. OO attached.	Appendix No. 5
			During tour nightly average of 10000 rounds fired on tracks behind enemy line; sixteen covered barrage positions constructed: five reserve dumps of SAA totalling 152000 rounds formed and 10000 rounds carried to each forward gun. Hot food taken to all sections (except that in POND) each night. Casualties during tour Officers 2 wounded (one gassed) OR 14 wounded 8 gassed shell "W"	
WATOU ~~[struck out]~~ AG 3	15		Moved by bus to ~~[struck out]~~ WATOU No 3 Refitting	[initials]
WORMHONDT	17		Marched to WORMHONDT "A" area	[initials]
	18		attached men returned to units. OO attached	Appendix No 6
GOUVES	19		Moved to GOUVES by train. O.O. attached	[initials]
			Training and refitting	
ST NICHOLAS	24		Marched to ST NICHOLAS - in divisional reserve	[initials] Appendix No 7
	do.		Training. Special attention to barrage drill - shooting - trench routine - gas precautions and precautions against trench feet - instruction of NCOs in indirect fire.	Appendix No.
	30		Total casualties during operations in WIELTJE SECTOR 5 officers wounded (inc 1 gassed) OR 2 killed in action 2 died of wounds 52 wounded (includes attached)	[initials] 8
			Strength 9 officers 179 OR (includes 1 attached Interpreter)	[initials]
			Drafts during month 5 off. 58 O.R.	

[signature] CAPT.
COMDG. 184 COMPANY M.G. CORPS

A5834 Wt. W4973 M687 750,000 8/16 D. D. & L. Ltd. Forms/C.2118/13.

Operation Order No 34. 4.9.1917.

Copy No [illegible] 184 Coy M.G. Corps.

(1)

Ref Map 28 NW 1/20.000.
FREZENBERG. 1/10.000.

1. The 184 M.G. Coy will be relieved in the line on the night of 4/5th inst by the 182 M.G. Coy and 183 M.G. Coy

2. The following dispositions will be handed over:-

To 182 M.G. Coy:-		To 183 M.G. Coy:-	
4 Guns	JEW HILL	1 Gun -	POMMERN REDOUBT.
2 "	POND FARM.	3 "	CAMEL FARM.
1 "	DONT TRENCH.	4 "	JASPER FARM.
1 "	C.19a 15.90		

3. Guides will be at H.Q. WIELTJE dugout at 7.30 PM as follows:-

2 Guides	JEW HILL	1 Guide	POMMERN REDOUBT
1 "	POND FARM	1 "	CAMEL AVENUE
1 "	DONT TRENCH	1 "	JASPER FARM.
1 "	C.19A.15.90.		

Each will have a piece of paper showing the gun or guns for which he is guide.

4 Full particulars will be given to in-coming detachts as to position of infantry posts.
S.A.A. in boxes will be handed over, but equipment and stores other than this will be brought out.

5 The visual station on JEW HILL will close when our detachments leave JEW HILL, and the lamp borrowed from O.C. Signals 182 Bde will be returned as soon as possible afterwards. A receipt will be obtained.

6. Reserve Nos of the following sections will report at H.Q at 7.30 PM as carriers.
No 1. No 2 & No 3 Sections. Dress:- Drill order. Steel Helmets. Box Respirators.
Arrangements will be made that they move from Camp forward by train or lorry.

7. Sections on relief will return to WIELTJE where a hot meal will be issued. They will then proceed by train to Camp at G 5.c. 6.4.
Special instructions to Section Officers are attached.

8. Completion of relief will be reported by relieved Section Officers, to H.Q. on arrival at WIELTJE, and to D.M.G.O. by code word:- ABDULLA

9. H.Q. will be at WIELTJE dug-out until the completion of relief, when it will move to Camp at G.5.c.6.4.

Acknowledge.

Issued at 11 a.m.

Copies to

1-4. Section Officers

5 Transport Officer

6 C.S.M.

7 C.Q.M.S.

8. 184 Bde.

9. 182 "

10 182 M.G. Coy.

11 183 M.G. Coy.

12 D.M.G.O

13. O.C. Signals 182 Bde.

14. War Diary

15 File

Instructions with copies 1/8. 12.14 & 15

R.I. McKay. Lt.
for Capt
Comdg. 184 M.G. Coy.

Instructions to Section Officers
Issued with Operation Order No 34.

4.9.1917.

1. Limbers will report to dump as follows:-
1 fighting limber containing 4 gun boxes will be sent for each section.

No 1
No 3 10.15 pm. No 2 10 pm.
9.45 pm No 4 9.30 pm.
H.Q. 10.30 pm.

2. No 3 Section limber will bring up to dump hot rations for the 4 sections.

3. Limbers when loaded will be sent back at orders of C.S.M.
He will be responsible that all stores at dump are sent back.

4. If section Officer No 1 considers situation allows he will signal for his limbers as soon as his relief arrives - the limbers will then move to VANHOELE FARM

[signature]
for Capt
Comdg. 184 M.G. Coy.

Copy No

Operation Order No 38.
184 Coy. M. G. Corps.

Ref Map "FREZENBERG" 1/10.000 4.9.1917.

1. Two sections of the 184 M.G. Coy will relieve two Sections of 183 M.G. Coy in the line night of 8-9th
2. The following dispositions will be taken over:-

FOUR GUNS - JASPER FARM. - No 1. Section
THREE " - CAMEL AVENUE -
ONE " POMMERN REDOUBT - } No 3 Section.

3. Detailed orders to Section Officers are attached
4. Guides will be at Dressing Station WIELTJE at 7-30pm on night of 8-9th as follows.

1 GUIDE - JASPER FARM.
1 do CAMEL AVENUE
1 do POMMERN REDOUBT.

5. All S.O.S. Lines, all SAA and all Trench Stores will be taken over but not guns or belt boxes.
6. Completion of relief will be report to Coy H.Q at WIELTJE by runner, and to 184 Bde + D.M.G.O by code word "STORM TROOP"
7. Coy H.Q will move to WIELTJE dug-out at 6-30pm 8.9th.
8. All guns of the 183 M.G. Coy in the line will come under orders of O.C. 184 M.G. Coy at 10pm 8-9th.
9. Acknowledge

Issued at

Copies to:-

No 1 S.O. No 1 Section
2 " No 3 "
3 Transport Officer
4 C.Q.M.S.
5 C.S.M.
6 S.C. 184 Bde
7 B.M. do
8 183 Bde
9 183 M.G. Coy
10. D.M.G.C.
11 File
12 War Diary

[signature] for Capt
Comdg 184 M.G. Coy.

Instructions to Section Officers
Issued with Operation Order 38. 4.9.17

1. Fighting limbers will dump guns + gun equipment at DRESSING STATION WIELTJE at 7 pm under Section arrangements.

2. It is possible transport of personnel from camp to ST JEAN may be arranged. Orders will be given later.

3. A Sub Section of No 3 Section under 2/Lt SIMPKIN will be prepared to take part in an operation on afternoon of 9th – this Sub Section will move in the first instance to CAMEL ~~[illegible]~~ AVENUE. Orders will be given regarding the operation later.

4. Each man of No 1 + No 3 Section will carry 2 days rations.

5. As usual a dump for rations, water and stores will be formed at DRESSING STATION WIELTJE under a L/Cpl to be detailed ~~[illegible]~~ by C.Q.M.S. Rations for Sections in the line for 11th will be drawn at that dump at 4.30 am on that day and at the same hour following days. Water can be drawn as required on signature of Section Officers.

6. The usual reports will be render at 9 am by Section Officers in the line.

F. L. Simmie for Capt
Comdg 184 M.G. Coy

SECRET

Operation Order No 39
~~184 M. G. Co.~~ TERROR

3

Copy No Spare

Ref map FREZENBURG $\frac{1}{10000}$
Sketch map 61 M 79 $\frac{1}{2500}$

9th Sept. 1917

1. ~~184 M. G. Co~~ TERROR will cooperate in an attack being made on German gun positions on HILL 35 on the 10th September 1917.

2. The attack is being made by ~~Oxfords~~ TEST. A company is attacking on the left D company on the right. The objective of A company being tree on left of position and No 1 2 and 3 blockhouses consolidating a line fifty yards east of the blockhouses. D company has for objective No 4, point P and No 5. They are to form a block in E.R trench and consolidate round No 5 throwing back their right flank.

3 Zero will be 4 p.m.

4 A subsection of No 3 section under 2Lt SIMKIN will report to O.C. ~~Oxfords~~ TEST at Batt Hqrs BANK FARM at 11 p.m 9/10th. The two detachments will move from there to positions chosen by O C ~~Oxfords~~ TEST as positions of assembly. From dawn on the 10th until zero no movement will take place and fire will not be opened on hostile aircraft. One gun will be placed in the vicinity of A company and one in the vicinity of D company.

5. These two guns will not move forward until the objectives have been secured except such short move as the Section Officer may consider necessary to avoid the hostile barrage after zero. On moving to objectives one gun will be placed at No 1 blockhouse to protect the position towards GALLIPOLI and one gun at No 5 to protect towards IBERIAN

6. O.C. ~~Oxfords~~ TEST will detail three men of his battalion to each gun to assist in carrying ammunition forward these six men will come under orders of Section Officer from 11 p.m 9/10th.

7 Ten belt boxes ~~[illegible]~~ four shovels and one pick besides gun tripod spare parts spare barrel and condenser will be carried by each detachment.

8 A belt refilling depot will be established at Dugout 61

9. As the position once gained is to be held at all cost in the event of one of the two guns detailed to advance being put out of action the gun now in POMMERN at D19a 65.10 will replace it. the remaining gun of No 3 section moving up from CAMEL AVENUE to the position vacated

10. The section at CASPER FARM will stand to on its SOS barrage line at zero and will not stand down until the situation is normal.

The guns in position in the vicinity of SOMME and at POND FARM will from zero onwards deal with any patrols of the enemy seen near AISNE or GALLIPOLI

11 Reports will be sent to battalion headquarters at 90 and thence by visual to GALL RESERVE

Section officer moving forward will report on occupying objective and afterwards as the situation demands.

Copies to

1 Section Officer No 1
2 do do No 3
3 do do POND FARM
4 TEST
5 TEAZE
6 Bm go
7 War Diary
8 File

[signature]
Lt
for
Capt
OC TERROR M G Coy

"A" Form.

Army Form C. 2121.
(In pads of 100.)

MESSAGES AND SIGNALS.

No. of Message..............

Prefix.......... Code.............. m. | Words. | Charge.

Office of Origin and Service Instructions.

Sent
At..............m.
To..............
By..............

This message is on a/c of:
.... *Service.*
(Signature of "Franking Officer.")

Recd. at .... m.
Date..............
From..............
By..............

TO [illegible]

Sender's Number.	Day of Month.	In reply to Number.	AAA
* G82	9		

ZERO
4 PM
[illegible]
10th
ACKNOWLEDGE

From [illegible]
Place [illegible]
Time

The above may be forwarded as now corrected. (Z) [illegible]

Censor. Signature of Addressor or person authorised to telegraph in his name.

* This line should be erased if not required.

(3198.) Wt. W 12953/M1294. 375,000 Pads. 1/17. H. W. & V., Ld. (E. 818.)

THE BATTERY POSITION HILL 25

(1) [illegible]
(2) [illegible]
(3)&(4) behind crest
(5) is 65 yds from wrecked plane

Copy No 5

Operation Order No 40

Ref MAP FREZENBURG 1/10.000 12.9.1917. 4

No 1. Two Sections TERROR will relieve two sections TOMMY in line night of 12/13th Sept

2. The following dispositions will be taken over:-

2 Guns - JEW HILL }
2 " CALL RESERVE } under 2/Lt WOMERSLEY No 4 SECTION

2 Guns - POND FARM }
1 " DONT TRENCH } under Lt CASWELL
1 " D19a 1.9. } No 2 SECTION.

3. Guides will be at Dressing Station Dump at 7.30 pm as follows:-

1 GUIDE - JEW HILL
1 " CALL RESERVE
1 " POND FARM.
1 " DONT TRENCH
1 " D19a 1.9.

Each guide will have a piece of paper shewing position for which he is guide.

4 The following will be handed over at positions:- MAP. FREZENBERG - Range Cards - tabulated particulars of position - Sketch - S.A.A. - and 10 belt boxes each position relieved.

5. Completion of relief will be reported by runner to H.Q WIELTJE and to D.M.G.O. by code "ALWAYS"

6. Instructions to relieving Section Officers attached.

Copies to:

No1 - S.O 1. TERROR
2 - 2 -
3 - 3 -
4 - 4 "
5 - 2 TOMMY
6 - 4 "
7 B.M. TEAZE
8 O.C. TOMMY
9 D.M.G.O.
10 FILE
11 WAR DIARY
12 CQMS
13 C.S.M.

Issued at 4 pm

[signature] Lieut
for O.C. TERROR

Instructions to Section Officers
Issued with Operation Order No 40

12.9.1917.

Limbers will dump guns & gun equipment of Nos 2 & 4 Sections TERROR at DRESSING STATION DUMP WIELTJE at 4.15 Pm. under Section arrangements.
The man per ~~Parties~~ detachment will be sent with limbers.

Section Officers TOMMY on relief will dump guns and gun equipment at DRESSING Station Dump WIELTJE in charge of a loading party and will then return to Transport lines TOMMY

Sections No 2 & 4 TOMMY will proceed to dump under Section arrangements.

Rations for 13th will be taken into the line. Rations for following days at Dump 6.30 pm as usual.

[illegible] Lieut
for O.C. TERROR

Belt boxes.
Range finders.

Obtain Guide }
our Guide } Jew Hill
Messenger } CALL RES

Hand over + obtain receipts.

Take out {
Guns
Tripods
Spare parts
any spare belt boxes
2 Range finders
}

1 Dump them at Dressing Station near WIELTJE
2 + Leave two men as Loaders Limber arrive at 10.30
3 others march back under L/C Morgan.
4 Self + Smith report to [illegible] + leave sketch.

SO

No 2 Tommy

CALL RES.

Copy No 10

OPERATION ORDER No 41.

Map Ref. FREZENBERG 1/10.000.

5 — 14.9.1917

1. TERROR will be relieved in line by INCLINE on night of 14th–15th Sept. 1917.

2. The following dispositions will be handed over:-

2 GUNS	JEW HILL	1 GUN	D19 a 2.9 (Hill 35)
2 "	POND FARM	4 "	BOSSAERT FARM. (CALL RES)
1 "	DONT TRENCH	5 "	JASPER FARM.
1 "	PEMMERN REDOUBT		

3. Guides will be at H.Q dugout WIELTJE 4.15 pm as follows:-

1 GUIDE	JEW HILL	1 GUIDE	D19 a 2.9 (Hill 35)
1 "	POND FARM	1 "	BOSSAERT FM. (CALL RES)
1 "	DONT TRENCH	1 "	JASPER FM.
1 "	PEMMERN REDBT		

Each guide will carry a piece of paper showing the position for which he is guide.

4. The following will be handed over at each position:- S.O.S. LINES – Position of Infantry – MAP FREZENBERG – RANGE CARDS – tabulated particulars of position – S.A.A and 16 Belt Boxes each gun.
Receipts will be obtained in duplicate and forwarded to H.Q on completion of relief.

5. No movement will take place in forward positions prior to 8.15 pm. ~~in~~ Carry bodies of pairs at 50 x's distance.

6. T.O. TERROR will obtain from T.O. INCLINE. the Belt Boxes at the Transport lines of the latter.

7. Instructions to Section Officers attached.

8. Completion of relief will be reported by out-going Section officers at H.Q and to Bde and D.M.G.O. by Code Word. "DIFF"

Issued at:- 11am

Copies to

No 1 Section Officer No 1 + 3.
2 " " 2
3 " " 4.
4. Transport Officer
5 C.Q.M.S
6 C.S.M.
7 INCLINE
8 TEAZE
9 D.M.G.O
10 FILE
11 WAR DIARY

[signature]
Lieut
for O.C. TERROR.

Instructions to Section Officers
Issued with Operation Orders No 41.

14.9.17.

1 On relief Sections will proceed to WIELTJE where hot food will be issued and orders given about proceeding to camp.

2 Limbers will report as follows:-

No 1/1.	9 pm.	3/1	10 - 15 pm.
1/2	9 - 15 pm	4/1	9 - 30 pm.
2/1	10 pm.	H.Q	9. 45 pm.

and will return to Transport lines at orders of C.S.M. when loaded.

3 All fighting limbers will be empty and except 1/2 will carry 4 gun boxes.

4 No 4/1 Limber will bring up hot food.

5 ~~All spare numbers at Transport lines will report to CSM at of 5 pm. Dress. Drill order. Box Respirators. Steel Helmets.~~ Cancelled

[signature]
Lieut
for O.C. TERROR.

184 M.G. Coy.
Operation Order No 42

(6)

16.9.17

Ref Map. Sheet 27 1/40.000

1 The 184 MG Coy will march tomorrow 17th to WORMHOUDT "A" area to billets at C2&C

2. Starting Point. X Roads K14b 5.8. facing N.E at 8-25. Route – HOUTKERQUE. HERZEELE – WORMHOUDT.

3. Order of March: 1.2.3.4. H.Q.
Fighting Limbers – 1.2.3.4. – Water Cart – NO 3's – H.Q. – Cooks Cart. – G.S. Wagon.

4. There will be a halt of 10 minutes before clock hour. The strictest attention will be paid to march discipline.

5 2/Lt Jones and 2 O.R's to be detailed by C.S.M. will proceed on Bicycles to the WORMHOUDT to be there at 8 Am. 2/Lt Jones will report to O.C. Company for instructions at 6 Am 17.9.17.

6 Sgt Smith will report at Bde H.Q. at 9am to proceed by Lorry to DUISANS area. He will report to O.C. Company at 6 Am for instructions. He will take rations for and including 20th inst.

7. Transport officer will hand over huts in the present Camp to the Billet warden, and forward receipt to Coy H.Q as soon afterwards as possible.

Copies to
No1 S.O's. CSM. CQMS.
2. File
3 War Diary
Issued at 10.30 Pm

[signature]
O.C.
184 M.G. Co

Copy No 5

184 M.G. Coy.
Operation Order No 43

7.

13.9.1917.

Ref Sheet 27 1/40000

I The 184 M.G. Coy will entrain at ESQUELBECQ (13 b d central) 17.9.17

2 Starting point forked Roads at C 28 a 5.9 for transport and horse holders at 8.30 Am.
For Company less transport at 10.15 Am

3 Route - Cross Rds C 21 d 6.9 - forked roads C 21 d c 3 - Cross roads C 20 b 9.9 - ESQUELBECQ - cross Roads B 14 b 4.8.

4 Order of march - Transport - Horseholders - Fighting Limbers No 1.2.3.4 - No 3's 1.2.3.4 - HQ - Water cart - cooks cart - G.S. Wagon - Supply wagon.
Company less Transport: 1.2.3.4. HQ Bicycles in rear.

5 C.S.M. will detail 1 brakesman each ~~limber~~ vehicle not already provided with one and in addition a party consisting of 1 Cpl and 15 O.R. who will report to Transport officer at 8 Am. This party with the brakesmen will act as horseholders as detailed.

6 Transport with horse holders will arrive at B 14 b 4.8 the entrance to Station Yard at 10 Am
Company less transport will arrive at same point at 11.30 Am
Neither party will pass that point until all is clear for it in the Station Yard

7 The Water Cart will entrain full.
Drag ropes will be used as breast lines in the Wagons
No lights will be lit on the train.

8 The probable length of the journey will be 7 hours all ranks will be ready to detrain on arrival at detraining Station. Sections will form up clear of the Station Yard without delay, prior to moving to billets

9 2/Lt Horrocks will report to R.T.O at entraining Station at 9.30 Am. He will provide the R.T.O with a marching in state of the Unit.
He will obtain detailed instructions as to entraining and will make them known to the unit as it arrives.

Copies to
No 1 Section officers
Q.M.S. C.S.M.
2 War Diary
3 B.M. 184 Bde
4 Transport Officer. 5. File

[signature] Capt.
COMDG. 184 COMPANY M.G. CORPS.

Copy No 1 — Operation Order No 4 A — 184 Coy. M. G. Corps. — 23. 9. 1917

Ref Maps FRANCE 51B and 51C 1/40.000

I The 184 MG Coy will move to Camp in ST NICHOLAS area on 24th inst.

2 Starting Point - Road Junction K15 b 9.0 at 4.3 pm. Route - AGNEZ LES DUISANS - DUISANS - L9A4.0 - G21a 3.6. - G15d1.2. - G21 b 4.7. - G16c 5.5.

3. Order of March 2. 3 4 1. H.Q Cyclers. Fighting Limbers 1. 2. 3. 4 - Nos 1. 2. 3. H.Q. Water Cart. G.S. Wagon

4 The following distances will be maintained - 400 yds between units - 200 yds between companies and between the two sections into which the transport will be divided.
There will be a halt of 10 minutes before each clock hour.

5. C. S. M. will detail a runner to obtain Brigade Signal time and report back by 2 pm. He will also arrange that Cooks Cart and No 3-4 Limbers proceed at 1-30 pm to new Camp and that tea is ready on arrival of the unit at about 4 pm.

6 An advance party will proceed earlier in the day - orders later. This party will provide a guide to meet unit at G. 16. c. 55. and conduct it to Camp.

7. The unit will not enter the camp that is allotted ~~to them~~ until the unit that is being relieved has moved out.

Copies to:-
No 1 Section Officers ✓
2 Transport Officer
3 CSM & CQMS
4 184 Inf Bde.
5 War Diary.
6. File.

Issued at 2-30 pm

[signature] for CAPT.
COMDG. 184 COMPANY M. G. CORPS.

Section officers

1 61

Vol 17

CONFIDENTIAL

WAR DIARY
OF THE

184 COMPANY M. G. CORPS

FROM 1st October 1917 To 30th October 1917

VOLUME 17

WAR DIARY

~~or~~

~~INTELLIGENCE SUMMARY.~~

(*Erase heading not required.*)

Army Form C. 2118.

Instructions regarding War Diaries and Intelligence Summaries are contained in F. S. Regs., Part II. and the Staff Manual respectively. Title pages will be prepared in manuscript.

184 M. G. Co

Place	Date	Hour	Summary of Events and Information	Remarks and references to Appendices
	Sept 31 October			
St NICHOLAS	1	–	Still in divisional reserve. Training continued	Ref maps FRANCE 51 B NW 1/20000 FAMPOUX 7B 1/10000
	2 3		Line reconnoitred by officers and senior NCOs	
GREENLAND HILL SECTOR	4	.	Relieved 183 M. G. Co in GREENLAND HILL SECTOR south of GAVRELLE. O.O. attached. A·A guns at ANZIN withdrawn before proceeding to line. Firing carried out by night on tracks behind enemy lines.	App. 1
			Dispositions taken over 1 gun CLAW ALLEY — 3 guns CHICKEN RESERVE 2 guns CHARLIE SUPPORT — 2 guns CHALK RESERVE 4 guns CORK SUPPORT — 1 gun CALF RESERVE 2 guns CONRAD TRENCH — 1 gun NAVAL TRENCH Nine guns forward system Seven guns reserve system.	
	5 6 7 8		Firing each night on enemy tracks and trenches. Average expenditure daily 6000 rds	
	9		2/Lt J.P. WOMERSLEY to Hospital – struck off strength.	
	10		Guns in reserve system relieved those in forward system. O.O. attached	App. 2
	11 12 13 14 15		Usual night firing carried out each night. Areas behind enemy lines kept under fire. 6000 rds expended nightly	
	16		Dispositions altered. Eight guns concentrated to a position H6c21 as a barrage battery. Four guns in reserve. H6d7598, H6d6210, H6d4005, H6a8525. Four guns in forward system I7 b1025, I7 a7035, I7 b3005, I1 c5550 Emplacements selected for reserve and forward guns away from trenches. Battery position sited in a disused trench and camouflaged. OO attached	3 & 4

A5834 Wt. W4973 M687 750,000 8/16 D. D. & L. Ltd. Forms/C.2118/13.

Army Form C. 2118.

Instructions regarding War Diaries and Intelligence Summaries are contained in F. S. Regs., Part II. and the Staff Manual respectively. Title Pages will be prepared in manuscript.

WAR DIARY

~~or~~

~~INTELLIGENCE SUMMARY~~

(Erase heading not required.)

Place	Date	Hour	Summary of Events and Information	Remarks and references to Appendices
GREENLAND HILL SECTOR	Oct. 17		Work on new positions continued. Usual night firing carried out	Map Ref. GREENLAND HILL and CHEMICAL WORKS SECTOR 1/10000
	18		New targets engaged	
	19			
	20			
	21			
	22		Interaction relief between reserve and forward groups and the right guns of Battery group. OO attached. Usual night firing	
	23		Co operated in raid by 2/5 Glosters by firing a barrage – eleven guns used. 17500 rds fired	
	24		Co-operated in raid by 2/4 Royal Berks. Barrage fired 26750 rds.	
	26		Work on positions continued. Usual night firing carried out. 6800 rds nightly.	
	27		2nd Lt J.D. LANE reported arrival.	
	28		Relieved in line by 12 noon by 182 M.G.Co. The new dispositions handed over as above.	
ARRAS			Marched to billets in ARRAS. Co quartered in LEVIS BARRACKS. OO attached	App 6
	29		Resting. Baths and refitting. Transport inspection.	
	30		Resting. cleaning guns and equipment.	
			Statement of prisoner as reported in Corps summary to the effect that as a result of M.G. fire by night the enemy troops are forbidden to proceed overland in the forward areas.	
			Strength at 30th Oct. 1917 10 officers 166 O.R.	

W Napier CAPT.
COMDG. 184 COMPANY M. G. CORPS.

2449 Wt. W14957/M90 750,000 1/16 J.B.C. & A. Forms/C.2118/12.

Copy No 9 Operation Order No 45 3-10-17.

184 Company M.G. Corps.

A

Ref Sheet France 51B N.W. 1/20000.
Fampoux Trench Map 1/10000.

1. The 184 M.G. Coy will relieve the 183 M.G. Coy in the line 4th.

2. The following dispositions will be taken over.
Right front No 3 Section under 2/Lt Allen and 1 detachment No 4 positions 1/ 6a. 6. 12. 13.
Left front No 1 Section under 2/Lt Jones. Positions No 16. 15. 8. 14
Right rear. No 4 Section less 1 detachment under 2/Lt Womersley positions No 24. 23a. 23.
Left Rear No 2 Section under Lt Caswell. Positions No 27 26. 25. 24a.

3 One guide per detachment will meet incoming sections at TANK DUMP H11 a 5 7. at 8 am 4th.

4 Trench Stores. S.A.A. belt boxes, Maps, Barrage lines, orders for sentries and full particulars will be taken over at each position. Receipts in duplicate will be obtained and one copy forwarded to Coy HQ without delay.

5 2/Lt Allen with 16 Nos 1 will report at HQ 183 M.G. Coy at 3 pm 3rd these Nos 1 will move immediately on arrival to the positions their detachments will occupy.

6 CSM will report to CSM 183 M.G. Coy at 9 am on 4th to take over SAA dumps. Receipts in duplicate will be obtained.

7 HQ personnel will report to CSM at HQ 183 M.G. Coy at 10.30 am

8 One fighting limber each section loaded as below.
For each detachment 1 gun complete, tripod, spare barrel, cleaning rod, oil case, spare parts case, rations for 4th - 5th. one petrol tin.
For each Section 1 Rations for Section Officer and batman, 2 petrol tins, 1 dixie, 2 spare parts boxes, range finder, clinometers. with 1. NCO & 3 men each section will report under 2/Lt Bass to T.O. 183 M.G. Coy at the transport lines of the latter at 6.30 pm on night of 3/4th.
These stores will be dumped in the vicinity of TANK DUMP and will remain under charge of NCO's until the incoming teams arrive on 4th.

9 One fighting limber will report to 2/Lt Taff at A A positions ANZIN at 4 am 4th. He will withdraw with the detachments at that hour, reporting at Company HQ at 5 am.

10 Completion of relief will be reported by runner by Code word "RATIONS"

11 Company HQ will move to H11 b 80 95. at 10.30 am 4th.

Issued at 4.30 pm

Copies to

No 1/4 Section Officers No 1. 2. 3 & 4 Section
5 Transport Officer
6 CSM
7 6 G M G
8 184 Bde o/c War Diary

Capt.
COMDG. 184 COMPANY M.G. CORPS.

Copy No 12

Operation Order No 44.

RUTH

9.10.1914

Ref Sketch Map H/1 1/4,000 – M.G. Dispositions

1. The sections in reserve will change places with the forward sections on 10th.

2. Detachments will relieve as follows:-

Detachment at position No to Position No

2/Lt Tapp	23 23A 24	2/Lt Allen	6 6A 7
2/Lt Ball	24A 25 26 27	2/Lt Jones	14 8 15 16.

Detachments at No 12 and 13 will not move and will come under orders of 2/Lt Tapp on completion of relief

3 The No's 1 of the positions detailed for relief will exchange today. This exchange will commence at 3 pm and finish by 4 PM.

4. Full particulars will be handed over at each position. Lists of stores at positions will be checked on taking over and reported correct to H.Q.

Gun + Spare parts cases will move with detachments, all other stores will be handed over and receipts obtained in duplicate.

5 2/Lt Johnson, 1 N.C.O and 8 men at the Brigade school will report at HQ at 10 Am 10th, proceeding there from to their sections.

2/Lt Allen, Cpl Henderson and two men from each section to be detailed by section officers will report at HQ on completion of relief to proceed to Brigade school.

6. Guides will be arranged by Section Officers concerned. Reserve guns will commence to move forward at 11 Am. relief will be completed by 1 PM at latest.

7 Completion of relief will be reported by each section by wire, by code word "FORM". and by HQ to Bde by same word.

8 Receipts and reports under para 4. will reach HQ 6 pm 10th inst.

Issued at. 11 Am.

Copies to:-

F. Lomax Capt

Comdg "RUTH"

No1	Section Officer No1	No 7	6 Inf
2	" " No2	8	C.Qm.S
3	" " 3	9	Brigade
4	" " 4	10/11	War Diary
5	Sub " " 3	12	File.
6	Transport Officer		

SECRET.

Copy No 11

Operation Order No 48

15.10.17

Ref Map 51 B N.W.

1. Machine Gun dispositions will be altered on 16th as follows:-
(a) One detachment of No 3 section will relieve No 12 detachment at I 4 b 1.3 at 2 pm 16th. The detachment relieved will proceed to Battery Position at H6 c 2.1. Field of fire will be altered to 50° - 90° Grid.
(b) No 6 & 6A detachments in CHARLIE SUPPORT and No 7 in CLAW ALLEY, will withdraw at 2 pm to Battery positions at H 6 c 2.1.
All equipment and Gun Stores to be brought out.
(c) An Emplacement will be made about I 4 a 95. 45. for No 13 gun. This emplacement will be commenced at dusk and will be occupied during night. The gun team will continue to live in present dug out. Field of fire will be 90° - 120° Grid.
(d) One detachment of No 3 will take up position about I 1 c 80.05 at dusk. Gun team will occupy dug out in BRICKFIELDS. An Emplacement will be dug at dusk and occupied during night.

2. All Equipment except Guns & Spare Parts will be handed over on relief. Lists of stores handed over will be forwarded to H.Q. on completion of relief

3. All other details will be given to Section Officers verbally and will be arranged by S.O's concerned.

4 Completion of ~~Relief~~ move will be reported by wire, by code word "SCHULER"

Acknowledge.

Issued at 9.30 pm

Copies to

1/4 Section Officers 1.2.3.4.
5 Bde
6 DMGO
7 Renown
8 Research
9 Rodent
10 Rex
11 War Diary
12 ~~Bde~~

W Napier Capt
Comdg. [illegible]

SECRET

Copy No 12

Operation Order No 49

(D) 16.9.17

(1). The following alterations in M G dispositions will take place on 17th inst. Moves to be completed at dusk on that day

(A.) No 1 Section. The 3 guns in CHICKEN RESERVE Nos 24. 25 + 26 + one gun in NAVAL TRENCH No 27 will withdraw to Battery position at H 6 c 21

(B) No 2 Section. Gun No 16 at I 1 a 5.5 will be relieved by one detachment of No 3 Section. Field of fire of this gun will be altered to 120° 160° Grid. Guns No 14. 6 + 15 in CORK SUPPORT will withdraw + take up positions in Reserve as follows:

No 3	1 gun	H 6 d	45	96
No 4	1	H 6 d	62	10
No 6	1 ..	H 6 d	40	05
No 5	1 ..	H 5 a	85	25

(C). (1) Teams of Nos 3, 4 + 6 will for the present live in CHICKEN RESERVE positions to be manned at night only.

(2) M G Battery at H 6 c 21 will be composed of 8 guns Nos 1 + 4 Section under the command of 2nd Lieut H. G. Jones who will be responsible that the Battery is laid on the S O S line by dusk on 17th

(3) Lists of trench stores handed over + remaining in old positions to be made out + sent to Coy H2 on completion of move.

(4) Section Officers will report completion of move to Co. H 2 in writing

ACKNOWLEDGE

Issued at 9 30 pm

W Harper Capt
OC [illegible]

Copies to 1/4 Section Officers
5 Bde
6 D M G O
7 Reserve
8 Reserve
9 Rd
11 War Diary
12 Filed

(F)

SECRET
Copy No 8

E.
21.10.17.

Operation Order No 50

I. An inter section relief will be carried out tomorrow 22nd inst details to be arranged by Section Officers concerned.

(a) No 1 Section will relieve No 3 Section in the following positions commencing at 1 pm

No 7	I 7 b	0550
No 8	I 7 a	9075
No 2	I 1 c	7500
No 1	I 1 a	5050

(b) No 4 Section will relieve No 2 in the following positions commencing at 3 pm.

No 3	H 6 d	7598
No 4	H 6 a	7020
No 6	H 6 d	4005
I II	H 5 a	8622

(c) On completion of relief Nos 2 & 3 Sections will move to Battery position H 6 c 21.

II 2nd Lieut H G JONES will remain in command of the Battery and 2nd Lieut W.T. JOHNSON will take over command of No 1 Section in the forward position

III Guns & Spare Parts only will be taken up on relief and ~~the remainder~~ a list of all other equipment and stores handed over will be signed by both Section Officers and a copy forwarded to Company Head Quarters.

IV Completion of relief to be reported to Company Head Quarters in writing

ACKNOWLEDGE

1/4 Section Officers
5 Bde
6 D.M.G.O.
~~7 [illegible]~~
~~8 [illegible]~~
~~9 [illegible]~~
~~10 [illegible]~~
7 ~~11~~ War Diary
8 ~~12~~ Filed.

[signature]
Capt OC Batty.

C. [initials]

Copy No 11

Ref.

SECRET Operation Order No 51

184 M G C.

26th October 1917

F

GREENLAND HILL and CHEMICAL WORKS SECTOR 1/1000

FRANCE 51B N.W. 1/2000

1. 184 M G Co. will be relieved in the line by 182 M G Co on 28th Oct.

2. The following dispositions will be handed over.

MG Nos I 7 b 0530 No 5 I 7 a 9075. No 6 I 1 c 7500 No 7 I 1 a 5050	Forward group	No 8 H 6 d 7598 No 9 H 6 a 4020 No 10 H 6 d 4005 No I 4 H 5 a 8622	Reserve Group

Eight guns H 6 c 21 Battery group

3. All S.A.A. belt boxes maps S.O.S lines trench stores and the fullest possible particulars will be handed over but not guns tripods, spare parts, clinometers and other equipment on charge of sections.
Detailed receipts in duplicate will be obtained by section officers.

4. The numbers one of 182 M.G.C will proceed to gun positions during afternoon of 27th inst and will remain there. One guide will meet them at CAM VALLEY at 2 pm on 27th inst and bring them to Headquarters where guides to sections will be provided.

5. One guide per detachment of Forward & Reserve Group & one guide per section of Battery group will meet incoming teams at CAM VALLEY at 8 am 28th inst.
Relief will be complete by 12 noon 28th inst.

6. Completion of relief will be personally reported by outgoing section officers to Headquarters and receipts for stores handed in at the same time.

7 On relief sections will proceed under Section Officers to billets in ARRAS. Transport Officer will arrange for one limber per section and one for Headquarters to meet sections at CAM VALLEY and for one guide per section to ~~meet~~ sections at ST NICHOLAS G16 c 57

8 LT CASWELL and two detachments of No 2 Section will by 5 pm on 28th inst occupy the anti aircraft posts at ANZIN G 9 c 71 and G 8 d 61. Completion will be reported by cycle orderly to Headquarters.

Acknowledge

Issued at 11 pm

Copies to GO's 1. 2. 3. 4
TO 5.
182 M.G. 6.
184 Bde 7.
D M G.O. 8
CSM 9
CQMS 10
File 11 ✓
WD 12. 13.

[signature] CAPT.
COMDG. 184 COMPANY M. G. CORPS.

F

Vol 18

C O N F I D E N T I A L.

W A R   D I A R Y

*** of ***

184TH COMPANY, MACHINE GUN CORPS.

From 1st. Nov to 30th. Nov. 1917.

Volume XV111.

*****

Instructions regarding War Diaries and Intelligence Summaries are contained in F. S. Regs., Part II. and the Staff Manual respectively. Title pages will be prepared in manuscript.

WAR DIARY

~~or~~

~~INTELLIGENCE~~ SUMMARY.

(Erase heading not required.)

Army Form C. 2118.

Place	Date	Hour	Summary of Events and Information	Remarks and references to Appendices
Arras.	Nov. 1/4		In divisional reserve. Training. Special attention paid to Barrage drill. H.J.	Ref map. FAMPOUX TRENCH. 1/10000.
	5		Training continued. Inspected by B.G.C. commanding Brigade. H.J.	
	6		Training continued. H.J.	
	7		Preparing for line. H.J.	
	8		Relieved 183 M.G. Coy in CHEMICAL WORKS SECTOR. (Operation order attached) The following dispositions were taken over:- "A" Battery, Copper Trench. (8 guns). 1 gun, Chemical Trench, Crete Trench, Cupid Trench, Chalk Pit, Embankment Cinema Trench, Cady Reserve & Calico Trench. Night firing on enemy communications & trenches. 4000 rounds.	App. 1.
	9		Night firing as usual. 8000 rounds. H.J.	
	10		Indirect fire on enemy's trenches & communications. 6000 rounds. H.J.	
	11.		Gas shell bombardment during night. Usual I.D.F. 6000 rounds. H.J.	
	12.		Coy Hdqrs shelled with gas shells from 3.30am - 4.30am. I.D.F. 6000 rounds. H.J.	
	13.		Night firing on enemy trenches & communications. 1000 rounds. H.J.	
	14.		Night firing on enemy trenches & communications. 2000 rounds. H.J.	
	15		Cooperated in raid on enemy trenches by 183 Inf. Bde. Usual I.D.F. 28000 rds. H.J.	
	16		Night firing as usual. 8000 rounds. 2nd Lt TAPP to hospital. H.J.	
	17		Night firing carried out. 12500 rounds. H.J.	
	18.		Smoke discharge 3 pm. Cooperated with raid by 182 Bde. 42500 rounds. H.J.	
	19.		Smoke discharge 6.20 am. Usual I.D.F. throughout night. 29000 rounds. H.J.	
	20		Orders to display "unusual activity" throughout 24 hours. 50500 rounds. H.J.	
	21.		Cooperated in raid by 2/1 Bucks. Gas shell bombardment of back areas. 39000 rounds. H.J.	

A5834 Wt. W4973 M687 750,000 8/16 D. D. & L. Ltd. Forms/C.2118/13.

Instructions regarding War Diaries and Intelligence Summaries are contained in F. S. Regs., Part II. and the Staff Manual respectively. Title pages will be prepared in manuscript.

WAR DIARY

~~or~~

~~INTELLIGENCE~~ SUMMARY.

(*Erase heading not required.*)

Army Form C. 2118.

Place	Date	Hour	Summary of Events and Information	Remarks and references to Appendices
CHEMICAL WORKS SECTOR.	22		Projection of gas at 3½ am. I.D.F. 9000 rounds. H.R.J.	
	23.		Usual night firing. 9000 rounds. FAMPOUX shelled. 3 O.R. wounded, 2 mules killed H.R.J.	
	24		Night firing as usual. 8000 rounds. 2/LT R. A MOON reported for duty. H.R.J.	
	25		Night firing carried out 10000 rounds. H.R.J.	
	26		Night firing carried out 14000 rounds.	
	27		Night firing as usual. ~~[illegible]~~ 8000 rounds. Total rounds fired during tour 32700 rds. H.R.J.	
	28		18th M.G. Coy relieved by 225 M.G. Coy, 45 M.G. Coy & 46 M.G. Coy. Coy returned to billets in ARRAS. Operation order attached.	
ARRAS	29.		Refitting H.R.J.	App. 2.
	30		moved to BERTINCOURT. (TO BAPAUME by rail; thence by bus.) O.O. attached H.R.J.	App. 3.
			Strength at end of month. 10 officers, 171 O.R. H.R.J.	

[illegible] Capt.
OC 18th M.G. Coy

A5834 Wt. W4973 M687 750,000 8/16 D. D. & L. Ltd. Forms/C.2118/13.

110.

Appendix 1

CAPT.

COMD'G. 184 COMPANY M.G. CORPS.

Appendix 2

Copy No. 14 Operation Order No 53 27.11.17.

Ref Map FAMPOUX and GREENLAND HILL TR MAPS $\frac{1}{20,000}$

1 The 184 M.G. Coy will be relieved in line on 28th by details of 45-46-& 225 M.G. Coys.

2. The following dispositions will be handed over.

No1. CHALK PIT
No13. EMBANKMENT } 46 M.G. Coy

No2 CUPID
No12 CHEMICAL
No14 CRETE
No3 CALICO
No11 CINEMA and AAP
No15 CAVIZ and AAP } 45 M.G. Coy

BATTERY COPPER 225 M.G. Coy

3 One guide per detachment of following guns will report to Coy H.Q at 7-30 am. No2 12. 14. 3. 11 & 15. They will then proceed to FAMPOUX LOCK by 8 am, where they will meet a guide to positions, the No 1 of relieving teams.

One guide per detachment of above numbered guns will report Coy H.Q. at 4-30 pm. They will meet incoming gun teams at H.M.G. 35 & guide them to respective positions.

One guide per detachment of No 1 & 13 guns will be at SINGLE ARCH at 8 am to meet incoming teams.

Guides from Battery will be detailed later

4 All trench stores. S.A.A. belt boxes - maps - & full particulars will be handed over, but not guns, tripods, petrol tins or equipment on charge of Sections - Detailed receipts in duplicate will be obtained from incoming teams.

5 Teams from No1 & No13 positions will on relief proceed out with the relieved infantry to Section H.Qrs.

No 1 Section | Details later
No 2 –
No 3 – for 1. 13. 2. 12. 14. 6 – 30 pm.
No 4 – for 11 – 13 – 15 6 – 0 pm.

7. Coy on relief will proceed by sections to Billets at LEVIS BARRACKS ARRAS.

Belt boxes for those in exchange for those handed over in line will be collected by T.O. from T.O's of 45 46 and 225 M.G. Co. on 29th inst.

9. Completion of relief will be reported by outgoing Section Officers to Coy HQ personally. Relief of No 1 and No 13 by runner.

Issued at 11 45 pm.

Copies to 1 – 2 SO 1 SO 2.
3 – 4 SO 3 SO 4
5 T.O.
6 7 CSM Q/C QMS
8 – 184 Bde
9 – 45 M.G. Co
10 – 46 M.G. Co
11 – 225 M.G. Co
12 – DMGO.
13. 14. War Diary.
15 – File

ACKNOWLEDGE

G. [illegible] Lt.
for Capt
184 Co M.G. Coy.

War Diary

SECRET Copy No 2 Appendix 3
184 M.G. Coy Operation Order No 26.

"SECRET." 29.11.17

Ref map. 51b. $\frac{1}{10000}$

" LENS $\frac{1}{10000}$

1. The 184 M.G. Coy will move on 30th to LECHELLE area. Transport will proceed by road. Company less transport by train.

2. Transport will rendezvous under B.T.O. at Cross Roads ST. NICHOLAS at 7.45 AM & will move to new area under order of Major H.S. BENNETT 2/4th Oxfords.

3. T.O. will arrange to move fighting limbers from LEVIS BARRACKS at 7 A.M.

4. Starting point Cross Roads ST NICHOLAS G16c79 at 8.10 A.M.
Route — ROND POINT. RUE DE LILLE. E GATE of SCHRAMM BARRACKS. BOULEVARD CARNOT BAPAUME

5. A distance of 200 yards will be maintained between head of Transport & rear of unit in front. The usual halt of 10 minutes before each clock hour will be made. There will be a halt of 2 hours for food & water. Orders regarding this will be given later.

7. Company less transport will arrive at R.T.O's hut RUE LAMARTINE G28c13 at 8.45 a.m. It will move.

to that point via RUE LAMARTINE
8 Company less transport will detrain at BAPAUME & march to LECHELLE AREA Route LE TRANSLOY ROCQUIGNY
The usual 10 minute halt before each clock hour will be made.
A distance of two yards will be maintained between the Company & rear of unit in front.
9 LT CASWELL will report to R.T.O ARRAS at 8 am to meet entraining officer – He will know exact entraining strength of unit & will ascertain where men are to fall out prior to entraining
10 CPL SPADEMAN will be at PORTE BAUDIMONT ARRAS at 8-30 Am. to guide a lorry to billets & mess
Coy & mess Cooks will act as loading party & proceed with lorry to NEW AREA
11 2nd LT BASS will report at 6.15 Am at Bde H.Q & proceed to new area as billeting officer

1 Officers, CSM 4.5 – War Diary
2 T.O. / a/CQMS 6 File
3 Bde

Vol 19

C O N F I D E N T I A L

W A R   D I A R Y

*** of ***

184TH COMPANY, MACHINE GUN CORPS

From 1st Dec. to 31st Dec. 1917.

VOL. XIX.

****

Instructions regarding War Diaries and Intelligence Summaries are contained in F. S. Regs., Part II. and the Staff Manual respectively. Title pages will be prepared in manuscript.

WAR DIARY
or
INTELLIGENCE SUMMARY.
(Erase heading not required.)

No 184 MACHINE GUN COMPANY
1/12/17

Army Form C. 2118.

Place	Date	Hour	Summary of Events and Information	Remarks and references to Appendices
BERTINCOURT.	Dec 1		Moved by road at 11.30 AM to FINS, where we bivouaced for the night.	
FINS.	2		Moved off at 10.0 AM to HAVRINCOURT WOOD. 2/Lt JACKSON admitted hospital	
HAVRINCOURT WOOD	3		Coy moved into the line. No 4 Sect [illegible] 2 Sec of 182 Coy in DUNRAVEN TRENCH & FIFTEEN RAVINE [illegible]. Considerable artillery activity shown by both sides.	
GONNELIEU SECTOR.	4		Usual Night Firing carried out.	
"	5		184 M.G.Coy relieved 183 M.G.Coy in the line. The following dispositions were taken over. Left Sector: [illegible] 1 gun — PEAK ALLEY; 2 guns — SURREY ROAD; 1 gun — MONUMENT. Right Sector: [illegible] 1 gun RILEY Rd; 2 guns FAIRLEY T[illegible]; 1 gun FARM RAVINE.	[illegible]
"	6		Barrage Fire from Battery in co-operation with artillery.	
"	7		Usual Indirect Fire. Hostile Trench Mortars active against Right Front Forward Sector.	
"	8		Marked Hostile activity around GONNELIEU & LA VACQUERIE. Usual Indirect Fire 1,000 Rounds. A/C.Q.M.S. ~~Ha~~ HODGKINS proceeded U.K. for commission.	
"	9		Usual Night Firing 6000 rounds. Pte FREATHY [illegible] Killed.	

(A7092). Wt. W12839/M1293. 75,0.0. 1/17. D. D. & L., Ltd. Forms/C.2118/14.

Army Form C. 2118.

Instructions regarding War Diaries and Intelligence Summaries are contained in F. S. Regs., Part II. and the Staff Manual respectively. Title pages will be prepared in manuscript.

WAR DIARY
or
INTELLIGENCE SUMMARY.
(Erase heading not required.)

Place	Date	Hour	Summary of Events and Information	Remarks and references to Appendices
GONNELIEU SECTOR	Dec 10		Usual Trench Firing. Hostile artillery active round reserve position. 2 O.R. Killed. 1 O.R. Wounded.	[initials]
"	11		184 M.G. Coy relieved by 183 M.G. Coy & 182 M.G. Coy. 1 O.R. wounded. Lt LISMORE [illegible] M.C. transferred to command 208 M.G. Coy. Coy on relief moved to billets in METZ less the 182 Sub. which occupied Reserve position on BEAUCAMP RIDGE	[initials]
METZ	12		Coy occupied in rest & cleaning.	[initials]
	13th		Ditto	[initials]
	14		New position taken on BEAUCAMP RIDGE	[initials]
	15th		184 M.G. Coy relieved 182 & 183 M.G. Coy in the line. Right Forward Sector 5 Guns under 2nd Lt [illegible]. Left Forward Sector 3 Guns under 2nd Lt [illegible]. B Batty 8 Guns in FIFTEEN RAVINE under command of Lt CASWELL. B Batty relieved by 182 M.G. Coy came under the tactical control of 184 M.G. Coy	[initials] Ref. [illegible] 1/20000

(A7092). Wt. W12839/M1293. 75,000. 1/17. D. D. & L., Ltd. Forms/C.2118/14.

Instructions regarding War Diaries and Intelligence Summaries are contained in F. S. Regs., Part II. and the Staff Manual respectively. Title pages will be prepared in manuscript.

WAR DIARY
or
INTELLIGENCE SUMMARY.

(Erase heading not required.)

Army Form C. 2118.

Place	Date	Hour	Summary of Events and Information	Remarks and references to Appendices
	17 Dec			
GONNELIEU S.6.a	16		Day quiet. [illegible] [illegible] [illegible] of [illegible] commenced. [illegible] co-operation with artillery. 8000 rounds fired.	[illegible]
"	17		Day quiet. [illegible] [illegible] [illegible]	[illegible]
"	18		Hostile artillery [illegible] [illegible] [illegible] [illegible] [illegible] [illegible]. Result of [illegible] [illegible] [illegible]. "B" Battery [illegible] [illegible] [illegible] [illegible]. "A" Battery [illegible] [illegible]	[illegible]
"	19		Day quiet. [illegible] [illegible] [illegible] [illegible]. Rounds fired 7500	
"	20		15th M.G. Coy relieved in the line by 183rd M.G. Coy [illegible]. On completion of relief Coy returned to [illegible] in METZ [illegible] [illegible] [illegible] which [illegible] returned to HAVRINCOURT WOOD	[illegible]

Army Form C. 2118.

WAR DIARY
or
INTELLIGENCE SUMMARY.

(Erase heading not required.)

Instructions regarding War Diaries and Intelligence Summaries are contained in F. S. Regs., Part II. and the Staff Manual respectively. Title pages will be prepared in manuscript.

Place	Date 17	Hour	Summary of Events and Information	Remarks and references to Appendices
METZ	Dec 21		[illegible]	[illegible]
"	22		[illegible]	[illegible]
	23		[illegible]	[illegible]
"	24		[illegible]	[illegible]
SUZANNE	25		Voluntary [illegible] Service at 12.00 noon [illegible]	[illegible]
"	26		[illegible]	[illegible]

(A7092). Wt. W12839/M1293. 75,000. 1/17. D. D. & L., Ltd. Forms/C.2118/14.

Instructions regarding War Diaries and Intelligence Summaries are contained in F. S. Regs., Part II. and the Staff Manual respectively. Title pages will be prepared in manuscript.

WAR DIARY

or

INTELLIGENCE SUMMARY.

(Erase heading not required.)

Army Form C. 2118.

Place	Date	Hour	Summary of Events and Information	Remarks and references to Appendices
[illegible]	Dec 27		Training as per Programme attached	
"	28"		Training as per Programme. 2 Lieut [illegible] proceeded to U.K. on leave	
	29"		Training as per Programme [illegible]	
	30		[illegible]	[illegible]
	31		[illegible]	

[illegible]

(A7092). Wt. W12839/M1293. 75,0.0. 1/17. D. D. & L., Ltd. Forms/C.2118/14.

Vol 20

C O N F I D E N T I A L

WAR DIARY.

of

184TH. COMPANY, MACHINE GUN CORPS.

From 1st. January 1918 to 31st. January 1918.

(Volumn XX).

Instructions regarding War Diaries and Intelligence Summaries are contained in F. S. Regs., Part II. and the Staff Manual respectively. Title pages will be prepared in manuscript.

WAR DIARY
or
INTELLIGENCE SUMMARY.
(Erase heading not required.)

Army Form C. 2118.

Place	Date 1918	Hour	Summary of Events and Information	Remarks and references to Appendices
VRELY	Jan 1	—	Training. Tactical Exercises. Lecture by O.C. on "Barrage Calculations"	
"	2	"	Training Range Work & Tactical Exercises	
"	3	"	Tactical Exercises with 2/5 Gloucs: All officers & N.C.O.s attended a Bde Tactical Scheme under the B.G.C in the afternoon	
"	4		Tactical Scheme with Ox & Bucks L.I.	
"	5		Tactical Training (Defence)	
"	6		Range Work, & Tactical Training	
"	7		Moved by road to PARGNY	
PARGNY	8		Physical Training & Baths	
"	9		Moved by road to BEAUVOIS. 2/Lt CASWELL & 16 O.R. proceeded in advance into the line	
BEAUVOIS	10th		184 M.G.C. relieved the 224th French Regiment in the line on the night 10th/11th inst. Vide Op: Order	
FRESNOY (Sector)	11th		Quiet day. Work done: Cleaning & Repairing of Trenches	

(A7092). Wt. W12839/M1293. 750,000. 1/17. D. D. & L., Ltd. Forms/C.2118/14.

Army Form C. 2118.

Instructions regarding War Diaries and Intelligence Summaries are contained in F. S. Regs., Part II. and the Staff Manual respectively. Title pages will be prepared in manuscript.

WAR DIARY
or
INTELLIGENCE SUMMARY.
(Erase heading not required.)

Place	Date 1918	Hour	Summary of Events and Information	Remarks and references to Appendices
(S: QUENTIN)	Jan. 1918			
FRESNOY.	12"		Quiet period. Work done. Cleaning & Repairing of Trenches	
	13"		Hostile Artillery Slightly more active than usual. Principal Target. CEMETERY FRESNOY.	
	14.		Quiet period. Usual work on Trenches & Emplacements.	
	15.		Retaliatory fire by our M.G.s Considerable movement observed during the day at THREE SAVAGES.	
	16.		Quiet period. Usual cleaning of Trenches, etc.	
	17		Considerable hostile artillery activity from 12 noon until 7.0 PM FRESNOY received great attention from "5.9s" & 4.2s	
	18.		Hostile artillery shelled valley in M.15 b with H.E. Shrapnel Our MG's fired on Three SAVAGES, & on suspected DUG-OUTS	

(A7092). Wt. W12839/M1293. 75 ,0.0. 1/17. D. D. & L., Ltd. Forms/C.2118/14.

Army Form C. 2118.

Instructions regarding War Diaries and Intelligence Summaries are contained in F. S. Regs., Part II. and the Staff Manual respectively. Title pages will be prepared in manuscript.

WAR DIARY
or
INTELLIGENCE SUMMARY.
(Erase heading not required.)

Place	Date	Hour	Summary of Events and Information	Remarks and references to Appendices
FRESNOY.	1/am 1918 19.		Enemy Snipers active in GRICOURT Sector. Usual Cleaning & Repairs of Trenches, Emplacements, & Dug outs.	
	20		Hostile M.G.s active during the night on all approaches to GRICOURT. Our aircraft very active.	
	21.		Hostile Artillery – usual concentration on FRESNOY CEMETRY. Enemy sent up an extraordinary no. of coloured lights on Bde front at 4. P.M. presumably in order to draw our S.O.S. Worked not reply.	
	22		Quiet period. Usual cleaning, & repairing of Trenches & Emplacements.	
	23		Hostile M.G.s active during the night. Our M.Gs retaliated successfully.	
	24.		Quiet day. Visibility very low.	
	25		Our Artillery shelled TRRES SAVAGES at intervals. Visibility low.	
	26.		184 M.G.Cy relieved by 182 M.G.Cy. Very quiet relief.	

(A7092). Wt W12839/M1293. 75,0 0. 1/17. D. D. & L., Ltd. Forms/C.2118/14.

Army Form C. 2118.

Instructions regarding War Diaries and Intelligence Summaries are contained in F. S. Regs., Part II. and the Staff Manual respectively. Title pages will be prepared in manuscript.

WAR DIARY
or
INTELLIGENCE SUMMARY.
(Erase heading not required.)

Place	Date 1918	Hour	Summary of Events and Information	Remarks and references to Appendices
VAUX.	Jan. 27		Day spent in cleaning, & settling down	
"	28		Day was spent in Overhauling & cleaning equipment, & making up Deficiencies.	
"	29		Two A.A positions were taken over at BEAUVOIS from the ROYAL BERKS. Day spent in cleaning limbers & training. Lieut T. E. Goode was appointed second-in-Command & resumed duties on this day.	
"	30		Training. 3.2 General overhauling	
"	31		" 2nd under Section Officers	

C O N F I D E N T I A L

W A R D I A R Y

*** of ***

184 COMPANY, MACHINE GUN CORPS

From 1st Feb.1918 to 28th Feb.1918.

VOLUME XX1.

******

Instructions regarding War Diaries and Intelligence Summaries are contained in F. S. Regs., Part II. and the Staff Manual respectively. Title pages will be prepared in manuscript.

Army Form C. 2118.

WAR DIARY
or
INTELLIGENCE SUMMARY.
(Erase heading not required.)

Place.	Date	Hour	Summary of Events and Information	Remarks and references to Appendices
In the Field	1.2.18	–	Small tactical schemes were done during the morning	
	2.2.18	–	The O.C. & Section Officers visited the right sector. Guns were prepared for the line.	
	3.2.18	–	The 184 M. G. Coy. relieved the 183 M. G. Coy. in the line. Company moved off from billets at 2.30 p.m. & marched by sections, 200 yards interval being maintained. Relief was reported complete by the O.C. at 7.55 p.m. by the code word St. QUENTIN. Nos 1 & 3 Sections were in front, No 2 Section in "BROWN LINE". No 4 Section in reserve, & acting as the mobile section.	
	4.2.18		The ground between FAYET - FRESNOY ROAD - NAMELESS COPSE was shelled between 11.30 AM & 12.30 p.m. with 5.9s. Small bursts were fired during the night. Individual movement was observed in the vicinity of St. QUENTIN Cathedral. Emplacements, dug-outs etc. were cleaned & trenches cleared.	
	5.2.18		There was not so much shelling as on the previous day. FAYET received a great deal of attention during the night from Enemy M.G's. Two red lights & one white were sent up by the enemy in quick succession from the region of St. QUENTIN, but no apparent action followed.	
	6.2.18		The O.P. on MANCHESTER HILL was shelled during the afternoon, two direct hits being obtained. One red & one white light were sent up by the enemy at 1.30 a.m., & M.G. fired [illegible] on the right of St QUENTIN. Individual movement was noticed about St QUENTIN	

(A7092). Wt. W12839/M1293. 75,0.0. 1/17. D. D. & L., Ltd. Forms/C.2118/14.

Instructions regarding War Diaries and Intelligence Summaries are contained in F. S. Regs., Part II. and the Staff Manual respectively. Title pages will be prepared in manuscript.

WAR DIARY
or
INTELLIGENCE SUMMARY.
(Erase heading not required.)

Army Form C. 2118.

Place	Date	Hour	Summary of Events and Information	Remarks and references to Appendices
			during the day – Several of our Flying Squadrons managed to cross the enemy's lines during the afternoon in spite of very heavy A.A. fire. A new emplacement was made for No 5. gun, & sentry post was constructed for Nos. 6. 7 & 8 guns.	
	7.2.18		The enemy managed to get several direct hits on the road running from FAYET to FOX COVERT. Enemy M.G. fire was very active during the night, FRANCILLY-SELENCY receiving much attention. A.A. emplacements with pole mounting were constructed, & fresh emplacements made at new positions for 6 & 7 guns.	
	8.2.18.		The front line & FAYET were shelled during the day & night. SAVY - ST QUENTIN was engaged with enemy M.G. fire. Several red lights & one green one were sent up by the enemy about 3.30 a.m. One red one was sent up in ST. QUENTIN as though in answer, no movement was taken as far as is known by the enemy.	
	9.2.18.		The ground between FAYET & NAMELESS COPSE was shelled very freely about noon. Direct hits were obtained on the road running through FAYET. Our guns (M.G.) fired during the night in answer to enemy M.G's, which soon became much quieter. At dusk enemy sent up numerous Red lights N. of ST QUENTIN, Red lights were also seen in ST QUENTIN as though in reply, no apparent operation followed these ~~indicated~~ individual movement on the roads near ST QUENTIN was heard. About 9.30 a.m an E.A. crossed our lines, but was fired on by 2 A.A. M.G's & was forced to return. Three A.A. positions (pole mountings) were erected.	

(A7092). Wt W12839/M1293. 75 ,0 0. 1/17. D. D. & L., Ltd. Forms/C.2118/14.

Army Form C. 2118.

Instructions regarding War Diaries and Intelligence Summaries are contained in F. S. Regs., Part II. and the Staff Manual respectively. Title pages will be prepared in manuscript.

WAR DIARY

or

INTELLIGENCE SUMMARY.

(Erase heading not required.)

Place	Date	Hour	Summary of Events and Information	Remarks and references to Appendices
	10.2.18		FAYET & valley were shelled during the morning & also HOLNON–ST. QUENTIN Road. In the afternoon the FRANCILLY–SELENCY Rd was shelled. Usual night firing by M.G's was done by both sides. Very little aircraft were up owing to the weather. Nos 1 & 2 positions were improved. AA emplacement (Pole mounting) was constructed at No 2 Position. A fire was noticed in ST. QUENTIN about 6.30 p.m.	
	11.2.18.		Very quiet day. Planes were not active owing to bad weather.	
	12.2.18.		The [illegible] in the morning. [illegible] artillery [illegible] in the afternoon. MANCHESTER HILL was shelled with [illegible] FAYET [illegible] attention. [illegible] heavy [illegible] M.G. fire during day & night. [illegible] ST. QUENTIN. [illegible] AA (pole mounting) position constructed at No 5 Position.	
	13.2.18.		[illegible] very quiet during the day, no shelling [illegible] M.G. [illegible] the weather being unfavourable for any observation.	
	14.2.18		[illegible] MANCHESTER HILL was shelled during the morning with 5.9". Very little enemy [illegible] No 17 Position. [illegible] emplacement constructed [illegible]	

(A7092). Wt. W12839/M1293. 750,000. 1/17. D. D. & L., Ltd. Forms/C.2118/14.

Army Form C. 2118.

Instructions regarding War Diaries and Intelligence Summaries are contained in F. S. Regs., Part II. and the Staff Manual respectively. Title pages will be prepared in manuscript.

WAR DIARY
or
INTELLIGENCE SUMMARY.

(Erase heading not required.)

Place	Date	Hour	Summary of Events and Information	Remarks and references to Appendices
[illegible]	15.2.18	–	[illegible] was not [illegible] but our own was very active between [illegible] 5.30 p.m. [illegible] our [illegible] and [illegible] opposite. About 6 pm. a number of E.A. [illegible] were engaged by A.A. guns [illegible]. One of the enemy planes flying very low, [illegible] one of our [illegible] at FAYET.	
	16.2.18		The enemy shelled [illegible] HOLNON about [illegible] [illegible] fired on targets in ST. QUENTIN during the night. About 7.15 pm [illegible] were observed from different parts of the enemy line. [illegible] followed. [illegible] planes were brought down in the direction of HOLNON.	
	17.2.18		Our artillery shelled St QUENTIN during the day [illegible] fire during the night. [illegible] was put up in front of No 1 [illegible].	
	18.2.18		Several [illegible] lights were observed [illegible] our lines. E.A. planes were very active during the night, bombs being dropped on our lines during the night.	
	19.2.18		[illegible] relieved by [illegible] Coy. [illegible] at 10 a.m. [illegible] FINES. [illegible] the company marched to VAUX.	
VAUX.	20.2.18		[illegible] the company.	
	21.2.18		[illegible] the morning [illegible]	

(A7092). Wt. W12839/M1293. 75,0 0. 1/17. D. D. & L., Ltd. Forms/C.2118/14.

Army Form C. 2118.

WAR DIARY
or
INTELLIGENCE SUMMARY.
(Erase heading not required.)

Instructions regarding War Diaries and Intelligence Summaries are contained in F. S. Regs., Part II. and the Staff Manual respectively. Title pages will be prepared in manuscript.

Place	Date	Hour	Summary of Events and Information	Remarks and references to Appendices
VAUX.		22.2.18	The Coy paraded for C.O.'s inspection [illegible] The following hours were allotted for training. 9.0 a.m. – 9.30 a.m. Close order drill. 9.30 a.m. – 12.30 p.m. under S.O.s. Lt. G. R. Bass + 2 guns of No. 4 section relieved 2/Lt. A. G. Jones + the 2 gun teams of that section at BEAUVOIS on A.A. duty. The [illegible] were inspected at 9.45 a.m.	
		23.2.18	The Coy paraded for C.O.'s inspection at 9.0 a.m. 9.30 a.m. – 12.30 was [illegible] on the range.	
		24.2.18	The Coy paraded at 10 a.m. for Church parade.	
		25.2.18	Nos. 1 & 3 Sections moved up to the Battle Zone, [illegible] at LATTILLY. The remainder of the Coy continued training under Section Officers.	
		26.2.18	The two A.A. guns at BEAUVOIS were relieved by the 183 ~~Bridgade~~ Brigade Lewis Guns. Nos. 2 & 4 Sections were on the range during the morning.	
		27.2.18	The 184 M.G. Coy relieved the 183 M.G. Coy in the line in the ~~[illegible]~~ [illegible] ST QUENTIN Sector. Relief was reported complete at 9 p.m. by the code word "CAPSTAN".	
		28.2.18	Shelling during the night was not active except on the left where the enemy shelled heavily for 3/4 of an hour.	

T. E. Goode[illegible] CAPT.
COMDG. 184 COMPANY M.G. CORPS.

(A7092). Wt W12839/M1293. 750,000. 1/17. D. D. & L., Ltd. Forms/C.2118/14.

www.ingramcontent.com/pod-product-compliance
Lightning Source LLC
Chambersburg PA
CBHW080915230426
43667CB00015B/2682